NOODLE TRAILS

a travel memoir

*Fair Trade, Dung Trade
and Travels in Thailand
and beyond*

Eileen Kay

First published in Great Britain in 2014

British Library Cataloguing in Publication Data: A catalogue record for this title is available from the British Library.

1.   Travel (Thailand, Cambodia, Hanoi, southeast Asia)
2.   Memoir, Autobiography (Eileen Kay)

British Library Cataloguing in Publication Data: a catalogue record for this title is available from the British Library.
Library of Congress Catalog Card Number: on file.

ISBN: 978-1505948530

Cover design: Marius Trandafir

Although this is based on real events, much is fictionalised and dramatised.

www.noodletrails.com: author's website with present day tales of icky fauna, life in a jungle hut, and noodle-shaped journeys through other territories

Contents

Earth Calling Bangkok

"First time you come Thailand?" It's Bangkok airport, and my cab driver is the chatty type.

"No. I've been here before. I love Thailand."

"Oh, thank you, thank you! How many time, you come Thailand?"

I am jet-lagged and dizzy enough to need to count on my fingers. "Seven?" I'm guessing. It might be six. I have lived in sweet, lovely Scotland for seven years, and every winter I go somewhere very, very hot. This wonderful luck is now at an end, and this trip is my last hurrah.

"You holiday? Or you business?"

"Both. Some holiday, some business." Both things used to be true. This time I'm not sure.

"Good-good! Have fun, make money. Good-good." If only. For now, "so-so" will do.

1

"Where your husband?"

"What?"

"Only you?"

"Yes. Only me."

"Oh."

No "good-good" this time. He has his doubts. I bloody do, too. Two months ago, my partner of many years announced it was all over, out of the blue. Amidst the immediate devastation emerges a practical question: What do we do with the air tickets to Thailand we bought months before, just like we've done for years? He's going anyway, itinerary unchanged. Someone writes to sympathise with me about the end of the relationship and for having to stay at home. What? I sob at the very idea. It's out of the question. I've done business there for years, after all. I have every right to go – even though I'm almost broke and my business sold next to nothing last year.

Why go on a business trip when clearly there's no business to do? I have no idea. Therefore I go. While I hesitate to do something I'll regret it's worse to think I'll regret not even trying. So I decide to try. Or rather, to paraphrase Bart Simpson, "I can't promise I'll try, but I promise I'll try to try."

I change the departure date, abandon the itinerary and focus on creating a new one. All I know is that suddenly – within less than a year – I have no income, no business prospects or obvious abilities, ongoing poor health, no close family, a cold and damp house filled with frogs and slugs which I really must vacate, and then, when all its heating shut down and I had nowhere to stay in freezing winter, this is exactly when my beloved partner of seven years announced he doesn't do bad times, and ended it with a note.

Best of all, it is the start of the winter of 2008. The year in which the entire UK is just waking up to the realisation that this is not just a recession: this will be a long, tough one.

I'm not usually rash, but on absorbing this latest bit of world financial news, I go straight to my bank and empty my savings account – all two thousand pounds. The clerk raises her eyebrows but I don't care. I change the ticket to open-ended – and would have made it one-way if that were cheaper. Would I rather be miserable in frozen Scotland, or miserable in the tropics? At this point in time I am too confused to know. Thank goodness some great invisible magnet pulls me in the right direction, by which I mean any direction away from where I am. If it has to be a grieving season, at least in the tropics you can weep at night and thousands of cicadas will join you. In daylight, tears wash away when you swim, when you sweat, when mango juice dribbles down your chin. You're always dripping wet in the tropics. What're a few tears thrown in?

The cabbie turns up the radio, bringing me back to now. Sugary pop music chirps away. It's a high-pitched Asian version of the Osmond family, only sweeter if that's possible. It's such a happy, pinky-girly accompaniment to my downfall, as I see it, that for irony's sake, if nothing else, I thought I should buy the single. We crawl towards the city centre, into the dense, vast jungle that is Bangkok rush hour – oozing like molasses, and shimmering in the blinding heat. This is going to take a while. The cabbie starts humming.

Scores of unfinished skyscrapers loom, started decades ago in the boom before Thailand's currency suddenly crashed. These half-made monsters hover, rusted in place, unfinished towers crowned with abandoned cranes, glass windows looking rickety, the whole skyline a raggle-taggle herd of dinosaur skeletons overshadowing the city.

Billboards blare preposterously enormous images of every computerised gizmo you can drape a girl over. Advertising psychology gets more sophisticated every year, drumming its message into hip urbane Thai professionals that whatever foreign blond executives do is the New Cool. As long as the skyscrapers stay up, that is.

I, on the other hand, work in Fair Trade. It's the poorest of the poor who get my custom. Some urban Thai people enjoy a good standard of living: better than their neighbours in Cambodia or Laos or Vietnam, and certainly better than those out in the countryside – the ones with whom I've been trading. This year, though, I won't see many remote rural suppliers and trading partners.

Normally I see my suppliers every winter. Proper big business, yes? Yes and no. Business: yes. Big: not at all. It's a one-woman, one-van, one-spare-room operation. I import earrings, cards, novelties and gifts. I sell them wholesale to shops and retail on a website. I joined the British Association of Fair Trade Shops and the World Fair Trade Organization. I do slide show talks to schools and church groups. I do market stalls and festivals, and people are even starting to know me. I write "importer" on my landing card and Immigration don't laugh or arrest me. It's all true. It just sounds more substantial than it was. Is. Could still be if the economy wakes up. Or, I could be homeless in a caravan this time next year, not unlike some of my Third World trading partners.

So this year, I email most of my suppliers to say that business is so poor (down 90%) that I simply cannot place an order this year. Maybe next year, I offer, not really knowing. Some write back sympathetically, hoping to see me next year and wishing me luck.

Others are more adamant. "Come anyway," they say. "We understand. Business is like that. Ups and downs. We can still talk about design, quality control, plans for the year after next. We will be happy to see you. Please come?" At the risk of sounding corny, Fair Trading is not just business. It attempts to be more considerate, more humane and more personal. These people all run small businesses, like me, and we all face the same global giants. I just worry they're expecting too much of me.

I'd love to see my old pals – the recycled paper people, the elephant dung people, the rice bag people, lots of jewellery people – but I'd especially love to see two groups I've always wanted to meet but never had the chance because we only traded through an intermediary: the coconut people, and the tsunami people. I want to photograph them, not only because this is always useful in promotions, but also – it could be my last chance. There is no logical or financial reason to go, that's for sure. Perhaps there are times in life specifically meant for doing things that make no sense, like some kind of test you can undertake on faith alone. So, I will go, admittedly on a flimsy life-raft on a sea of doubts and misgivings, and I promise to try to try.

In Bangkok, traffic is hotting up. Sharp hooting, steam rising, air-conditioning panting and struggling. I lean my head back and, even with my eyes shut, I need sunglasses against the glare. I can't sleep. I keep wondering, "How on earth did I end up here? And where will I end up next?" This entire trip, however many months it takes, will provide the answer to this. I hope.

Oh yes, I almost forgot: I'd like some laughs too, please. I haven't had many of those in a while. And so, with that prayer, in the back seat of this steam bath of a taxicab, I finally fall asleep.

Fruit Guy and Other Reunions

"Home!" says the taxi driver. "Madam. Wake, wake. Home."

"What?"

"Home. You home."

Oh, home. The old neighbourhood. An alley of nondescript, low-budget, cheap-but-cheerful guesthouses. These are not rock bottom accommodation but more lowish mid-range, which means adapted Thai food but European toilets. I've only been here a few times, but it's familiar. Home-away-from-home. Every little shred of familiarity is a comfort.

We turn the final corner, off the mega-boulevard and, oh joy of joys: Fruit Guy lives! I am so pleased he's working the same corner as always. He's senior street vendor on this patch. Every year I buy fruit from him. It's the first really proper, luscious tropical fruit of my year.

This has been a favourite since, as a child, I drew pictures of coconut palms, and there aren't many of those in New Jersey. Fruit Guy is at least eighty, but I want to believe he's a hundred and fifty. Extremely skinny, he's nothing but wire, and tough as old boots. Long, white, wispy goatee, flip-flops and shorts, backwards baseball cap, and no shirt. I have never seen him in a shirt. He may not even own one. He doesn't speak a word of English, and I hope he never does. He will be my first port of call, after check in.

Check-in is a terribly sweet affair. The staff are mostly the same. I remember most of them. Some even remember me, and welcome me back. I remember how to say "hello" in Thai. They praise this and giggle, and I protest and giggle, and we all love this game. It's like applauding a dog doing party tricks. It amuses them, another new dancing dog.

Miss Main Receptionist bows and bestows upon me, as one of their sacred returning customers, the privilege of not having to pay in advance. This is unusual and I am highly honoured. I bow back, incorrectly. She changes the subject diplomatically.

"Single room OK? Where your husband?"

This is going to happen again and again, and I am going to have to get used to it. I take a deep breath. "This time I am travelling alone."

"Oh," she says gently, kindly changing the subject again.

Later that afternoon, I've showered and powdered myself into a summer dress I haven't touched for twelve months. Now it's imperative I stay awake until bedtime, which should rocket me forward eight hours, if I'm lucky. Time for a stroll. See that old gang of mine, down Foodie Alley. It sounds like a 1950s radio comedian. "At eight o'clock: Foodie Alley, in Don't Touch that Plate."

Let me tell you what I love about Fruit Guy. A few streets away, tourists buy fruit from exquisitely constructed pyramid displays, each one sculpted into intricate, filigree rosettes. More functional offerings are the pre-cut packages, with a small bag of dipping mix (sugar, salt, chilli). With my guy, minimalism rules. Gritty old card tables support fruit displayed plain and simple, straight onto newspaper, while he reads a fresh newspaper seated on a plastic beach chair. He always keeps odd bits of fruit to one side to throw in free extras if he wants. They might be from yesterday, but they're always fine. He chucks them in as a parting shot with not exactly a wink, but a discreet nod, and a look that could come from somewhere between your guru and your granddad. He sets up when he likes and goes home when he feels like it, which is my idea of a perfect business.

There are over ten different varieties of banana in Thailand. I start with my favourites, "finger-bananas", delightful little fellows. There are twenty or thirty of them to a bunch, reminiscent of plantain but with a tanginess all their own. I add mangoes, and he adds a free orange.

Mangoes come in many varieties – and all stages of ripeness. I pass on the crunchy, tart green ones, and instead go for the luscious softies, the ones they use for "sticky rice and mango" – a dessert for which I would faint in homage. I get four, then six, and he throws in another orange.

Then I see rose apples, one of my favourite discoveries. Shaped like bright red pears, they have a crisp skin and a sharp apple taste, but inside is a feathery light, juicy texture, something like a lacy watermelon. I add half a dozen. He throws in a papaya and we're done. Fruit Man does the Granddad Yoda wise-nod thing and I thank him in Thai, which does not impress him in the least. I may rename him Uncle Guru. I adore him.

I wish I could eat my body weight in tropical fruit. Could a new law of mutant physics please make this possible? I guess that's my second prayer of the trip so far. Oh, beloved mangoes. I'd move here for a good mango supply. Still, there will be time to eat my fill. Creamy custard apples. The purple-skinned mangosteens with their clusters of syrupy, velvety, lychees. The big fluorescent pink artichoke-shaped dragon fruits with sandy white kiwi insides. I'll never learn all these Thai names.

There are always things I've never seen before, and they're always next to those Chinese star-shaped things I've never understood. I might even try a durian, spiky rugby balls so infamously stinky that they're barred from most Asian airlines, many air-conditioned buses and some hotels. People refer to them the way North Americans talk about skunks.

Enough fruit. Now dinner.

Our alley is lined with tiny noodle bars, rice bars, roasted banana grills, sweet potato grills, kebab grills, and soup cauldrons of all sorts. Many are mounted on motorcycle sidecars with cats crawling underneath. I'm only here for two nights, but I will eat all my meals out here, crouched under the sun umbrellas – the only one sweating – alongside the neat office girls, the macho cab drivers, and other local workers who either stare at or simply tolerate foreigners on their turf, at their soup bar.

Here's where I wish I'd studied more Thai phrases. I am lazy, and people here can be very accommodating. Meals involve pointing and smiling. Everything is delicious, so it hardly matters. What matters is that I see meat on ice. It may be pork noodles for breakfast, but not when Miss Piggy's been hanging in the sun all day. I have made that mistake before.

I approach Soup Woman and her cauldron. At the last second, instead of pointing at a chicken, on impulse I say, "Moo?" I do not mean beef. In Thai "moo" means pork. Or rather: moo-oo? It rises up like a question. All Thai words come in one of five tones: low, middle, high, rising or falling. Get the tune wrong and they will not know what you are singing. We speak, they sing, and that says a lot about both peoples. I say, "Moo-oo?" and Soup Woman pays me the ultimate compliment. She nods and makes the soup as if I am normal and no big deal. I adore her too. She is the spiritual cousin of Fruit Guy.

Every food stall on this alley is authentic. Even if it weren't full of Thai people, you can tell by the condiments. Real Thai place? Dry chilli powder, chilli oil, chilli vinegar. Fish sauce, garlic, sugar, ground peanuts. A box with soup spoons and chopsticks. Tourist place? Soy sauce, ketchup, brown sauce, salt and pepper, knives and forks. A Thai would never dream of letting knives out of the kitchen. A meal that needs a knife is just not civilised. If it comes to ripping things to shreds, you pick it up in your hands. Everyone, therefore, supplies toothpicks. You're meant to claw bits out while hiding this action behind your hand, or pretending to.

Soup Woman is on the case. Of the one million types of noodle here, she has five, and I go for the super thin ones. They're loaded into her big basket ladle and lowered into the broth, but not for long. One by one, she adds assorted fine-chopped greens and bean sprouts, in between slicing the meat thinly and preparing the bowl with seasonings, spices, powders and heaven knows what magic potions that wait to one side like the tools of a surgeon. Into this sauce goes the broth, then the noodles, then the meat laid out prettily on top, finished perhaps with a sprinkling of toasted garlic or spring onions and some other nicety, and there you are: all beautiful, in one minute, for under 50p. You need not speak any Thai to eat well here. You could wander wordlessly, pointing at things and eating them, and it would all be delicious.

I want to eat Thailand, starting with the things I can't pronounce.

In the meanwhile, I have my ratty but trusty pocket language guide, complete with emergency card. Key phrases are written in Thai for you to point out to people; statements like "Driver, slow down or I will throw up." I don't know how you show him at ninety miles an hour. In any case, every year I try to pick up a few new phrases, but soon they're gone. I wonder, what do I now remember spontaneously, from a year ago? "Hello", "Thank you", "Fish sauce", "1-2-3". Not bad, I think, getting food into the top three.

I'm full and sagging, but it's still too early to go home. It's time for a relaxing stroll on the main boulevard, which is crashing with noise and filthy with fumes. Bangkok's pride and air-conditioned joy – the Sky Train – roars past a city of shopping plazas. No one notices the half-completed skyscrapers and their cranes dangling from top floors. Everybody's busy shopping.

There's some kind of festival on, with special stages set up everywhere. A Thai country-and-western band strums their heavily accented version of "Bad Moon Rising". They wear checked shirts and straw hats, and radiate an easy-going, slightly stoned sort of attitude. When they give the same treatment to "Rolling on the River", I move along. It can only ever be Tina's version for me.

Next door a kickboxing demonstration draws a bigger crowd than the stoned cowboys, yet it's all strangely sluggish. Kickboxing can be an electrifying martial art – choreographically dazzling – but these lacklustre boys only deliver a high kick now and again, and without much zing. I'm not sure who this show is aimed at, Thais or foreigners.

I have nearly killed enough time. My knees are weak and my vision blurry. Time to collapse. On the way back to my bed, I pass a fellow foreigner and try not to stare. He's a young, thin, pale-skinned black man, wearing a tee shirt with the face of Barack Obama, who he actually resembles. There's one bold caption on it: "Hope". It's like some odd apparition.

Back down Foodie Alley, I collect roasted bananas, a roasted sweet potato and a skewered sausage of pork, garlic and minced vermicelli – a delicacy I've enjoyed before – to stow away in my mini-fridge, or perhaps eat the second I get into the room. With my final purchase of the day, I remember how to say good night to Sausage Lady, who grins and gives me the thumbs-up. I will sleep well tonight. I am on Thai time now.

Day Two. I am quite, quite ill – and so is my computer. We both have terrible symptoms. I have a migraine and vomiting, convulsive sobbing, and a long list of other alarming and inexplicable surprises. As for the computer, it won't connect to the internet. The manager tries, a staff member tries, and fellow traveller – Kevin from Ireland – tries, all to no avail.

Kevin from Ireland turns into my fairy godmother, in more ways than one. He's going out and lends me his computer, which is just like mine. I am gobsmacked, but he just smiles. He says he trusts me. He can tell I'm OK. (Am I? Really? I wonder if he's right.) He places it in my hands and saunters up the alley.

That day – through the magic of Wi-Fi and this miracle loan – from my sick bed, I can contact the outside world. I confirm business appointments, a train journey, upcoming accommodation, and so on, but those aren't the main things I spend my time on. The main priority of the day is medical research into the poisonous sleeping pill I took on the plane, prime suspect for my most pressing problems.

Sleeping pills are new to me. I am suffering every side effect this one offers. There wasn't much information on the packet, but there's plenty on the internet. I soon learn I am probably not going to die, but it has been known to happen – especially with my symptoms. I should stay in bed and near a phone and be on the lookout for strokes, heart attacks, suicidal impulses and other lethal possibilities. Otherwise, see a doctor tomorrow if it doesn't stop.

Day Three. It stops.
I flush the pills down the toilet. I suppose someone else

would have sold them, or given them to those for whom it's entertainment. If I change my mind and fancy some kind of replacement, it could be arranged. There is enough available over the average chemist's counter here to shock most European nurses.

Last night I tried to return Kevin's computer, but he wasn't in. Kevin is a carouser, knows the city and loads of people. He was out way past carousing time, but I know he has a train to catch. Am I about to inadvertently steal his laptop? No! I return it at breakfast – which is rice soup for me and strong coffee for him. Then he tears off, hung over and half-packed, racing for his train. Kevin from Ireland, I salute you.

In my remaining hours in the city, I eat as many street snacks as possible. I can now remember how to count to twenty and beyond. I go to the shopping plaza and have business cards made for the next twelve months, because it is half the price and they are very good at it. It's also a half-hearted gesture to say that I believe I will still be in business for another year.

As for my ailing computer, I spend head-splitting amounts of time in Pantip Plaza – a gigantic techno-mecca that looks like a science fiction film set. I find a bloke who fixes it; oops no he hasn't. I find another bloke, then it works; oh no it doesn't. It works, it doesn't: it works, it doesn't. I take it home like a friend who's had painful but inconclusive tests in hospital.

Tonight, I see dangling cranes of skyscrapers from my

tiny, dingy, crummy little window. My whole life, including my own teeter-tottery business, feels every bit as precarious. Tomorrow is my train journey south with my Thai exporter colleague, Soo. My trusty old suitcase is more ready than I am. I'm reminded of one of those cartoon characters who wanders off a cliff. They keep walking into thin air until they look down. I think that's where I am – about to look down. It's only when they do look down that they plummet – and not all at once. First the boots go, elongating the legs, which pull down the torso, and then the head, followed by chattering teeth, bugged out eyeballs, and lastly the shocked eyebrows and fright wig. Then, after the long fading whistle, there is a thud and a distant little puff of dust.

This is as ready as I'll ever be.

The Coconut Trip

The plan is to visit a group who make arts and crafts out of old coconut shells and wood. They are called the Padang Coconut Products Group, from a small town called Padang Besar in Songkla province near the south-east coast of Thailand, not far from Malaysia.

I am to meet Soo, my Thai exporter and translator. She has a typically lengthy Thai name, and Soo is my shorthand. We're booked on the afternoon train down south, which will travel all through the night. I've not been on many sleeper trains, and still think it's a game. I'm smiling, thinking it's like a scene out of *Some Like It Hot*.

Unlike most places, trains here are often slower than buses. Bangkok is more of a boat and bus town. The main train station is touchingly small, with a huge TV screen jumping with female kickboxing, its rapt audience sitting in front of a hundred picnics on mats.

Our train is the next to depart. The queue fizzes with all the excitement that precedes an extra-long journey, the kind that takes days. Our train terminates in Malaysia, and there are plenty of people in Muslim dress in the queue. I suppose they are a mix of Thais, Malaysians, and other nationalities, judging by the variety of skin tones and facial types. This is a side of Thailand that I have not seen before.

Muslims in Thailand make up about 3 or 4% of a 95% Buddhist country. The few locals I've spoken to refer to their minority religion neighbours in a nervous, embarrassed way. It reminds me of 1960's American whites talking about "Coloureds" and "Negroes", insisting some of their best friends were, but you wouldn't want to marry one, and that sort of thing. There's plenty in the press about a few extremists sullying the reputation of thousands of peaceful, industrious and studious people.

I don't see any white tourists in this queue. There is a young school party, mostly Muslim. They're peering at the train, trading snacks, playing games, and itching to go.

We get the signal to board and find our places. Our seats are filled with a large, chubby Buddhist monk stretched out and snoring, dressed in traditional orange robes with the usual shaved head and lack of baggage.

There is general hesitation about waking him. No one

wants to poke a monk. Females must never touch them, for any reason. Soo gets the guard, who gently shoves him with some friendly chat. The monk wakes, shunts over to the seats opposite, and grins at me.

"Good morning!" he bellows heartily. It's nearly evening.

"Hello."

"Good morning!" he snaps with a sort of mad authority. I switch to his clock, dialect and world view.

"Good morning," I agree.

"Where you go?"

"Padang Besar. And you? Going home?"

His face falls like a child's. "No," he answers glumly, "I go back to the monastery." He's as miserable as a kid after the school holidays.

Most of our carriage is filled with Chinese Malaysians. They boarded in groups of twos and threes, but quickly introduce themselves to each other and merge into one large swell. By the time the train leaves the station, twenty of their bubbliest members are cackling around one table as if at a family reunion. They are unbelievably noisy, their eruptions, shrieks and screams painfully ear-piercing. Everyone else is cringing. The Thais show great forbearance. I sense there could be historical references here, but I am not privy to them.

The ringleader is a female in her fifties. "Oh sorry, sorry! Too loud," she shouts, gasping and guffawing – a real pantomime dame. "We the Laughing Club, hahaha!

Sorry, we be quiet now. Very quiet, see?"

They wait a few seconds and burst out screaming again, wiping away tears of mirth. This lasts all afternoon and well into the evening. At the last moment, a guard glides in and points to the "Quiet after 10pm" rule on the wall with one firm thump of an index finger. He is silent and eloquent in this balletic gesture. He exits. One by one they all shut up.

A dormitory has been efficiently and meticulously assembled by the train attendants. We climb into our private cocoons and pull the curtains shut as the train rattles on into the dusty, hot night towards the even hotter south.

It's six o'clock on a Monday morning when I wake up. We're still gently trundling along. A mix of humans in contrasting conditions stumble out of their train berths. I zigzag unsteadily down the aisle and attempt to brush my teeth and wash my face in the same sink as various others while waiters dart in and out creating forty-two breakfast trays, pre-ordered last night.

One loo is sit-down European, while the other is Asian squat style and has a shower, which exerts a profound allure. However, I decide not to push my luck. Surely I would soak both what I'm wearing and what I'm trying to change into. Only trained staff or locals possess such skills.

Back at my bunk, the curtains opposite whip open to

display my venerable monk neighbour in splendid near-nakedness. He sits in a perfectly casual, chubby half lotus, all jiggling and jollity, chatting with a young waiter, flirting. The boy looks uncomfortable. Mr Monk giggles skittishly in a high-pitched, almost hysterical way, his voice singsong and girlish. Maybe camp. Maybe mad. Maybe both.

Some say religious communities get more than their share of the mentally unstable, and don't have the heart to turn them away. Where else can they go? Some think inner peace magically awaits them. Little do they know, going through those gates, they are not escaping life. It follows them in there, condenses and intensifies. Bon voyage!

This fellow, we later learn, doesn't live in a monastery. He lives with a Chinese man in Malaysia. We stop asking questions after that. We start admiring the scenery.

There are miles and miles of iridescent green rice paddies. They're lined by muddy drainage ditches deep enough to be dotted with cows cooling off in them. In between each stretch of paddy, the land teems with luscious plants and trees of all sorts. Some I've seen pictures of and some are totally alien. I recognise rubber and eucalyptus trees, both of which are beautiful.

Rubber trees are slender and straight, with a blotchy bark that looks like a map wiggling with rivers. The blotches range from delicate and refined creams and off-whites to tans and pale earth tones, like desert camouflage designed by Grace Kelly. Eucalyptus leaves are long like willows, one side green and the other silver. The wind turns them into shimmering shoals of fish.

There are floppy banana trees, scratchy coconut palms, red trumpeting hibiscus, red hot pokers and more, in mile upon mile of tangled jungle vines. Soo has seen it all before, but I think it's a fairy world. She's absorbed in her book: *Introduction to Meditation.* She gave me a copy too. She thinks I should study meditation, and doesn't seem to believe me when I mention various studies, books, retreats and courses I've read and taken over thirty years. She is fervent about her new teacher and wants me to do the same retreat she did. She wants everyone to do it. She's got it bad. I remember that. We have interesting mirror-image stories.

Soo has a large Thai Buddhist family and had a Catholic education. None of this involved meditation, but recently she attended a couple of ten-day retreats to learn more.

I, on the other hand, had a deeply unpleasant Mafia-style fascist Roman Catholic upbringing, from which I fled in my teens. I encountered Zen Buddhism in my twenties, then Tibetan Buddhism in my thirties, and have been hanging around Buddhist neighbourhoods intermittently ever since.

My brain replies to her, "I've studied this for thirty years. I have my favourites, thank you. Am I telling you who you must read? Please don't tell me what to read?

Please don't ask me to switch to your guy?" My mouth, however, says, "Thank you. Oh my, so many teachers. I might get confused." Her book stays in my bag.

Approaching Hat Yai train station, we pass the "Chief Permanent Way Inspection Office". Buddhists promote the idea that nothing is permanent, so maybe we're in Muslim country now. It's a longer stop than usual, with lots of coming and going, during which time the main feature arrives: the food sellers.

These energetic professionals leap aboard and zing up and down the aisles, bearing wide hoop baskets full of fresh and fragrant goodies, singing out lustily what's on offer. It all smells wonderful, especially the fried chicken.

These girls wear plain Muslim headscarves, wildly colourful beach shirts sporting palm trees and dancing dolphins, super tight jeans, and very high-heeled sandals. My monk neighbour buys some chicken, lays the money on the couch and sits well back. Miss Chicken-seller waits a key second or two, and then takes the money. That's the custom. A woman and a monk can't even touch either end of a banknote at the same time for fear of distracting his poor weak mind into mortal thoughts. This is even if the monk is as camp as Frankie Howerd and truly only wants the chicken.

The train, which limped most of the way, is now crawling as if infirm and seems to give up the ghost in a deserted little side yard where it looks like we're being abandoned to obscure Badland Bandits. There is a long wait. Is it our stop or isn't it? No one seems to know. It doesn't look like a real station – more like a disused platform in the middle of a dry, dead field.

To find out, we step off the train, shoving past and even climbing over some of the Chinese Malaysians, who hang out the windows waving us back in. "Wrong stop! No stop!"

This is it. Padang Besar. Suddenly my arm is grabbed by a tiny, excited birdlike lady, who seems about to take flight, she's so excited. I'm startled at first, but Soo introduces me to Boon, our host and the organiser of the Padang Coconut Products Group. She is talking a mile a minute to Soo, like a parakeet on caffeine. She weighs about half what I do, yet has no problem grabbing my bags like they're a couple of twigs and scooting us away to a pickup truck where her driver husband is waiting.

Boon chatters away while her husband keeps his careful eye on the road until we're out of town. The road in town is cracked and bumpy dried mud, and has deep, deathlike ditches on either side. After that, it's just smooth, thick dust, although the deathlike ditches remain. Boon is so thrilled. She yacks breathlessly, holding my hand and squeezing it eagerly, talking faster than Soo can translate. We must have passed through the modest little town of Padang Besar, but all I remember is the main street lined with interesting and great-smelling food stalls run by ladies in head scarves, ready for hungry people on their way to work and in need of a breakfast soup or a grilled chicken leg.

Soon we are on a jungle road to Boon's home deep in the middle of a rubber plantation, owned by other members of her extended family. We turn off the two-lane dirt road onto a one-lane dirt road, which takes us past her father-in-law's place to their house.

The clean, upright lines of rubber trees are all around. From each trunk hangs a bowl made from half a coconut shell. A spiral is cut into the trunk's bark, leading the thick white sap into the bowl for collection once a day, after which the spiral is cut afresh. It reminds me of the old-fashioned bucket collections of maple syrup in New England. These rubber trees cast a cool, dappled, silvery shade which I find magical.

The rubber industry is not in such poetic rapture. Prices have plummeted and small farmers, like Boon's father-in-law, are getting squashed by huge competitors. It's not unlike my own situation. For small farmers and sole traders, it isn't always a game.

The group's workshop is an open-air shed about four times the size of a two-car garage. In front is a big sign, in Thai, announcing they are approved by the Ministry of Industry. They've been employing people in this area for years, along with the rubber farmers and a handful of cafés and shops. It is not a densely populated area, and there is not much work. Very few tourists come here.

There are huge piles of coconuts everywhere: green ones, old dry ones, halved ones, quartered ones, slivered ones, hairy ones, bald ones: every stage of coconut imaginable. It is phenomenally dusty work, and the entire area is covered in deep drifts of brown coconut-coloured dust. Brush against anything and thick clouds engulf you. The workers wear face masks at all times.

One machine sands off the hairy part of the shell, another cuts it into pieces, another polishes it to a smooth shine, and another drills holes to create mosaic designs, borders, patterns, and other decorations. These are used to produce candle holders, decorative bowls, and slotted spoons, amongst other items. It's their combination of prettiness and practicality I especially love.

I always dreamed of eating my meals out of coconuts. I may have seen too many Jungle Jim movies as a kid perhaps, but there was also that one desert island book which ruined me forever: *Island of the Blue Dolphins*, a wonderful novel by Scott O'Dell based on the true story of a real girl Crusoe, abandoned by accident when she was a teenager, and who lived for many years on a deserted island. I've gone everywhere with a pocket-knife ever since.

Twittering birds fill a long row of beautiful ornamental cages made from reeds, bent wood, and other local materials. This is Boon's husband's business. She says they never intended to have pet birds. He just liked making the cages, started selling them, and people started giving him birds. Now they have a whole array, each cage unique and attractive, each bird singing a different tune.

Two eager puppies chew our toes, and then their slower moving mother lumbers in. The morning is growing hotter, and they repair to the garage, underneath the truck, now cool after our journey earlier. The luggage is taken in, and we follow.

The first large room we come to is filled with their products, in cartons and trays of finished and nearly finished stages. There are serving spoons, salad sets, spatulas, and ladles with handles made of coconut wood and the main piece of coconut shell. There are necklaces and earrings made from coconut shell beads hanging from display carousels. There are coconut shell mobiles, candleholders, boxes, bowls, incense holders, lamps and lampshades.

Boon has cold water, juice, and biscuits ready by the time we each emerge from a much-savoured shower to wash away the train journey. We sprawl onto chairs around the snug kitchen table, drink and recover. Soon there is also breakfast: omelettes, and rice and mangoes.

I love the vibrant kitchen floor, tiled with an assortment of shapes and colours – no two alike, all dynamic and cheerful. Their son, in his twenties, is a talented and imaginative artist whose paintings are on the walls, and also in the local temple. He masterminded their striking, plant-laden bathroom, featuring a massive gnarled wooden branch, with naturally shaped pegs, nooks, and mini-shelves for towels, toothbrushes, and even a tiny toy gorilla super hero.

The house is assembled from corrugated tin roofing, plaster walls, and rough timber joists, many of which extend outside. There's a sideways door leaning against the kitchen entrance to keep the dogs out.

The room we share is tidy and piled high with laundry, a TV, a non-working computer, and the family photo albums Boon has selected to show us. There's the married daughter and son-in-law who are so incredibly good-looking, even she's amazed. The artist son lives at home and also helps with their other businesses, the coconuts and the rubber trees. The unmarried daughter lives and works in the city. A fortune-teller said she'll marry a foreigner and emigrate. She has just met a Canadian man, so all eyes are glued to them. No pressure there, naturally.

We're cooler now. We're fed. The journey has been shaken off. We've met the family. Now we can talk.

Their news is worse than mine. Their business had a very bad year. Unlike me, they are not new to their line of work. They have a good set-up, a long track record, lots of experience, a fine reputation for quality and honesty, and a decent and helpful exporter representing them. What they don't have at the moment are any orders. They haven't had any for three months.

The year started with business down by a third and it dwindled from there. I am in a similar position. For example, the year before I supplied forty gift shops. This year it is down to five. My takings have plummeted about 90% in one year.

Here, the neighbouring families who usually work with them are instead collecting used glass bottles and returning them for the meagre deposit. If it continues like this, nobody knows how they'll get by.

Instead of selling their wares, this group (and I too) have to lend out stock to shops, hoping to be paid later if it sells, on a sale or return basis. It's no one's preferred way to operate, but there's no cash. At least if we can get this stuff out on the shelves, there's a chance it will sell, which is better than it collecting dust in a warehouse.

Boon, therefore, provided a load of stock on sale or return to various outlets, but her people needed a wage in the meanwhile. She managed to get a loan from a bank, since she's a trustworthy figure in the community. Then sales dropped, and now paying this loan will be difficult. Anxiety is ravaging her voice.

She has to live next door to the people she feels she has let down. If my neighbours have a run of bad luck, they head for the dole queue. They don't have this in Asia. They have beggars, or people who migrate or move in with others, or we just don't know what happens to them.

I love this group's coconut wares so much I over-ordered grotesquely last year. Their products are popular and admired, but I still have a lot of stock. I may order again the year after next, after this backlog goes, but no sooner. I hate this fact, for their sake, but that's how it is.

She shows me some new samples. We talk over a few small points in design, like how to best secure utensil heads to their handles. People tell her to use nails or glue, but that's neither traditional nor natural, both of which are high priorities for her.

I take loads of pictures. I am swept up in her effervescent enthusiasm. She grabs my hands, shows me around, and drags me here, there, and everywhere. She is a dynamo. You cannot stop a river this strong. I like her immensely. That's why this is painful.

This trip will not pay for itself. I also worry I'm wasting their time and giving them false hope when I have no real money to spend. Now, though, I see this visit is injecting energy into her tired, frazzled frame. This lady – and many like her – fear they are forgotten. I have disproved this. I have travelled sixteen hours on a rattling train next to a half-nude mad monk just to meet her and make a statement of moral support. A nice fat order and some nice fat income would be better, but moral support is all I have to offer, for now.

Back to reality and lunch, which is pink papaya salad with plenty of chilli, a shrimp and crab dish declared "not spicy" (meaning very spicy, just not lethal), with a fabulous sweet and sour dressing. Later we snack on batter-fried bananas and sweet potatoes, and sugar cane juice on ice, all of which is delectable, and which I eat with gusto.

Boon loves food and is a very good cook. She's taught many a cookery class. Food keeps appearing when I least expect it, and then more food appears. This is quite wonderful. At one point there is a sort of mixed grasshopper and insect pâté. This is less wonderful. I try a cautious spoonful, and crunch on what may have been a wing or a husk or armour or some other tough metallic material. I hit a cultural border at this point. Reassuringly for me, Soo hits one too. Evidently not all Asians eat insects. Boon just passes round other dishes. At least I can now say I have ingested insects, and need never do so again.

Suddenly she bursts out laughing, having noticed her tee shirt is inside out. She doesn't change it, but just giggles and shrugs it away. Then we have a visitor – the local Immigration officer – who wants to talk to me. Should I be nervous? Have I done something stupid? No, it's a friend of hers who works on the Thai–Malaysian border. He wants a photo of us all. With our permission, he will use it to publicise this area, encourage visitors, and show how tourists really do come here. They feel perfectly safe and thoroughly enjoy themselves. I assure him I do, and I am. He says to smile and he snaps the picture.

Danger is relative. The nearby train and bus stations have been bombed by extremist Muslim separatists. Teachers are often the targets, because they're seen as operatives of the State. It's estimated that over one hundred and fifty teachers have been killed in the last ten years. The assassins work in trios, placing three fingers on the trigger, one apiece, to share responsibility and confound prosecutors. I've been to the Middle East, Zimbabwe, and even the old New York City subway system (which is better now, I'm told), and this doesn't feel anything like that. Still, a place gets a black mark sometimes, and this area has been unfairly slurred. Tourists should come back, and I hope they do. We laugh at the idea that my face will be famous on the Thai–Malaysian border crossing.

Boon wants to show us the local temple, so we pile onto her motor scooter: "No need helmet, very safe, I go slow." She tears down the road, and I am very scared, which she finds immensely funny and laughs all the way there.

This temple is really a series of temples, carved straight out of the mountain. Its name has forty-eight syllables that I couldn't even begin to write down. We creep through weird and wonderful dripping caves and bizarre rocky shapes, past dozens of statues and murals. It is immense, stony, echoing, slippery – and mercifully much cooler than outside.

Once we emerge, we pass stalls and souvenir stands, all locked up and empty. There used to be a steady stream of visitors, but not now. Today we're the only ones here. On our way back to the scooter, we pass a local policeman on his way in. Boon goes quiet and scowls. She says they come to demand rice from the temple. A sort of protection racket, she explains contemptuously. Bribery is endemic enough, but stealing off a temple does seem low. It's been going on for as long as she can remember.

Back at the house we have more cool drinks and bananas in the shady, chummy kitchen. An odd hissing emanates from the bathroom. Boon gently captures in her palm what they call a hissing beetle, an enormous creature that reminds me of a North American June Bug, big as a fist, and hard as metal. Its wings rise and inflate, shaking forth a loud, weird hissing noise. It waggles crab-like pincers that look like they could slice off your finger. She releases it, and it buzzes about clumsily while I duck and cover my hair. They love this, and take it into their hands. It looks like a tank, but it's harmless. Now we exchange confessions of creatures we fear. Boon is allergic to the bite of a centipede. Her son can't stand cockroaches. I volunteer bats. Soo proposes rats, a popular choice. Snakes unite us all.

Supper is a truly wonderful squash stuffed with rice and minced pork, fish soup, and fried mixed vegetables. No insects, minimal chilli, and mouth-watering flavours that are nothing like what I am used to. It doesn't get much better than this.

We'll be up early for our departure in the morning, so tonight's chat takes on a reflective tone. Boon says she'd like to get a loom, a small portable one like those at the Saori project – the weaving and textile group we're visiting next. She wants to weave things out of banana leaves, coconut palms and other plant fibres, as people have done traditionally for centuries in this part of the world.

She says it's a second job she can do in the evenings, after her long working day is done. I think this woman can turn her hand to anything. She is devoted to the idea of using natural or recycled materials, and not just because they're free. She is determined to turn around their situation, but doesn't yet see a clear path ahead of her. She has more energy than anyone I can think of, and is determined to save her neighbourhood and all the people she once employed. If it isn't the coconut business, then it will need to be something else. Whatever it is, she can organise it.

Boon admits she's aware of getting older and slowing down, and I know what she means. She's forty-nine and I'm fifty-one, which makes us a Chinese dog and rooster, respectively. We don't feel that dynamic, but maybe we can do more than we think. When I used to be a teacher, I was forever saying this to people. "You can do it! You can!" Why do I not believe it about myself? We complement each other on looking younger, but we both sigh with fatigue.

She is familiar with Saori, the tsunami survivors' group Soo and I are visiting next. Boon is a passionate person and cannot contain her feelings. She speaks of the lavish amount of aid, volunteers, money, press, job training, and other help that was given to tsunami survivors – which she does not begrudge. However, she also points out that plenty of groups around the country have struggled all their lives and also need help with their businesses too.

Padang Besar doesn't have a groovy hippy beach reputation to offer, let alone chic luxury resorts. Is that what it takes to draw volunteers? I think it was the sheer scale and emotional drama of the 2004 tsunami that drew so much aid and support – that and the loss of the King's grandson. Long-term poverty just isn't as thrilling. It doesn't make the donor, as the saying goes, "feel good about themselves". It's more satisfying to rescue a helpless victim. It's not as heroic to help set up trade, and do business as usual. I, on the other hand, feel great to have met these fine people, and feel equally miserable that I am neither the expert nor the investor they need and deserve. At least they're well served by two exporters, who I hope will bring them more trade.

Breakfast is tasty but pensive. We need to go soon. Minutes are ticking by, and we have a long day of travel ahead of us. Boon pours out everything she hasn't said yet. She asks what we know about "Home Stay" tourism. She wants to find people (probably students and young adults) who will come and live with them for free room and board in exchange for teaching English or just helping out at the local school, and perhaps elsewhere in the community. I've read about this. I think there's an infinite range of possibilities, and it's a good idea that's getting more popular all the time. I promise to do some research and send it to them. I promise that if she gets set up properly, she can advertise on my website. Her face lights up, and I ought to warn her that this is not the advertising billboard of the century. We can cross that bridge when we get to it. As long as she leaves insect pâté off the menu, I think it's a goer.

Boon is choked up with fear about her English, about her future, about the future of all the people for whom she feels responsible, and about her debts and no way to pay them. I don't even mention mine or I'll get fearful and tearful too.

Her husband waves that he'll wait in the car. "My darling," she calls him. "He is good man, good father. He works hard, he's happy, he doesn't drink much, only smokes a little, helps with the business. He is good man."

"You're lucky," I say, and she nods.

"Come back next year," she says, "and next time, bring someone – bring someone special!" She has no idea what an open wound this is, and that I am still reeling from shock. I nearly got through an hour today without thinking about any of that. I don't want to get started. Now suddenly I need to stock up on extra tissues, essential for getting through another day.

I excuse myself, saying I need the loo, where I collect myself and the fresh tissues.

Tears do not help do business, but they do connect us as humans. Now when I use my coconut utensils in my kitchen at home, as I do every day, I can picture buzzy, zingy little Boon, her darling, decent husband, and their dusty, industrious workshop – and no dole or safety net.

Her Darling drives us to the bus. In the waiting area, we have pally girl fights over who will buy whom which snacks. We each refuse to let the others pay. We stuff gifts and money into each other's pockets, bags, down the backs of shirts. It's wonderful to be silly. It releases some of the fear. It is unusual for Thais to hug in public, but women sometimes do with each other. We embrace without hesitation, and we are both very close to tears.

I want them to survive. I wish this were within my power. For now, we wait for the bus.

High Ground Above a Tsunami

The next leg of our journey looks short on the map, but it isn't. In the spirit of Italy's boot, and the UK's begging dog, we are down the southern end of Thailand's dangling elephant trunk. We need to traverse from one side of the trunk to the other – east coast to west coast – along a sharp diagonal: on small roads, with several bus changes. This will take all day and part of the evening too. I wasn't aware of this at the time, and that's just as well.

Our destination is Kaolak, in Pangha Province on Thailand's south-west coast. It's just north of its more famous neighbours, Phuket, Krabi and Pipi, and the other darlings of the jet-setting beautiful beach people. At first glance, there is far more money on this coast than on the other. I read there's also more rain, more lush scenery, more Muslims, more tourism, and more inflation.

The small town of Kaolak suffered 90% of the damage done to Thailand by the 2004 tsunami. In a way, my entire trip revolved around this fact. If I'd stayed home in Scotland this year, the main local event, besides Christmas (which I have to fight fierce opposition not to celebrate), was the twentieth anniversary of the Lockerbie air crash, which happened just before Christmas 1988. Instead I rescheduled my trip to Thailand. A non-Christian does quite well in a predominantly Buddhist country, after all – in general and especially at Christmas time.

Also, the Thai tsunami happened just after Christmas. I've been trading with a tsunami survivors' group called Saori, but have never had the chance to meet them. Maybe now is the time, on the anniversary of their loss, and their founding. If they can get through that, I can get through this. I did not tell them my personal troubles, but we made contact and they were happy to receive me. I decided to spend Christmas and New Year in the tsunami zone, and build the rest of the trip around that. Thus a shaky new itinerary was born.

So that is why I'm in the Hat Yai bus station, waiting with Soo on an open-air bench next to two monks who look like ex-cons. Make no mistake, a tiny percentage of them are ex-cons. They span the gamut of drink, drugs, crime, prison and who knows what else, and then – in a last ditch effort – they show up at a monastery's door with nothing to lose but their hair. Good luck to them.

In this particular case, the younger one smokes his cigarette out the side of a tough scowl. He's rubbing his calves, which are covered in tattoos of knives, blood, and images of violence. The older monk looks like the thug who taught Junior everything he knows. Uncle Thug and Junior Thug-in-training.

Across from me sits a girl in a cap with the glittery slogan "Christian Audio" above a picture of three flaming skulls in a heavy metal style. Below the skulls is the caption, "All You Need Is Love". Other than this, she and they look quite normal. I decide to take a walk around the block.

I buy a cold drink and terrible snacks from a lovely man so eager to speak English that it's absolutely touching. I want to talk to him and his entire family all day, and possibly move in with them. On the way back, I pass the "Brilliant Progress Company" and wonder what kind of brilliant progress they provide.

We get loaded into a minibus, which takes us to the main bus, and somewhere along that long hot day we change buses again. We wait in a little roadside café, full of various Thai people trying to assist a mad-looking, badly sunburned Italian. He's dressed entirely in fluorescent colours that match his luggage. Many items he's wearing have price tags hanging off them. Perhaps he's been selling things all day on a market stall with no hat? He wants directions to an island no one has heard of. No one can find it on his map, either. There's a bit of froth at the side of his mouth and he seems delirious. People start backing away.

As I'm the only other European there, I become the sole recipient of his heartfelt but unintelligible outpourings. They were in mostly Italian, some in English, all in badly garbled yet passionate pronouncements regarding (I think) the subjects of God, the Bible, the Catholic Church, Italian culture, getting a Thai visa, drugs, and the end of the world – quite possibly in that order, but we are not certain. Finally he appeals to the crowd to recommend another destination, since his choice was imaginary. Somebody suggests Ranong, several hours up the coast. This is a popular idea with the crowd. Ranong is a port town full of boats that take you elsewhere, to nearby little islands, either Thai or Burmese. I've only ever known airports and newsreaders use "Myanmar". Every Burmese person I ever met called themselves just that.

Thousands of tourists every year do the visa run: an extremely organised operation in which tourists in Thailand take a few steps over the border into Burma and hand over a crisp ten dollar note. (No more, no less, and no change. Two people must pay two tens: a twenty will not be accepted.) Within seconds they step back over the border into Thailand, with another two weeks on their passports, or maybe more if they're lucky. There are foreigners who have stayed in Thailand for decades on this basis. This is why it could change.

Near Ranong are loads of little islands to choose from. Our Italian nut likes the sound of the area, and seems to think he can find another island on which to really complete the insanity process. The crowd points him towards a distant bus stop and we wave him goodbye – every single one of us.

Soo whispers, "Was he drunk?"

"I think it's drugs," I surmise, "and lots of them, and for many years."

The owner of the café asks me to write a sign in English for him: "Give donations here to help stray dogs". They pay vets to neuter them because of their annoying, noisy numbers. The ones around here are typically diseased, underfed, and fight aggressively over garbage and limited territory. Fewer of them is a good idea. I write it, he tacks it to a pole, and everyone smiles. Not every white person is barking bonkers. Some of us have our uses.

On the opposite side of the highway are the backpackers going south to Phuket. We will go north – up the west coast, following the sea, the palm trees, the pristine white beaches and the cruddy local shacks alternating with the posh tourist villas – until hours later when it's too dark to see. Into a muggy blackness, we are deposited near a small dark driveway with no one around but cicadas.

Instantly, two silhouetted women appear magically to collect us. One is heartrendingly sweet and shy, and is renting us her bungalow. The other is taller and more senior, graciously composed and dignified, and she is our driver. I cannot pronounce, or rather sing, their names properly. Instead I name one Mrs Sweet, and the other Mrs Elder.

They gesture to the vehicle, a motorcycle with a sort of cage fashioned as a sidecar. You see them everywhere around here: making shop deliveries or sometimes selling food cooked on an entire mini-kitchen with street stall and canopy built in. They are the very definition of rickety.

"It's safe, it's safe," they chorus when they see the look on my face. Does it look or feel safe? It does not. So we all climb in and rattle our way down the road.

At a cute little café full of Thais, who are surprised to see my white face, we enjoy fish cakes, seaweed soup, and Chinese broccoli with salted fish. It's all lovely, so unlike the usual tourist stuff, and I wish I could eat like this more often. Our two hosts have already eaten because we arrived so late. I feel a bit awkward, but I'm also famished, having lived all day on weird crisps and cheap doughnuts. I devour everything with gusto and without a single thought for my table manners, which I know are appalling when I'm enthusiastic. I can only hope they are tolerant, or maybe take it as a sign of appreciation.

Then I remember something I learned from the entertaining book *Mai Pen Rai Means Never Mind* by Carol Hollinger. As a white person (and North Americans need to get used to being called Europeans here), you will always look like a barbarian. Even if you clean up your act and learn some of their customs, it won't work. You are white. You will never seem civilised to them. I'll do my best, but will keep my expectations low.

After the meal, we are delivered in the cage, like so many meat parcels, to our accommodation – the tidy modest bungalow of shy Mrs Sweet. It's in a place called ITV Village, which was built after the tsunami, using donations gathered via ITV, one of Thailand's national television stations. Several hundred families are now housed several kilometres inland in rows of terraced bungalows, with concrete floors, and reassuringly strong walls and ceilings.

There is one large front room, divided in half by a huge wooden unit with wardrobes and storage drawers, plus the centrally sacred TV and sound system area surrounded by family photos. To one side – on the entrance wall – is their shrine to the Buddha, and to various Buddhist monks and revered teachers.

Behind all this is the sleeping area, from which a door leads to the kitchen, laundry, and bath areas. Former foreign visitors have left a large Canadian flag, a lurid poster of a woman in a bikini, and a few group shots of football clubs. We settle in. Soon we are showered, exhausted, and aware of our early start tomorrow.

Here, it's another working day for most, while elsewhere in the world it's Christmas Eve to some. We are reloaded into the cage and set off down the main road, where to one side there are sand dunes, coconut trees, and elegant driveways to posh resorts. On the inland side there are bus stops, shoddy wooden huts, and soup kitchens surrounded by sleeping dogs and dust.

We turn up the driveway and pass the nice new community centre, inside of which a gaggle of teenage boys is excitedly trying to be a pop band in, what looks like, a minuscule recording studio-cum-broom cupboard. This whole block looks well cared for and well financed. It centres on a big grassy common with a pond, and pretty hedges skirting the U-shaped lane.

The Saori Workshop is big, new, airy, spacious and well-constructed. A bold banner gives details in English and Thai about their Japanese sponsors. It's almost all open air, which means their manager sleeps there, as do most small café and shop owners. In the main central area about twenty women work on their small portable looms, which fold up easily at the end of each day.

A Japanese monk who had used weaving looms as a tool for meditation sent some looms to this group of grieving widows. It was meant as a therapeutic tool to keep their minds occupied and positive. It helped greatly. They created a group, worked alongside one another, had some companionship and solace, learned skills, created individualised products, and began selling them.

After the tsunami hit, tons of clothing were sent there from all over the world. With everyone in tents, there wasn't room for it all. Ironically, the overload became a problem. They took some of the excess donated clothing, unpicked the threads and wove them into new patterns, more than mindful of the symbolism of trying to reweave the threads of their lives. They also created patchwork fashions. They still use as many recycled and scrap materials as they can: for economic reasons, to be green, and for the emotional symbolism too. They now employ about forty people.

To the left of the main central area are: a sewing room, a shopping and display room, and a storage room. Centre back is a raised platform and shrine, which looks like it can serve for formal occasions, or as a prayer or meditation area. There is information about the group and their charity sponsors linked to a temple in Japan. Next to that is a small office with a computer. Other storage areas burst with rainbows of colourful fabrics, and fat spools of thread, yarn and ribbon. The kitchen is around one corner, and the toilets and showers are around another – behind the ironing area and the sleeping cat.

Everyone is smiling, but shy. They are all female. Jobs here are open to anyone and the management has encouraged men, but only women applied. These are traditionally female crafts. By the same token, a traditional village fishing industry is uniformly all male, and here they were all wiped out in one go. There are many tsunami fishermen's widows, and this group is one of many. First we look at new samples. I buy a few smaller ones, aware of my budget and my storage limitations at home. With my inventory overload, I need to sell that off before I can place any more orders. They know this. They understand. I still feel lousy. They still look hopeful.

Soo finds a great pair of trousers for herself, and we photograph a few dozen new designs. They've mostly expanded their range of shoulder bags, but there are also many more tee shirts, skirts, and trousers than before, as well as a big new range of dolls. UK health and safety rules about importing foreign toys are so strict and hard to understand that I shy away, but I love the idea.

After lunch (fried noodles – very nice) there was more photographing, with completely different sunlight and shadows. The women are nice about having their pictures taken. They nervously try to work normally, but are relieved when we're done. A few let me come close and peer at each unique bit of work on the loom. The young slim ones all sit in the front row. Wiser elders are available in the back row, for the occasional second opinion.

In the office, Soo tries to change their screen saver to pictures of their own products.

I ask whether there will be any public ceremony tomorrow, on the anniversary day. They say yes, but no one knows any details. They'll be home with their families. They're sure there's something, somewhere. I'd like to find out but the internet doesn't have much information. I also don't want to invade their private day, and they're not exactly handing out invitations.

Only weeks ago the shoe was on the other foot when my hometown of Lockerbie marked the twentieth anniversary of the air disaster that still hangs over it like a dark cloud. There were various church services, and something quiet at the cemetery. Newspapers emphasised the phrases "low key" and "private". Everyone local I spoke to said they were tired of repeating this story. They want to leave it to rest. Their grief is a private matter. It's seems similar with these tsunami women.

We look at my website and find their products on it. We all know it's about marketing next, and this is not my strong suit. I also want to upgrade the photography, but this is not the main issue. I see two basic possibilities for next year. If all goes miraculously well, I might place a few small orders the year after that, or my business will close down.

"No!" they cry.

"I'm sorry," I shrug, "but it's a maybe. It's best to know."

They don't want to know. Both Soo and the workshop manager, whom I call Mrs Red, are completely incredulous at the thought of my business ending.

"It will be OK", they say.

I repeat, "It's a possibility. It's best to think of this when you do projections."

"'Where there is a problem, then there is a solution.' The Buddha said so," offers Soo.

"He also said nothing is permanent, that everything

changes, and that sometimes life is disappointing and one needs to accept this, sometimes," I reply, but she does not agree with this interpretation. Perhaps she has studied different themes of Buddhist teachings than I have. Well, we were reading different things on the train. She was into meditation, and I had a humorous travel book and a lot of business files. These are different journeys.

She announces, "It is not a problem. It is an opportunity!"

An opportunity to get the hell out of this dying business, I think. There is no point in arguing. Most small businesses close. It is not simply a matter of positive attitude. It is a fact of economics that small-scale businesses have a tougher road than large-scale ones.

By now I feel faint and sun-stroked, and they create a wonderful little sleeping area for me in a storeroom. I awake later to find Soo learning how to make a patchwork cover for a wallet. Now there's a slightly different light in the room, and I take another series of photographs. Later we are revived with fruit and tea, and coffee and cakes.

Mrs Red has an idea for a sound system so that, besides music, the workers can hear, maybe for an hour each day, teachings of the Buddha about meditation. I ask if the group wants this. Mrs Red says of course they will discuss it, and if the group likes the idea, then they will ask the management.

Soo says, "It's a good idea. Don't you think so too?"

"Are they all Buddhists?"

"No, some are Muslim."

"Wouldn't this be pushing Buddhism onto Muslims?"

"No! It's not a religion. It's international. It's for everybody!"

"Does everybody want it? It sounds like what American Christians do."

"Oh no, it's nothing like them. They dominate. This is just to teach."

I pause.

"What's the harm?" she continues. "They might benefit."

I am glad our host cannot understand us, though she seems to be getting the tone of the debate. I suggest there could also be a time to hear teachings of Muhammad. Soo looks like she thinks this is a joke.

"Why not?" I quote her back to herself. "What's the harm? They might benefit."

Communications don't seem to be connecting at this point. I shrug, "Well anyway, whatever we think, it's their choice." I wonder if it is. Is it the kind of choice where your boss makes a suggestion and you feel that you should agree, even if you don't? I'd like to find out if they did start this, and I'd like to know what the Muslim ladies really think.

I will read Soo's meditation book later, when there's more time. I'd love to recommend my favourite Buddhist teachers and writers to her, like Suzuki's *Beginner's Mind*, anything by the Dalai Lama, and Thich Nhat Han. Maybe that's too much. Maybe it's pushy. Maybe it's exactly what she was doing before, so annoyingly. Maybe it's retaliation. Maybe this is a contest to see who's the best meditator.

We finish the day with a big group photo. We are caged up and rattled off to a little market where we have noodle soup. I've tried all sorts and I have my favourites, but the soup gets ordered before I can tell them what I like. I keep forgetting that it's polite to let them choose for me. If they guess wrong you eat it anyway because otherwise it insults their telepathy, the bread and butter of ordinary local hospitality.

During the meal there is a lot of chat in Thai between them, which I do not ask them to translate. I am awfully hot and tired at this point, and have lost the energy to keep asking. I let them talk and lose myself in my thoughts, which seems to suit them. After all, Soo will have other things to discuss with them. With luck she will also be exporting their goods to other buyers, too. I meditate into my noodles.

I recall an American friend's story about first courting the Japanese woman who is now his beloved wife. He suggested they go to a film and she asked him to choose. He asked her what she liked. She said he should choose. He asked what she liked. She said he should choose. This went in circles until finally she explained the Japanese way: he was supposed to know what she wanted, magically without asking, and he should tell her that's what they're doing.

"Wouldn't it be easier," he asked, "if you just told me?"

I have asked many Japanese people whether this practice causes misunderstandings and they all said it did. One fellow student shrugged, "Of course, all the time. But it's more polite, and that's the main thing." Sounds rather British, actually.

Americans, at the other end of this scale, will lay it all on the table, whether you want them to or not, in the interests of the truth, the whole truth, and nothing but the truth, however gauche or inconvenient this is. This is because to them the main things are the truth and very loud talking. Honesty must always trump kindness, discretion, subtlety and diplomacy.

I am caught between the two styles. I am also very tired. I wish I could take a cool shower, read a book, and fall asleep by nine o' clock. I'd also like a beer – maybe even a large one. Maybe even two. But nice ladies don't do this. I haven't yet explained I am not that kind of nice lady. This evening, I am a beer-seeking grump. I slurp noodles and go over this odd day in my mind. I am brimming with suppressed doubts and questions about my usefulness to this group. I wonder how many visitors they get who love the drama of their story, but aren't actually useful.

Suddenly, before I know it, someone else has paid for the soup – which was delicious, but this makes me feel even worse. Now I realise that on top of everything – being broke, admitting my business is failing, having no loved ones nearby, my house and home and health uncertain, everything uncertain – that I am fighting back tears, because my whole life is rather a mess, but there is no need to burden them with it. I would rather not have to explain. That would just make it worse. I need, in short, some privacy, and a good night's sleep, neither of which is likely tonight.

I have become skilful at pretending to have a bad stomach to have a copious but quiet weep in the toilet room. If you are white in Asia, you can go to the toilet all the time and they don't question it. I decide to wait until we get home.

"Come, we're going now."

"Home?"

"No, somewhere else first."

"Oh. Where?"

"Tsunami Memorial, park and museum."

As the sun starts going down (and this is always exquisite) they take me to the beach where most of the tsunami's devastation occurred. Now it's the site of a public park, garden, memorial, and museum. Now my individual troubles are grains of sand.

We turn off the main road (rattle and convulse off it, more like), and start down a narrow, barely two-lane track, unpaved and rutted.

Our driver, Mrs Elder, points out how far the destruction came inland. Everything we are about to pass, from that point on, has been built afresh. We continue for mile after disturbing mile, every minute my incredulousness mounting at the scale. When we finally get to the sea, I realise the distance that wave covered is mind-bending.

All the new buildings are small, simple and crude. It is not a prosperous area. A few destroyed shells of buildings are left as they were, empty. Several boats that were carried miles inland by the force of the wave have been preserved where they were found, after their hard metal bows sliced through roof after roof after roof. One is high in a tree.

We finally arrive at the sea. Along the coast there is a park and no hotels have been allowed to rebuild there. For now, no one can. There is a lovely paved promenade, benches and play areas, a little market nearby, all nestled next to the pretty blue sky and the pretty blue sea; the same sea that rose up and smashed this place in a matter of minutes.

A walkway runs between two long curving walls shaped like the hull of a boat. Its walls display plaques commemorating some of those who died. Some have photos or quotes or poetry, and they're in many different languages – mostly Thai or German.

The museum's several rooms display floor-to-ceiling photography of the area before and after the Tsunami, as well as the rescue efforts and visits from numerous heads of state, VIPs, and even some celebrities. There is a mass of information about the event and its ongoing aftermath.

Outside, by the souvenir kiosks, a cute pop song is playing. Mrs Sweet's one-year-old girl wants to dance. So, the two of them sway a little on the promenade, until they become too shy to continue. The little girl is sturdy, strong-willed, intelligent, and energetic.

Mrs Elder checks the souvenir stall where they and other survivors' groups have their wares for sale. I ask if anyone moved away from the area after the flood. They say no.

Most people were born here, so they stayed and rebuilt. They wouldn't think of leaving.

We are quiet on the ride back. I thank them. It must be painful for them to keep bringing visitors to these sites. I thank them again.

Back home, I relax with a book in the back room, while Soo relaxes with TV in the front. It sounds like a soap opera, and I have to have a peek.

"I think soap operas look and sound the same all over the world," I suggest. "See, he's the villain no one can trust, but she will fall for his charms. And that couple? So sweet, so in love, something will destroy it. It'll never work."

"Oh no," says Soo. "In a Thai soap opera, the lovers suffer and have many obstacles, but there will always be a happy ending."

I think soaps are just the opposite in Europe. Viewers accept couples getting together, as long as something messes it up later. Is this revealing something about

Thailand and Europe, or about Soo and me, or about both? When I mentioned I might shut down my business next year, she insisted there must be a happy ending.

Asians share beds all the time, but I am not used to sleeping with people I don't know very well. The high-speed fan gave me a painful stiff neck last night, but it's unavoidable. In the middle of the night, I wake up tangled in the sheets, having somehow reversed my position, with my feet near her head. This is sacrilege in

the iconography of their culture. It's about the worst thing you can do, kick someone in the head while they're sleeping, accidentally or not. She took it with admirable patience and grace, and presumably meditated herself back to sleep. Did I snore, too? Probably. Poor Soo. I should have come with earplugs and a warning "Danger: barbarian in the area".

The next morning I am continuing my journey on my own up the coast. Soo will work a bit more with the workshop. My role here is done. We wait by the bus stop, each to go in opposite directions. Mine comes first. She has painstakingly rehearsed me to say the name of my destination, and I do try. She diplomatically suggests it's better if she talks to the driver. My bag and I are heaved in the back, and we wave farewell.

I have always wanted to top up my first-aid training, including water rescue. How do two drowning people save each other? They don't. One of them has to be on land, or they might both drown. That much I remember. So therefore, if my business is drowning, I can't really save theirs. I need to get to dry ground first. I contemplate how to noodle my way through this conundrum, as we bounce our way up the road.

Plummeting Down a Cultural Divide

Cripes, I'm on my own now. It's only a short bus ride today to the town of Bang-Niang along a dusty two-lane coast road. I'm on a local bus, which is not a bus. It's much more fun. It's what they call a song-taew, which means two benches. It's a kind of pickup truck with two long benches in the back facing each other, covered by a tough metal canopy and roof rack. There's a climb-up ladder at the back, which young lads hang off as we travel at high speeds. These vehicles ply a flexible route, go where people need to go, let customers on and off at will, and it's a fraction of the cost of a taxi – if you can explain yourself to the driver. That's a big if, for most visitors.

This one is typically filled with locals and shopping. As usual, everyone's nice about squeezing in one more person and one more bag. There's the usual curious but cute glance or two. As usual, if I smile at this point, everyone smiles back, and then we settle back into private thoughts again. If I say hello to any child – especially in Thai – this always scores a hit and often starts a chat, but today I am subdued.

In terms of our map of Thailand as an elephant's head, we are continuing north, up the west side of its dangling trunk, heading to its chin. I will stop in the town where the tsunami memorial will take place tomorrow, on what they call Boxing Day back in Britain. I don't know anywhere else that calls it that. I think it's to do with masters giving an annual treat to the servants, but this wasn't on my UK citizenship exam.

This bit of coast used to house some of the ritziest resorts in Thailand, and in many places it still does. Wrought iron gates guard white beaches and heavenly gardens that are filled with white people trying to brown themselves. They are beautifully well served by troops of graceful brown people who often cover themselves from head to toe, in an effort to whiten themselves. We are a strange species. I can only add that the local pharmacy sells "Nipple Whitening Cream", and other cosmetics promising similar bleaching properties. It's difficult, in fact, to find any toiletries without "whiteners" anywhere in this nation.

Soon these resorts become fewer and further between, and then there is nothing but thick jungle, until we arrive in the next conurbation, Bang-Niang. This looks like the place where tourists go if they cannot afford Kaolak, the last place I visited. It is not a gardened, palm-studded boulevard. It is a fast-moving highway, surrounded by a hodgepodge of small businesses and a lot of uneven, cracked concrete, with the din of high-speed trucks in the background. It reminds me of London's North Circular Road but with sunshine, or New Jersey's Route 22 but with palm trees.

No matter where you go in most of tourist Thailand, you will probably be dropped off at one of the ubiquitous Seven-Elevens, or "Seven" as it's called here. If you are looking for any sort of bus stop or taxi rank, or anything really, like street vendors or drug dealers, you simply proceed to the nearest Seven. This may not take even thirty seconds. Sometimes there are two branches at either end of one block, or so it seems. I drag my things off the truck and into a clutter of concrete and dust, populated by covered-up Thais and all-too-uncovered fat Europeans. This is my destination. Merry Christmas.

In front of me are the Seven and the road to the sea. Behind me on Terrible Highway is something in a bilious, nauseating green called Motel Reg. I yank out the handle of my pull-along suitcase, put the motel and the highway behind me, and trundle down Seven Street towards the water.

It's not far to the Welcome Guesthouse, pre-booked for me by colleagues, and it's very easy to find because it is vividly festooned with alternating garlands of German and

Swiss flags. OK, it's late afternoon, and I am not shopping around for places now. This will do for tonight. I venture in and meet the German husband and Thai wife who run the place.

There's a mix-up with my name. They recognise it, but for some reason were expecting an English man and are confused at getting me instead. This is OK, they decide. I can have his room since he didn't show up, and is also fictitious.

The room is not ready but it will be soon. I am invited to sit down and peruse the menu. It is three times the price of anything I have eaten so far, even in the city. I peruse as well as I can while coaxing my eyebrows back into a polite position. It is delicious and plentiful, but I can't get over how just up the road I can eat this, for a third of the price.

At each of the tables sits one man. They're all white – very white. They are various ages. Some look like students, others like well-padded pensioners. Most are reading something in German. None of them are talking to each other. Every single one is smoking. The owners' little boy, about two years old, is happily running up to each of them in turn to show off a toy or tug at a sleeve. Each in turn looks, smiles, and maybe pats the little head before going straight back to reading or smoking, or both. Seven different little trails of smoke arise, one from each table.

On every table are brown sauce, ketchup, and ashtrays.

On the menu are wiener schnitzels and bratwurst, as well as the usual modified-for-tourists pseudo Thai stuff. Later I learn that not all their clientele is German or Swiss. Some are Japanese. I'm going to fit in just great.

Mrs Welcome tells me my room is ready, and asks is there anything else I need? I need to find out when and where the memorial ceremony is, the next day. I mean the public one. She does not know and asks her husband, whose English is better anyway. He says it used to be on the beach (he gestures vaguely down the road with his cigarette), but not now. He is not sure where it is this year.

Time to drag my stuff upstairs. I can hardly lift it, and it is not that heavy. I am just so very worn out. Mrs Welcome apologises about the key, which she says is a copy of a copy of something that you have to wiggle a lot to get the door open. In actuality, the lock is so wiggly a toothpick would open it. I thank her, drop my bags, shut the door, and feel tremendous relief.

I haven't had a second to myself in I don't know how long.

It's so lovely to take my time with the settling in rituals: the sniffing around of new digs, the setting up of the bedside table with those things which must sleep by your side, and the territorialising of sink and ablution areas. There are things you do anywhere – home or away – and these things must happen, like the shower and the laundry.

Checklist time. Happy column: tidy room, desk and chair, fan, bedside table. Not so happy column: toilet and shower are down the hall, despite request and high price. Key in lock is very easy to pick open, and there is no lock-up. It is also an oven, twenty degrees hotter than the hallway, with only one window, and that is facing a wall. There is hideous music drifting up from the place next door, which will be a late night scene, naturally. Earplug job, for sure. Possibly eyeshades too. I spotted loads of blinking fairy lights and mirror balls.

Downstairs check list? Boy cute, clientele awful. Pool table fantastic, but the men hog it and it costs money – appalling. Oh, this is all silly, it's only for a day or two, come on. Remember the occasion tomorrow. Pay your respects. For now, go look around, find some grub, meet the neighbours, and go to bed early. Then put on your best clothes first thing tomorrow. Tomorrow we pay respect to the dead.

This is where I get rather a large surprise. It all happens so suddenly. One minute I am sorting clothes, and plop myself down on the (quite good) mattress. The next I collapse in floods of tears. I now see they've been storing up for days, actually more like months. I've been putting on brave and polite smiles, but that only works for so long. The force of this storm is shocking, but it's over quickly. Necessary, if exhausting.

I was right not to make any more business appointments yet. I have a pained conscience about those appointments I cancel. This is no longer a business trip. Where there is no money, there is no business. I am officially now On Leave for Rest and Recuperation.Quite a radical decision. Now what?

"Food," is the obvious answer, and it comes from deep inside. I pull myself together and get out the door, locking the humorously flimsy lock while reassuring myself the owners' room is right next door, which may or may not be a theft-proofing factor. My laptop is worth very little, but I'd be heartsick to lose her. It, that is, it. I did not name the thing.

Mrs Welcome delicately wonders if I might want dinner later? I'm not sure, but I'd like to go for a walk, I say. Maybe later, I say, but I will most certainly look for somewhere else to have dinner. I proceed past all the wieners and don't look back.

Funny, not once so far has anyone said "Merry Christmas". And today is Christmas Day. I don't celebrate it, but it still strikes me as unusual, especially from all the Thais who usually have to shovel it out to the tourists. Maybe it's a Jewish place? That would be a refreshing change at Christmas. Somehow I don't think so though. I think those were classic porky Teutonic bratwursts I saw on those plates – and we are what we eat, after all.

Swiss and German flags are everywhere. You could easily forget which continent you're on. Seven Street, the road to the beach, is lined with pizzerias, sausage houses, plastic toyshops, and rack upon rack of garish shirts, holiday hats, and bikinis. The only Thai people are the ones working in the tourist shops. The beach is filled with bratwurst men, with not a single Thai person in sight. If it weren't so cluttered, it would be eerie. There is also a lot of rubbish strewn about, such as burger wrappers and beer cans.

Also at every street corner are emergency information posts, showing you which way to run in case of flood. There are stripes carved up each post, colour-coded, to show the relative safety of being one kilometre away, or two or five or ten, and therefore how many seconds you have to run the length of a football pitch to survive. The post is not round but four-sided, and the information is in Thai, German, English, and Japanese.

For my personal tourist dollar, and in terms of my evening meal, this is wiener heaven and rice hell. Where can I eat? To find anything I can stomach I must turn away from the sea, go back across Terrible Highway, scurry past lurid Motel Reg, and wander into the modest and hidden bits of town where the really good food is – and where some locals probably wish I wouldn't find them. However, there is always one nice noodle lady who doesn't mind feeding me, so long as I look harmless and docile, say hello in Thai, look bathed and am wearing sleeves.

I find today's lady fairly easily. She speaks very little English, but exclaims "Oo!" when I pronounce "vegetable noodle soup" intelligibly in Thai. Her young daughter appears around the corner. I say hello. The girl says hello and runs away giggling. She reappears, and we repeat this. We repeat it more quickly, and with more giggling. Mother Soup clearly approves, so Toddler and I repeat this a few thousand times.

Mother Soup then opens her home to me properly by snapping on the telly and a cheesy soap opera. We all settle in happily. You really can understand the story, without knowing a word of what they're saying. Soap opera characterisation is perhaps the one common language human beings share. It's like today's silent films being readable anywhere. This theory requires another book a specialist must write.

Mother Soup brings a bowl of bean sprouts (juicy and thirst-quenching) and chillies (small, scary and I don't touch them). These are to munch while I wait the whole two minutes it takes to make the soup, and the three it takes to cool down. I am so very happy to eat in a place like this. Even more so since she did not hang out any Christmas tinsel, unlike the wiener joints.

I love choosing which book comes travelling with me. There is usually one by my side and a backup in the suitcase. The travel guide with maps doesn't count. I mean the stuff I love reading. This time I am travelling with Pete McCarthy's *McCarthy's Bar*. How I adore and miss him and the books he would have kept writing if he were still with us. I'd have bought one after the next without fail. This trip more than any I needed to pack an all-time favourite so that whatever mood I got into, I could count on someone to make me raise a smile.

Here he's explaining how much he likes eating out alone with a book, especially in the evening. He does not feel pathetic. He is only pretending to read and is eavesdropping on everybody else. Bravo, I say. I do this too. It's great fun. I pretend to write letters when really I'm writing down everything that's happening in the room. Of course, I can only guess from the tone of voice what's going on. It's a bit like following foreign soap operas.

Pete goes from bar to bar, but I don't really drink much without getting stomach ache and falling asleep early. I don't spend much time in bars. I've never found it socially straightforward to go into a bar all on my own. That's when it hits me. I will go from noodle bar to noodle bar instead. This somehow gives me a road map for the rest of the trip. Follow the Noodle Trail. If in doubt, seek the Noodle Connection. Food is going to answer all my questions, I have decided. My grocery list is my map. Follow not men into their saloon bars, but women to their noodle bars.

Mother's noodle soup, by the way, comes with extra crispy fried garlic, and sweet yet pungent dark green kale with sharp scarlet veins. Removing some of this afterwards with my toothpick, as is the custom, I recall the phrase "noodling it out" means to gently work out a puzzle, or untie a knot, as in, "let's noodle out the answer". My thoughts and path are both noodle-shaped at the moment. I shall noodle my way through the female network.

"Delicious," I tell her as I pay, and she giggles and bows. I point vaguely around the neighbourhood and say, "Bungalow? Small bungalow? Four hundred bhat? Five hundred baht?" At first she doesn't get it, and then a light goes on. I have just plugged into the Noodle Network.

She drapes a graceful hand over my arm and guides me to the side of her little patch, waving towards a tiny alley a few doors down. "Bungalow," she says, "small." Then I see the very small sign for Sweet Mango Bungalows. A food name. I walk straight for it.

It's one of those little alleys you could easily miss. You'd never know anything is back here. The alley opens up into a small courtyard with two resorts. For some, the word "resort" conjures up grand, luxurious images. Here, it means one guy has a few bungalows and his sister has a few more across the road. There's a little garden, too.

The Sweet Mango door is opened by a nice fellow who got out of the shower specially – suds still all over him and a smallish towel around his lower half. The Sweet Mango Bungalows are full. They look a bit too smart for me anyway, all air-con and fresh paint. He asks me to sit while he rings his sister, who runs the simpler huts across the way, called Fair House Resort. She'll be right over. Would I like to wait? Oh yes I would.

He adjusts his towel and leans on a chair, asking what business I am in. I tell him, to cut a long story short, that it's importing silver jewellery from Thailand to the UK. However this year, all of a sudden the middle class women of the UK have no such money for gift shops. How is business for him? It's down by more than half, but that's better than most of his neighbours. They rebuilt fast, cheap, and furiously after the tsunami damage – now four years ago. The worst hit business in his extended family was their rubber tree plantation, and that's nothing to do with the storm. Global prices are literally starving small farmers. Sister Mango arrives and shows me a pleasant hut, up on the usual stilts to stay cool and to be above rats, snakes, rabid dogs, etc. It has a private (cold) shower, a fan, and a small balcony with chair and clothesline, all for six pounds per day (that's eight euros or ten dollars). This is less than half of what I am paying for my noisy wiener oven. The views are of palm trees and the garden. It is a surprisingly quiet courtyard, and most of my neighbours are friendly Dutch bikers. I am home. I pay in advance. I will move in first thing tomorrow morning.

I stroll back considerably more relaxed, past the Porsche Bar, with a front fender as décor. I don't know what Pete would say. Too much chrome and glass for his taste, perhaps, but I think he'd have a drink with them, and get both a laugh and a good chunk of a chapter out of it.

I breeze back into the Welcome Guesthouse, past a clutch of sleepy, beery, fair-haired gentlemen, and I wave at Mrs Welcome and her nice Niece Helper in the kitchen. I climb the stairs, wiggle-waggle the lock with the ill-fitting eighty millionth copy of this key, and enter the sweltering furnace with the Donna Summer disco soundtrack.

I shower, tidy up and pack. I have still not found out exactly where this ceremony is, but it is tomorrow, and it is somewhere nearby. I have a couple of hours to work out how to record pictures and sound, and also take notes and not trip, faint or mortally offend anyone.

As I fall asleep, I wonder what to do tomorrow? The question circles like a hawk over a bay – round and round – as I drift away into a steamy coma. I've blocked out the nightclubs with earplugs, and the neon signs and fairy lights with eyeshades. Soon it's like drifting backwards into a dark, hot, but safe little cave. We will try to try to be ready for tomorrow. We will find out what the best way is to go about tomorrow. Any advice? Anybody?

Hello?

NOODLE TRAILS

Trying to Try to Get Ready to Get Ready

"Just go."

This is the first cogent sentence to traverse my brain upon waking. "Just go," it repeats. "Just go. Just look, just listen. Just go!"

In no time, I am packed and ready to pay and go, but no one is up at the Welcome Guesthouse. They are a Stay Up Late Place and therefore not a Breakfast Place. No signs of life until lunch, I expect. No send-off coffee, not a noodle in sight, all deathly calm. Eventually Niece Helper shuffles in and adds up my bleary bill. By the way, I never had that cola. I never would. I hate the stuff and all it stands for. But I want to go, so I pay. I treat whoever it was that drank the evil brew. She sweetly unlocks the back gate to let me out, locks it behind me, and I hope she goes straight back to bed.

I trundle along Terrible Highway for a few blocks: past a lawyer, an internet place, several travel agencies, and a row of noodle joints, then turn down Sweet Mango Alley. It's bumpy and rutted, and strewn with building rubble. I long for a travelling bag with both rolling wheels and rucksack straps, as if I could lift that now! Old Faithful has been with me a long time.

I bump up to the Fair House breakfast porch. Two laid-back Dutch biker couples are finishing an English breakfast prepared by Sister Mango and Younger Cousin Mango, both of whom are very cheerful. Instant coffee is produced instantly, and my breakfast put on the grill. Too bad it's English. They're puzzled to be asked about rice vegetable soup, two beautiful bowls of which steam to one side, but to which I am not entitled. Younger Cousin gets the key and my bags while I dine amongst the tattooed. I'm feeling better already.

Sister remembers my question from the other night and produces a hand-drawn map to the Boat Park. She also gives me a small leaflet detailing the day's events, mostly in Thai but there are a few bits in English. She explains that the public memorial ceremony will not be on the beach this year, as it was in the past, because now the entire beach is owned by a string of private hotels. There is no public beach left. The hotels jointly decided the bereaved could relocate. Perhaps it might interfere with the cooking time of their pink, roasting customers. She did not say that last bit.

In the morning is a private wreath-laying ceremony for those directly involved. After lunch, the area is open to the public. The main presentations are in the evening. This means I have time to settle into my new gaff, get ready, and even go look for a sun hat. I faint without them, so I need to do this early in the day. A scorcher is already in the making. Soon I am fortified with greasy eggs and dry white bread. I'm ready.

For research purposes only, I wander through the lanes to the sea and find various simple hats for five and six pounds. I try a big place on Terrible Highway and see a straw one I rather like. He wants ten pounds. I turn to go. He runs after me, grabbing my shoulder and spinning me around, demanding, "How much you pay? How much you pay?" This is very uncharacteristic of Thai sales people; in fact, completely out of character. Then I see he is not Thai. I do not like being grabbed by strangers so I exit quickly. I pass by later and still like the hat, but can't hand my money to that sort of behaviour. One of the reasons I come here is because, by and large, people behave beautifully to their guests. Even to the worst of the idiots.

Now it's getting hot and I need cheap hat advice. I go back to the guesthouse and find both Sister and Cousin folding laundry. They ask where I've been, as Thais love to do – "Where you go?" I tell them, adding that I can't find a simple cheap hat and I don't like Seven (neither do they). Younger goes inside and comes out with a hat to lend. What a sweetie. The hat is unusual. It is extravagantly wide-brimmed, with a lavish, long ribbon, all in frothy bridesmaid pink.

In truth, Thai hospitality offers millions of thoughtful little moments like this. Perhaps they're also extra kindly because of the occasion. They may think I am one of the bereaved. Again, what leaps to mind is the parallel with Lockerbie. Before I moved there, I visited for years, several times a year, and always at the end of the year. I escaped London's Christmas by going far north to a Buddhist centre in rural Scotland. To me this was the obvious solution to the Christmas question.

One year, due to blizzards, very few supplies got through to the centre and its three hundred guests, and things were getting desperate. Once the roads cleared I offered to drive into the nearest town, Lockerbie, to get provisions.

At the supermarket checkout, boy scouts were helping bag groceries. I didn't realise it was the time of the Lockerbie bombing anniversary. There's always a ceremony at the cemetery, foreign (mostly American) visitors and press coverage, which is always local but sometimes national and international as well, depending on the anniversary. I didn't know any of that. However, the moment these boys heard my American accent, they suddenly went quiet. So did the cashier. The boys could not make eye contact with me. They bagged my things with their heads bowed. The cashier, a lady about my age, chatted a bit, gently, and quickly worked out I was not connected to the crash. I was there visiting friends. I was there for happy reasons. I holidayed there a lot and thought it was a beautiful area.

They all relaxed and quizzically bagged up my twenty sacks of flour, twenty cartons of eggs, twenty cartons of milk, etc. I joked I was making the biggest chocolate fudge cake ever, enough for three hundred. The cashier was impressed. I probably said it was for the Buddhist place up the road, which now I know is not something you admit to absolutely all of the good folk of Lockerbie. It's possible not all of Scotland embraces Lord Buddha, I'm told.

Bedecked in Cousin's sun hat, it's time to get ready for the ceremony.

On any long trip, one can only really pack One Nice Thing. This year it's my golden outfit. It always gets glowing admiration, although it's simple cotton. It's the lovely colour, the simple lines, and the excellent custom-tailored fit by some delightful Nepali girls in Kathmandu.

The thing is, it's in a Hindu style, which means most Thai people think I'm Muslim. This complicates matters unnecessarily, but it's the best I've got. Besides, this design is very flattering to the figure, even with the Barbie pink bridesmaid's hat. What's more, even Barbie has security issues. Underneath my clothes, I've hidden my money belt deep inside the billowing trousers and a small drawstring bag around my neck, with my room key and an extra stash of cash.

In, on and around my rucksack is a water bottle, notebook and pens, camera with extra-long zoom lens, tape recorder, sweet snacks, and a map. This is over the big golden Indian cotton shawl, over a golden flowing dress and fulsome trousers, topped with an absurdly frilly pink hat. Do I look like a sweaty, insane, bag lady? Of course I do. Do I look like that sun-stroked, drug-addled Italian nut we met at the bus stop? Perhaps not that bad. More like his American cousin. Nonetheless, if I do look insane, please could it keep away weird men and pickpockets? Surely there are perks to looking like a mad bag lady?

That's not even the worst of it. I am not with a group. That's phenomenally unusual around here. Right away that marks me out as a mad bag lady, or a Muslim extremist, or an old burned-out druggie hippy, or a silly lady do-gooder in a Scarlett O'Hara hat, cut adrift from her charity volunteer post.

I am strangely nervous about going at all. I am trying not to falter in my moral support of the Saori women. How humbling that they're surviving their tsunami far better than I'm surviving mine.

I think it's the last time I'll travel with a camera this heavy. Everyone else, except the professionals, is on lightweight digitals. I can do my public talks about Fair Trade on PowerPoint if requested. However, many community halls and churches have nothing but walls and chairs, no fancy projectors, and I can't afford one either. That's when I use an old-style slide projector. Some may scoff, but if the scale is large enough, I can cover the entire wall with bold, vivid, colourful images of these faraway people and places, and the impact is dramatic enough to make the audience gasp out loud. This is even with nice Scottish ladies, who are normally quite gentle and dignified, in my experience, especially the churchy ones. But today my back hurts, from toting an excellent zoom lens.

The public talks have a very satisfying result, whatever the format. For example, the Saori girls couldn't believe it when I reported to them that there are ladies in Scotland who are asking how they're doing. How are the kids? How old are they now? Are they managing with their businesses? I travel, I take pictures, I gather stories, and I come home and tell people what I saw on the other side of the world. I'm delivering postcards from one set of mums to another. "That's why you're here, you ninny," I scold myself. "Now get out there."

Right. Last minute outer rucksack pocket check: first-aid and toilet kit, loo roll, spare water and juice, spare pens, paper, batteries...did I say spare water? Check. Now, chant the motto. I will not faint, I will not faint, I will not faint. I have fainted before, which is why I chant this. Silently, not out loud. I am nervous but not totally nuts.

I exit with a quick wave to the Mango family. There is time for lunch up the road. I return to Mother Soup and

Toddler and simply say, "Same, same", since now we have a relationship. She puts on the morning soap opera this time, does the routine, gestures to a table like I've been coming here for years, even calls Toddler to come out and play. I put my fabulous hat carefully to one side. Toddler stares at it.

Mother Soup brings extra bean sprouts, saying about the weather, "Hot, hot," and I answer, "Yes, yes." I show her my pocket language guide and point to the word "market". She nods enthusiastically. I display a list of the days of the week and she selects both Saturday (which is tomorrow – hurrah) and Sunday. On her fingers she denotes it opens at eight and closes maybe three o'clock, is up Terrible Highway, over the bridge, and on the right. 'It's big,' she gestures, 'you can't miss it.'

None of this is in English. It's all mimed and eager and clear. She is proud of her local market, which bodes well. The Noodle Network just gave me a map to their market, tomorrow's lunch and maybe a new hat, if I'm lucky. I adore a market. I love a morning of strolling and ogling.

I am closer to the Boat Park and the Memorial than I realise. It's a short walk back up Terrible Highway, past Seven and shabby Motel Reg, and over a small bridge over a small river. There are welcoming desks at the turn-off to a long dusty track. It's flanked by rows of stalls and tents, each housing different photographic or information displays. It's mostly in Thai but some headlines are in English.

There are videos showing water safety courses now taught to children in all schools, with documentation from the Ministry of Education. Further along are stalls selling goods produced by new workshops that sprang up after the disaster, like the Saori and Padang groups.

This group is selling some lovely woodcarving, which can often weaken me. The clincher is that this richly grained coconut and mango wood – as with the Padang people – is turned into useful things like plates and bowls, candle holders and lamps, some of which I buy. I have never gone wrong with one of these as a gift. I keep the rest in my kitchen, if not.

I buy a DVD about the event and the area's reconstruction. There is also a magazine with a commemorative picture essay and the most dramatic photographs from the news coverage at the time, all of which is shocking yet moving and sobering.

Now come the ubiquitous cold drink stalls, the last before crossing the pretty, rickety little plank bridge, steep and curvy, like a semi-circle. The path curves to the left, leading to a large grassy field known as the Boat Park, so-named for its hilltop display of the Royal Navy vessel that was carrying members of the Thai royal family at the time of the flood. It may well have landed near this very spot. Most of those on board survived, but the King's twenty-one-year-old grandson was lost. Ever since, his mother remains the prime sponsor and patron of many post-tsunami building efforts.

The boat itself is painted a fresh pale grey. It looks like it could hold perhaps twenty or thirty people. Workers start stringing white fairy lights around its edges. Next to the boat is an entire pavilion dedicated to the young prince, filled with floral displays and photographs of him and his family, especially his clearly doting mother. These exhibits are open all afternoon, while teams of workers set up plastic chairs for the hundreds they expect that evening.

Next to the stage, other workers set up canopies and dozens of cushioned, white linen-covered chairs for the VIP pavilion, to shade and house the speechmakers, local dignitaries, Minister for Education and their entourages. A third canopied area is dedicated to the representatives from the three main religious groups involved, Buddhist, Muslim, and Christian. Each has sent a delegation with a leader who will offer their blessings.

The PA is being tested. A banner reads "Tsunami Survivors, Fourth Anniversary. Going Forward Together. 2008." At the other end of the field, packs of media men have instinctively parked themselves around a swamp. They hover, pace, smoke, and glare. It's early. Only sparse groups meander about, read displays, admire photos, pause for thought, and provide little action for the cameras.

Families and larger groups pose for pictures and take thoughtful strolls. Conversations are quiet, private. It's sweet, somehow. There are shy moments of eye contact with everyone, though, more than one sees normally. There's a kind of understanding. There is a lot of gentle kindness in the air. From high noon onwards, the steaminess thickens. Mid-afternoon, rain buckets down ferociously. Some people flee for temporary shelter. Others flee altogether.

The main ceremony isn't for hours, so I flee home too, home to Chez Mango. There's time for more sleep, more noodles, and more trying to try to feel ready. I still don't entirely know what I'm getting ready for. I'll just close my eyes for a few minutes. Then I'll just go.

After the Deluge

That evening, the return to the Boat Park has a completely different feel. The light is just starting to soften. It's merely intensely humid and hot, instead of suffocatingly humid and hot. There are three seasons here: hot, very hot, and hot and wet. There is no "not hot", except at the top of a mountain that's way up north.

The crowd steadily trickles in with a feeling of anticipation. It's that buzz of a special occasion. Gone is the strolling gait. People are walking with intent. Some are very dressed up, as if for church or temple, but not everyone, and there is certainly no feeling that it matters. There is a remarkable cross-section of human beings taking part.

Many small groups seem to cling to each other. There isn't really very much talk from group to group, but there are many tiny glances, hints of smiles, and warm looks of sympathy, however subtle, from every passer-by to the next. There are hundreds and hundreds of them, all affected somehow by this event. All these people who do not know each other have something extraordinary in common.

The boat has now been fully strung with white lights. Next to the main stage gather all the groups who will perform: several squads of dancers, the Navy jazz band, and several school groups too. Chairs are filling up. The media boys finally have more to do, and they are covering ground, just like me and a lot of other people. I love photography, especially this kind – on the hoof. There are dozens of us. Sometimes it's hard to tell who's a professional with national TV or newspapers, and who are the well-heeled dads using a broadcast quality family camcorder. The entire event is going to be very well preserved from every possible angle. It is interesting to see there are clearly some Thais are on a higher economic plane than their neighbours.

I aim to write whatever I can about this event, and yet am haunted by not being exactly sure why I'm here. I've often been advised to be a journalist, but I could never report news. I could never be objective enough. However, as celebrated war correspondent Martha Gellhorn once said, "Forget all that objectivity crap." Just say what you see. Tell the story that's right in front of you. OK, this I can do. This I can at least try to try to do.

So I, too, circle the area again and again from every possible angle, taking notes on paper and tape and clicking away. The media hounds can plainly see I am not "properly" covering the event, but am at best some wannabe "freelancer", i.e. an unemployed writer, which is true. The families, on the other hand, clearly think I am a pro, which could be due to the sheer heft of the camera. When they hear English, they say, "Are you BBC?" I used to work there as a sound editor, but not now. "No, I am not BBC", I tell them. I am independent (unemployed).

Here's how I tell everybody apart. The real media guys are in jeans and tee shirts. Dads are in smart dress trousers and white pressed shirts. Whereas earlier in the afternoon I was in a yellow and pink Muslim bridesmaid ensemble, now it's dark and I lost the hat. The new fashion statement is Not Mad Just Odd.

The main banner is in English, with Thai and Japanese subtitles. Most of the speeches are in Thai: speech upon speech upon speech, by local officials, event organisers, the Education Minister, the local Mayor, all herded on and off by two pretty female presenters. There is no shortage of speakers. On they pour like ants. By now kids are playing up and the rest of the spectators have begun to chat lightly amongst themselves. I think it's sort of a given, some evenings are full of speeches that aren't meant to be heard, but tolerated with due respect.

There are traditional dance groups with beautiful sarongs, fabulous gold headdresses and elaborate make-up, rotating their graceful wrists like unfolding lotus petals. The cool big band from the Thai Navy does loads of jazz classics extremely well, mostly early bebop. The King of Thailand is a great fan of jazz music, is himself a fine saxophonist, and has even released an album playing his own compositions. I'm sure people have tried to get him to jam with Bill Clinton. I'd certainly like to think so.

There is now the religious blessing, which is conducted by representatives of the three different faiths. Each group in turn sends their speaker to intone a prayer and then join the delegation in a song. I did not understand any of the languages they used, but the sound of prayer and chanting is remarkably similar. As for the songs, I'd say that musically speaking (and I do mean purely musically speaking) the Muslims rocked, the Buddhists grooved, and the Christians were slightly limp and lacklustre. They, at least, had a few women participants – and were the only group that did – but the lonely Kumbaya style guitar and struggling warble was just plain painful. I don't know any other job where you have to sing in public even if you really cannot sing. It isn't fair to anyone.

It all concludes with a Buddhist traditional invocation to make a dedication to extend all available blessings to as many other beings as possible. We are invited by the pretty presenter ladies at the microphone, first in Thai and then in English, to each make our own private dedications and prayers, while we light a lantern to launch into the night sky, along with hundreds of others. We will send our prayers out into the world, all together. A huge yet kindly army of volunteers now disperses throughout the crowds, in that meticulously organised fashion for which Thai hospitality is world famous. They distribute hundreds of huge golden lanterns. It looks like a magic anthill has sprung into action.

Magic lanterns, or make-a-wish lanterns, or so-called Chinese lanterns, are the shape and size of large barrels, nearly as tall as I am, over a metre around. They work like mini hot air balloons, or rather, hot air cylindrical lampshades. The wire frame is covered in strong, textured, golden translucent paper, with a wire contraption at the bottom holding a ring of compressed paper soaked in flammable oil.

Normally they are sold on the beach to tourists, lit and floated out to sea, where they rot or wash up elsewhere. On any New Year – European, Chinese, Thai, any will do – they are sent up en masse, which visually is spectacularly enchanting. It's a beautiful and touching choice for this part of the memorial ceremony. People are all over the field, waiting for the heat to rise enough to lift their lit lanterns into the air. Soon they start, at first one by one, to float up into the night sky, followed by hundreds of others, creating a massive sparkling spiral that disappears into infinity above. Tonight is unlike anything I will ever see again.

A girl materialises before me. She offers me a lantern, and indicates she will help me light it. Most of the time I wish I spoke more Thai, but this is one occasion when that's not needed. Suddenly, I know why I'm here. My dad's face springs to mind. He died more than twenty years ago when I was in my late twenties. I can picture him in a foggy silhouette. Inside, I say, "OK Dad, this one's for you," and imagine how he might wave back.

The girl now shows me how to open up the lantern to its full huge size and steady it while she lights the burner-ring. This takes a little patience. We sway with it, when the breeze picks up. She has it lit. Now we hold it together and collect the warmth.

The breeze bobs us about, like a subtle dance. I reminisce about kite flying when we were kids. While still imagining Dad's silhouette, immediately I see he is joined, in my mind's eye, by my two departed aunties, a late uncle and, sweetly enough, even a brother-in-law I didn't know as well, but surely felt for his kids when he died younger than expected. All four grandparents are there. I can picture my two favourite music teachers from college and secondary school, a favourite piano teacher and a favourite choir leader. There's a beloved childhood neighbour, a dear pal I lost about ten years ago, and a childhood classmate who died in a fire when we were teens. Everybody arranges themselves in a kind of photographic group portrait, in which they wave and smile, or give me a thumbs-up.

They're waving goodbye. Now it dawns on me what this is about. I never had much chance to say goodbye to these people, either before or after they died. I have not been able to attend the last few major funerals in my family. I was too far away, and news arrived too late. I have been travelling to faraway places for some years now. Some of these places need days and days to reach and even more to get back. It's as if I fell asleep years ago in a rowing boat and woke up totally adrift, out at sea, with no land in sight. I wonder if sometimes the news of a distant funeral doesn't really sink in fully. It might be like when people are lost at war, or in some distant place where they are never seen again. It's left hanging in the air somehow. One hasn't grasped it. You need a ceremony. Oh my goodness. That's why I'm here. I am borrowing their funeral because I missed so many of my own. This will be my private memorial and goodbye to my people, my clan, my gang who have gone ahead of me.

Thank you. That's my main thought. Thank you, thank you, thank you. Thanks for everything you gave me. I dedicate this evening to anyone and everyone who has had moments when they feel afraid to die, and pained to leave life and loved ones behind. Please help us seek bravery and calm, when it's time to take our turn.

The lantern becomes weightless. It slips from my hand and floats upwards, dances a little, and joins the many hundreds of others, winding slowly upwards, into a vast milky way of golden lights, disappearing into the swirling blackness forever. All around me on the ground, more and more lanterns are being handed out to the crowd. People are tying them together into groups to represent families.

Nearby, a frail elderly man has stepped to one side. He is white-haired and moves carefully. He waits for the lantern to warm and leaves his hand gracefully. He waves to it and blows it a subtle little kiss, and instantly I can picture a lady about his age and height.

By now it's drizzling steadily. I'm drenched and a flood of tears is inevitable. Then it's as if a huge ocean wave crashes over me. My knees collapse like jelly as my head spins. Somehow later, and I don't know how, I end up in the now-empty VIP area, flung over a wet linen chair. The crowds are filing down the path back to the main road, huddling against the rain or just walking normally through it, getting soaked. Workers are clearing up chairs. I stagger along behind the others.

We wind our way back up the now extremely muddy lane, back over the little curvy bridge now even more trodden, rickety and mud-caked. We disperse along Terrible Highway. I bring up the rear, a bit weak at the knees, and glad that the long scarves of Indian dresses are so handy as towel and tissue.

Police clear the last of the traffic. I need to sit down as soon as possible. My knees are about to give way. It's a distinctive feeling, and I promise you it sticks in the memory.

I cross Terrible Highway and head straight into the first café opposite. Though it's busy, there's a small table at the back (perfect), a bit secluded (ditto), next to the fan (thank you) and the foreign language bookshelf (extra big thank you with kiss). I get to the chair in time, and soon look so normal you'd never know I'll be incapable of standing unaided for at least another fifteen minutes. That's long enough for a beer and noodles, I think, as someone brings me a menu. Then I can stroll home, go to sleep early, and marvel at this remarkable day.

That's when I look around. Oh no. It's a wiener joint. German flags, large pink clientele, bratwurst everywhere, the lot. My prayer comes down in tone: feed me soon and get me out of here.

The guy at the next table is looking at me. Asian, stocky, maybe forty, not shy. He slides his chair directly opposite mine.

"Hello," he says, "I saw you at the ceremony, taking pictures. Are you a journalist?"

"No," I answer, "I'm a travel writer."

"Are you going to write about this?"

"Oh yes. And you? Are you a journalist?"

"Yes," he nods, "I'll write about it. I just don't know where to sell it. Do you?"

"No," I answer. "No idea."

He laughs, and shrugs sympathetically. "It's always like this. But I got an interview with the Minister of Education."

"Any good?"

He shrugs. "He didn't say much."

"Do you work for…?"

"I work for *The Democratic Voice of Burma*," he says, "as senior news reporter."

My mouth falls open, a car horn hoots, and he jumps to his feet. "That's my taxi," he says. "Here, have this." He hands me a book. It has his face on the cover. He asks for my name, writes a dedication on the inside cover, and signs his name: Htet Aung Kyaw. Then he says good luck and is gone.

It's the story of his life. It's called *Far From Home: Twenty Years in Exile*. I'm stunned. I stare at this gift, so unexpected. It's self-published, and also available on the internet. He's got an extraordinary CV as a freedom fighter and a journalist, and has had to live in exile from Burma for the last twenty years. He works on behalf of the cause of Burmese democracy, which is a very hard battle indeed – and not a very hopeful one, sad to say.

Maybe the grammar is not perfect in places, and maybe it wasn't edited by anyone who speaks English as their first language, but this doesn't matter. Reclaim my BA; I don't care. This has a compelling introduction, both astonishing and inspiring. I get all this from a few pages, as I eat what I am sad to report are the worst noodles I ever ate in Thailand. They are soggy, diluted mush in greasy dishwater.

He walked right up to me and gave me his book. I've

heard and read about self-publishing, and here is the most vivid sample I've ever seen. He has a story and he wants it out there. Now my story may not be so brave or extreme, but I too have stories. I've been collecting lots of stories from lots of amazing people I've met along my Noodle Trail. We all have our stories.

A few more pages in, he's in charge of several battalions of freedom fighters and has watched a friend die that day. He was just some guy at the next table. I'm on page four and I can't believe the life he's lead.

I'll admit that during my last few somewhat tough years, it did occur to me that there are people who reach a certain point, beyond which they reach for pills and gin and they just want done with it. I've never understood that impulse, though now I can almost understand how people get driven beyond the pale. Even almost understanding that disturbs me. All these thoughts linked up with the image of blades of grass. What's another blade of grass? I hound myself, over and over. If there's one blade of grass more or less in the world, does that matter so much? If I'm here or not, here for a little while or a long while, does that matter so much? Maybe it's time to let new shoots take my place?

Dad springs to mind. He presents me with the junior microscope and white lab coat I wanted for my tenth birthday. He invites me to look down the lens. What's under the microscope? It's a blade of grass, of course. It's beautiful, too, of course, with luminous colours, tiny veins and complex, beaded detail. It's exquisite and magical. It's unique, and simultaneously an absolutely identical twin to trillions of others. Herein lies the paradoxical lesson presented to me by the surrealistic new double act of my dad and a Burmese journalist. Anything on earth is utterly beautiful, if you look closely enough.

Now I don't even care if my noodles are cold. What an extraordinary gift! A sea of gratitude buoys me up. I've also had a beer on a severely dehydrated and empty stomach. So, I order another one, to counter-toast all my allies and comrades-in-arms across the world who have lent me moral support. I wish them the same and more in return. They are my clan on earth. Cheers, guys.

After I finish the disgusting noodle-porridge mush with a bit of a tooth picking, I indulge in a favourite ritual. I peruse the foreign language bookshelf, which is mostly in German. I try to noodle out the English offerings, but there are only two. There is a misery memoir by the mother of soap star Martine McCutcheon, of *EastEnders*, about how she survived childhood abuse. The other is called something like *How to Transform and Inspire Your Life*. I'll try that. I'll try anything at this point. I ask to borrow it and put it in my bag. I can always bring it back tomorrow if it doesn't transform and inspire me immediately.

I stagger back, and am glad to call Mango-land my home for the next few days. I will sleep much better in this room than the last one. It is amazingly quiet, considering what's nearby. There are three windows and a very pleasant and steady cross-breeze. There's a gentle fan that doesn't blow the hair off my head. There's a reasonable lock on the door. And I have had an amazing day, a once-in-a-lifetime kind of day.

As I pass into unconsciousness, I put in my order for breakfast, so to speak. I picture my people – my departed ones – and I pose them a question. What's the best way to go about tomorrow? I am not a great meditator, and I am not a great mind. But I do know that first thing in the morning, those first ten seconds of consciousness, are the most open-hearted. After that the chatter starts and it all gets too noisy. If, in those first few moments, I were to be granted some nugget of advice, or some sort of compass reading, I could steer my way through the rest of the day, unaided, and could probably do without any further handholding.

So, phone lines will be open. See you in the morning. Goodnight.

NOODLE TRAILS

Escape from the Tsunami Zone

"Lighten your luggage. Send business things home. Find an island with peace and quiet. Get better."

These are my first waking thoughts and I decide to agree. It now occurs to me: this is a new version of a Q&A game I often enjoy on a New Year's Eve, if I am not too inebriated. It doesn't really work then. If I'm reasonably sober, I ask for an inspirational theme for the year, and hope to awake with a new idea.

I went to post-graduate film school on this basis. I'd thought about it for years, then one New Year's Eve I fell asleep fervently asking for an answer. I woke up with the words, "Go. Go to film school." So I did, and never looked back. It was a great decision.

This technique makes a straight beeline for your deepest beliefs and intuitions, before you or anyone else (including your own history and habits) can talk you out of it or get in there first.

Other noteworthy examples include: "Don't let fear rule your life, and this goes double for spiders." Another year all I got was, "Order pizza." It was a good pizza, but maybe it pays to word one's enquiries with somewhat more scope.

I used to do this once a year but nowadays, feeling rudderless, I seem to be doing it on a daily basis. Compass readings are needed more often in stormy times.

Also, you don't have to obey. I could have had fried eggs for breakfast that time, instead of the pizza. It's not like following orders.

So, what was it again? "Lighten your luggage. Send business things home. Find an island with peace and quiet. Get better."

The ring of truth there is palpable, so I go straight into action. I divide all my belongings into two piles on either side of the bed. Every time the swing-fan goes by, they flutter excitedly, as if chattering about new destinations.

Business things go: heavy camera, sound recorder, much paperwork, technical paraphernalia, textiles and other samples – some of which may later turn into keepsakes for me and gifts for others. This fills four grocery bags and is bloody heavy. I'm even more eager to send it on its way.

The plan is to get enough cash to pay the Mangos,

post this stuff home, and find the quietest island available on which to spend a month or three. There are islands galore that provide exactly the peace I'm searching for. They have no roads, no vehicles, no engine noise of any kind. At most, they have one or two motorboat deliveries a day, and a slow-humming generator keeping a fridge going. That's it, for the electricity. Nothing but quiet, fresh food and swimming. This fits the bill.

I've researched such places off the coast of Ranong already, such as Ko Chang, Ko Phayam, Ko Kwayet. Any of them may have been the destination of our demented, sun-crisped, Italian traveller from the other day. There are enough islands for everyone, and they're not far from here. Ranong is a mere few hours away. I can be on a dawn boat tomorrow and in the quietude by lunch. This is a glorious plan. This is probably why it will not happen without a few hitches.

The Dutch bikers are off stage this morning, sleeping something off. I have the usual fried eggs with white bread, and instant coffee with powdered milk. I ask about a post office, but Sister Mango has to think. "Far," she murmurs, trailing away.

This doesn't bode well. She goes on. "Far. Difficult to find. Difficult to say to taxi."

I recall with embarrassment how in previous visits, I accidentally humiliated illiterate drivers by pointing into my phrasebook, clever me. It happens. Sister Mango brightens, however.

"I ask. I get direction, for you, in English."

"Oh thank you!"

"Sure," she smiles. "Easy," she adds. "We have time, before Monday."

"Monday?"

"Post office closed today, Saturday. Open 8.30 Monday morning."

"And the bank?"

"Same, same."

"Oh. But the cash machine?"

"Maybe full. Maybe not full."

True. Maybe it got emptied by the partiers of last night, which was a Friday, after all, although every night is party night when people are on vacation. Suddenly I'm even more glad than usual that these awful breakfasts are in small quantities. Over my white bread, I decide to visit Mother Soup for my main course.

On the way, a stop at the cash machine quickly confirms my fears. There is no cash to be had until Monday. Maybe there are other machines; maybe I can start a hunt, maybe. I have a deep instinct this is a stupid road to consider. I may have melodramatically packed up my entire life and career, heart and soul in a cardboard box, and made an invigoratingly radical decision – for me anyway – but I can't post it until Monday.

In the meantime, a check of my pockets reassures me there is plenty of money for food, if nothing lavish. Two breakfasts in as many hours is perfectly affordable, so I head for the non-touristed side of Terrible Highway. Mother Soup has seen me for lunch and for dinner, but never for breakfast. Now she knows I'm hard-core. Also, I have my phrasebook. I compliment the soup and point to the phrase "post office".

"Monday. Eight o'clock open. Forty baht, song-taew, no taxi." She gestures I should sit and wait, while she procures a neighbour speaking excellent English who, under her instruction, explains.

"Please go early, eight in the morning. It's very busy. Also, take a local bus, the song-taew, and do not pay more than forty baht. Do not take a taxi. They will ask too much! Too much!" This last bit is said in the tone of calling them bastards she'd like to spit at but it's more than they deserve.

"Thank you," I reply. These pleasures await me on Monday.

For now, I head to the weekend market, because I haven't eaten in over five minutes, and have no idea how to suddenly spend the weekend here, when I thought I was leaving in ten minutes time. Just for the heck of it, on my way over, I stop various willing participants and ask them about banks and post offices, thumping my little phrasebook. They all agree that nothing is ever open on the weekend. Ever. They each in turn thump the word "Monday" in my phrasebook. It seems I am here for the weekend, like it or not. I may as well eat my way through.

The market is just over the muddy little bridge over the

muddy little river, in the big dusty field that usually houses the taxi men and their air-conditioned vehicles. These are the men I have been warned about. They are not an inviting crowd, I must say. The market behind the taxi ranks, however, is a cracker. It's small, untidy, and perfect. It's perfect because it's for locals, and tourists can go hang. It smells very complicated and utterly wonderful.

There is plenty of food fried on woks on tripods, grills or barbecues. There is every sort of chicken, pork, fish, and shellfish you could imagine, each with a distinctively seasoned aroma. One stall pours sugar cane juice straight on ice – as basic as it gets. There are fresh metre-long barracudas hanging up next to pirated Elvis CDs. These are next to a mountain range of low-budget bras, which are next to plastic chopsticks and glitter nail varnish. The more incongruous the neighbours, the better I like it. I try as many foods as I can, wash up, and then spot a hat.

It's with the hardware and aluminium kitchenware, in a very dusty stack of the wide-brimmed hats you see on cleaners and building crews. I choose a shockingly electric leafy green one, and it costs about fifty pence (well under a dollar or a euro). I also buy some string to make a tie to keep it on my head. I am happy, well shaded and, yet again, look like a cross between a bag lady and a madwoman, I sashay home very impressed once again with the high quality and style of Thai everyday street food.

It's now time to get home, shower off the grease and sticky syrup, and snooze away my gluttony during the highest arch of the afternoon heat.

Later, I explore the other end of Terrible Highway, which is equally ugly and cluttered. Then I see a small sign to the "Tsunami Memorial Sculpture" pointing down a dusty red path. This is now my destination.

I am melting, but the corner shop mostly has alcohol. A scrawny, wizened lady appears, all bony smiles, but the only soft drink is a cola, which I despise in every way. Mark Thomas wrote an excellent book about this, *Belching Out the Devil*, although he said he wanted to call it *Gary Glitter Loves Coca-Cola*. It is funny and informative, but disturbing too. This is all the shop has. I take enough sips not to faint and, once around the corner, pour the rest into the dust.

The park is cleverly placed so that you turn a corner and suddenly spot the sculpture. It's instantly intriguing, and gently attractive, constructed of a dozen tall thin girders with softened edges and made from a gentle, pewter-coloured metal in a subtle matt texture. It's about ten metres high.

The girders lean at slight diagonals, tilted against one another. They look like they were dropped there from the sky. The shapes suggest either teepee sticks, or the rib cage of a ship thrown helter-skelter. It's called *Stability* and looks extremely unstable, as if a light breeze could make it topple. It looks fragile and pretty, a reminder that impermanence is the natural state of all of us, of all life, of all those buildings and boats and vulnerable creatures that were wiped away with one gashing wave.

The visitor is then treated to another skilful bit of planning by being delivered to the perfect vantage to see, hundreds of metres away, the washed-ashore royal vessel in the distant Boat Park. From this angle, it looks like a discarded toy. All the pavilions, sound stages, and exhibits have been swept away. It's eerie.

I wander back to the road. Two doors down Terrible Highway is a tiny sign, "Tsunami Museum". As I am feeling faint, this becomes the plan for tomorrow, Sunday.

I go home, nap, hose down, and re-emerge in search of dinner. Along Terrible Highway, I find a café full of Thai people, who neither welcome me nor glare, so I take a discreet table at the back and no one phones the tourist police. I also make sure to order something I can pronounce. This is not what I get. I am served a marvellously tasty and large plateful of chicken in oyster sauce with mixed vegetables and lots of kale on rice. I wish I had the nerve and vocabulary to look at other customers' food and say, "Can I have that, please?"

Seven Street is well lit at night with neon and spotlights. I cruise past my old home – the Wilkommen Inn as I now call it – and none of them recognise me. I head incognito to the beach, where the stone walls on each side of the road rise up to high corners, on which diners perch in the hope that people like me will not spoil their view. People like me are pouring forth onto the sand, all of us ruining their view. This is the trouble with beautiful blue water in the cooling-down evening hours. We all want a piece of it. Why else are we here?

These gardened terraces are draped with well-dressed people eating beautifully presented dinners adorned with wild orchids. Nearby on the sand, a young white couple impatiently try to light a hot air lantern. They shove it upwards too soon, and it falters and falls. They repeat this, more vehemently. They scowl, discuss and repeat a third time.

In theory, I could tell them to set it down on the sand to collect the heat, but it's none of my business. They give it one good almighty push, up and over the water, where it lands with a plop and a fizzle, drifting half-sunk out to sea. The couple slink away, grumbling.

Twenty metres away and twenty seconds later, another rich young white couple do exactly the same thing. Soon a third couple arrive and I almost laugh out loud.

It's so very, very weird to see no possible way to speak to any of the human beings in the immediate area. There are young German families, old German men, young German backpackers, me, and a few middle class couples too arrogant to fly a balloon. Invisible social bubbles keep them all separate.

On the other hand, none of that matters when you walk along a sandy beach, listening to the whispering surf, and splashing through the sea. Nothing much can spoil that. Back at the hut, it's time to see which two books have fallen into my path. One is the meditation book from Soo. It is sweet and wise, and would be a fine introductory guide for someone who has never travelled down this road before. The other book is the one I grabbed last night from the foreign language bookshelf at the wiener joint where I met the exiled Burmese journalist. This book, I now see, is highly recommended by Billy Graham, the right-wing extremist Christian evangelist, so I drop it like it's a scorpion. I'd rather have read about the heroic survival of the abused mum of the soap star. Maybe it's time for sleep. Any questions to ask? No, not really. Tomorrow, surprise me. Onwards, through the fog.

Still Adrift

"Leave this area tomorrow, come what may." That's my first waking thought. In no time, I have finished breakfast, again English but Thai-style. It's still early, and not too hot yet. I go straight to the Tsunami Museum.

The drone of traffic noise echoes sharply around the small concrete room, which is open air in front. It's about the size of a small shop, right on Terrible Highway. I shuffle along the simple but information- and photo-packed panels that cover the walls.

My perusal is accompanied by the sounds of huge lorries, tinkling ice cream vans, lots of boy-racers blasting pop tunes out their windows, and adverts for Thai kickboxing blaring from loudspeakers mounted on pickup trucks.

After five minutes of reading, I am surprised at the depth of a very long, deep sigh that seems to rise up from the soles of my feet.

These are the facts and figures I take away with me.

Casualties from the 2004 Tsunami were worst in Indonesia, numbering 130,000. Next came Sri Lanka with 35,000, India with 12,000, and Thailand with 8,000. Altogether 230,000 people were either killed or never found. Over 400,000 homes were lost, and over 100,000 fishing boats and livelihoods were destroyed as well, all in 24 hours.

The museum was created by psychology professor David Sattler, of Western Washington University, to help local people and to provide information. It's part of the Institute for Education and Culture, a non-profit organisation that helps schools. The Thais were faster than any other nation to rebuild schools and set up temporary ones. All Thai children, one way or another, were back in regular schooling about one month after the disaster.

This museum has won many awards, and it's very thought-provoking. That said, my last comment into my tape recorder was, "But this is all I can take." People who work in rescue services see this all day long. That astounds the rest of us. I can only collect the flip-flops I left at the entrance and plod back to my extremely fortunate existence.

Thoughtful, quiet, and walking tenderly, I make my

way across Terrible Highway again and head for the market.

First I cool myself with fantastically iced sugar cane juice. It's so luscious I have to have two. There are any number of Halal Muslim fried chicken stands, and I cannot resist the wonderful fragrance, even though it's a strange pinky-red, either dyed or radioactive. It's zingy all right, heavily salted, very peppery, highly and imaginatively seasoned, and admirably greasy, all washed down with coconut milk.

It's time to head for home and again sleep away the sweltering hours. This nap has one big difference. Under the comforting putt-putt of the gentle electric fan, I am seized with a truly agonising pain in my chest. It's almost impossible to breathe. It takes phenomenal concentration to keep breathing and asking my chest to please not implode. The muscles across my chest are trying to crush my lungs.

Do I really have to die like this? Who's going to find me? How will they send my stuff home? Maybe they'll sell my passport. They can keep it, why not at that point? Why am I thinking these things? I pound my chest, cough hard, push my ribs off my heart. I'd rather not die, not just yet.

Little by little, these waves of pain fade, each one smaller and smaller still. Air trickles back in. Was that a minor heart attack, or a record high in painful heartburn? I do not know, but I can breathe. I rest, I wait, I sleep. I'm fine now, and never again will I ignore people who tell scary MSG stories.

I try a test walk and do not die. I go to a shop to buy some film to shoot, before I send the camera home. The shop's front window is filled with amazing snaps of this building, before and after the flood. For some reason, the owner goes to a filing cabinet and gets a roll from there. It does strike me as odd, but I don't ask why.

Later it turns out my magic new roll of film, which he got out of the filing cabinet especially for me, has only got six shots on the allegedly thirty-six-exposure roll. I don't have the will to go back, let alone to argue my case. I pack the camera. I pack away this business and many years of endeavour.

"Lighten your luggage. Send business things home."

I look forward to the lovely practical Thai post office and its wonderful We Box Up Anything For You For About Fifty Cents department. Tomorrow, that is, tomorrow.

Tonight, now that it's cooler, I have my last ritual noodle soup from Mother Soup. She likes my new hat. I say I got it at the market and she likes it even more.

"How much?"

"Thirty-five baht."

"Good."

"At the Seven shop," I add, "this same hat is three hundred baht." She waves away the thought dismissively, and I agree. I say, in terrible Thai, "I don't like Seven. I like the Thai market. I like it very much." She beams and brings me extra bean sprouts.

The evening soap opera is already in progress. The smooth, oily villain now seems to have snared the eye of the unsuspecting young maiden, but her romantic admirer from afar can see what's going on, and so can her mother. The soup arrives just as mother and suitor exchange meaningful looks of agreement, cooperation and vows of revenge. Back in my reality, the soup is simple and tasty and perfect, and I fill the steaming broth with crunchy, cool bean sprouts.

I tell Mother Soup I will go to Ranong tomorrow. She says thank you, and goodbye and good luck. I say the same back. Mother coaxes Toddler to wave, which she does uncomprehendingly.

On the way home I stop by the wiener joint with the foreigners' lending library, and drop off the books. There's the preacher one, and *Meditation 101*. The soap opera one's still there. I return to the internet place on Terrible Highway to top up my sketchy list of islands, and even sketchier list of possible places to stay on them. I haven't really found my island of peace and quiet yet. There are lots of little pieces of heaven to choose from.

That night, there is one last small but tastily radical decision. I rip out my guidebook's sub-chapter on Ranong and its neighbouring islands, and leave behind all the rest. It becomes cushioning for the lenses. Something deep inside me clicks into place. It took a while to noodle out the right road, because we're on a Noodle Trail. No map, no recipes, just a spoon.

That next morning, I awake with the light and the instantaneous thought, "Go as soon as possible!" Now there's a sentiment to jolt one out of bed. It takes mere minutes to finish packing. The carrier bags are ready to nestle into crates and join the hold of the next freighter heading west. The phrase "nearest post office" is now underlined in my pocket guide, so I bound towards Terrible Highway in pursuit of enough cash for a month of retreat with an option for more.

The post office excursion is as everyone advised. The taxi drivers are aggressive in their touting, so I go further up Terrible Highway to escape them and wait for a two-bencher, confidently waving aside those who have followed me. They're like the soap opera villains from last night, twiddling their moustaches. However, I am not an innocent young maiden. I am an astute, experienced and crabby old bat, and soon they can see better than to mess with me. Nonetheless, I do it with a smile, because that is the Thai way. Plus it's also awfully, frightfully British, wouldn't you agree?

A song-taew pulls over. The driver squints at the "post office" note, and then explodes with merriment. "Ah, post office! OK! Sit here!" That's an honour, riding shotgun in front with the driver, usually reserved for family, mistresses, or monks. He bubbles with an eager but crazy salad of Thai and English, and convulses with joy at all his own jokes. "I need speak English. Please, speak English with me!"

We do greetings, where we're from, and the weather. Then we count to ten in unison, cheering ourselves afterwards. We pass another taxi rank, and he scowls.

"Taxi no good. Me no like. They Mafia. They try take my customer. They want finish my business. They make boxing, they make fighting." He mimes, punching the air, shakes his head sadly.

What a drearily sad and familiar story. Stories like this abound. I vow to take song-taews for the rest of my life when in Thailand. I have been mildly ripped off in taxis and in tuk-tuks, but never in one of these.

"You want speak Thai?"

"Sure."

"OK, we count," he challenges me. We count to twenty, while a few passengers in the back join in, and they all applaud when we get there. I've had this happen before. I don't know if it's peculiarly Thai, but it's endearing. He stops at the post office, the ones in the back help unload my four bags, and every single one of them waves, singing "Bye-bye! Bye-bye!"

It's like an old reliable pal, this department of the Thai postal service. It's exemplary, as usual. The guy there eyes up my bags, unfolds their largest carton, and frowns a bit pessimistically.

"Not sure. Maybe too small?"

"Can I try?"

He bows and hands it over. I retreat to a corner and, in the manner I find so disgusting in other travellers, I dump my belongings on the floor. I repack everything until I have created a perfectly shaped, totally cushioned and firm entity, snug and clever as a Rubik's Cube. It fits the box to the millimetre. The clerk gives it a thumbs-up, smiling. It weighs less than I thought, costs less than I thought and, when I hand it over to him, I suddenly feel a hundredfold lighter in the very heart of my soul. When I bound down the steps to cross the road for my return journey, I'm almost giddy to have finally reached the right road, the one that sparkles, the one that put this grin on my face. My own reflection startles me, I look so pleased. Suddenly I don't look utterly ill. Now, suddenly the foliage seems gorgeous, the world seems bright and big, and some kind of tide is turning. I even realise that my smile muscles are rusty from lack of use.

A song-taew pulls over almost immediately, and I confidently pronounce where I am going. The driver just stares and looks embarrassed. A nice elderly Thai woman seated in the back, wearing a wide, cone-shaped coolie-style hat is happy to deputise. She reads the phrasebook and yells something at him, which he seems happy to accept.

"Thank you."

"OK, OK." She and her pals drag me into the back and bang on the partition to signal him to move. As he drives, he snacks from a bowl on the dashboard, full of long, slim chillies. He holds them between his fingers like a cigarette, munching them steadily, one after another. He's a chain-chewing chilli addict. He consumes them non-stop during the half hour trip.

It turns out my destination was a lot further than the driver realised, so by the time we get there, the entire delegation has consulted, and their spokeswoman asks me to pay a little more. They smile as one when I make no argument. I thank them all as they disappear into the dust.

I get off at the Seven. Right behind me is a bus to Ranong. That means the next one is in about an hour. Fifty minutes later I'm standing there with my bags, in the broiling midday sun. I don't want to budge. I don't even want to buy a drink or use the toilet, because I've got to be on that bus.

A couple of bright pink backpackers ask for buses to Ranong, and some of us nod. When does it come? Maybe five or ten minutes, some say. Maybe soon, others say. "Cool," they reply, "we'll go get the provisions," and they disappear. The bus arrives immediately and we all climb on. The next one is in an hour, apparently, for the bright pink people who may be even pinker by then.

This journey is bathed in a feeling of freedom. I feel like a wrongly accused inmate finally pardoned and released from prison. It's an easy trip, only a few hours, right up the pretty coast. The road is all palm trees, modest villages and hardly any white people. It's absolutely lovely.

In earthy, grotty little port town Ranong, we are besieged by taxi drivers plucking up those doing the visa run to Burma and back. They are bored to hear I am not doing that, but wave me in the direction of the guesthouse.

I walk past the main bus depot and its ratty hippy hostel. I read about it and am now extremely glad I'm not staying there. I'll eat cheap food, but I will not sleep with fleas, rats or college students, and I certainly won't sleep with all three.

The resort is one big gorgeous mountainside garden, right on the banks of a river. It has groovy spa rooms as well as cheapies for the likes of me; very good for the price. The friendly, helpful family who run it are charming and they deserve a specific plug: the Thansila Hotspring Resort. What's more, even though I'm in the backpacker economy range, the boys offer to carry my bags, and that gets extra points for them.

Later, I return to the desk to ask the nice boy where I can eat. He waves me back to the main road. I enter the first place I come to, which is completely empty. I know that's a bad sign, but it's an odd hour: too late for lunch and too early for dinner. The girlies don't mind. They are eager to please, and indicate I can sit where I like in the big, empty, echoing, dusty room.

Mama Cleaver behind the counter is clearly not my biggest fan. I order a Crispy Pork and Kale, a classic basic, but it arrives as Soggy Pork Fat and Raw Garlic Salad with Uncooked Kale Stems Like Wood. It's only later I see on her counter of ingredients a large peeled aubergine covered in a carpet of ants. This is obviously after I've eaten as much as I can. Mama is surly at the stone mortar and pestle, pounding garlic like it's her ex-husband's face. Finally they remember that I ordered a beer, and it arrives, on ice, which I've never tried. The tin was in the window, and is seeringly hot. Beer on ice kind of works, in a diluted, sudsy way. I'd have drunk anything at that point.

Back at base camp, a sweet girl behind the desk is eating some fried chicken which smells delectable – far better than what I just swallowed.

"Hello!" she calls out. "Welcome. Can I help you? Where are you from?" She's happy to help and chat, and clearly likes her job. She has just moved back to Thailand after earning her business diploma in Germany. Her dad is nearby and explains, "She study there, then she comes back here. You see? She comes back, to work here, in our business." He wanders away, shoulders proud. Lots of them never come back, ever.

Her English is excellent, and she puts her chicken legs to one side until I tell her to go ahead and eat. She licks her fingers, and probably notices me drooling, so she tells me it's her mother's special chicken made with a long list of Thai spices I've never heard of. She has meanwhile found a second plate, put a drumstick on it with a little sweet and spicy dipping sauce, and gently pushes it over to my side of the table. It's delicious.

She knows these islands well, and describes the range.

The one that fits the bill I'm going to call Tainee Island.
She offers to help make phone calls, but her hands are
covered with sticky chicken grease. So I dial and hold the
phone to her ear while she licks and cleans her fingers.
She has a long and spirited conversation with a friend of
her mother's, which goes on and on until she mimes the
universal talking-fingers sign for too much yap-yap.

Finally she covers the mouth piece and whispers, "She
doesn't leave the island very much". She explains
sweetly and honourably: "She need the gossips first. OK,
for you she has a bungalow for four hundred baht, but it is
very – simple. No hot water, no electricity, no lights, no
fan. But, it's right on the beach, really right on the beach,
so there's strong wind and no mosquitoes. Is this OK?"

"OK? This is perfect."

"OK!" she smiles and confirms with Aunt Chatty. I
may have found peace and quiet at last.

"Can I go there tomorrow?"

"Sure. There's a boat at nine." She scribbles
something on a scrap of paper. "Take this to the boatman.
He's her nephew. He will take you to her. And he," she
says gesturing over to an Equally Honourable Younger
Brother, "will help you get to the pier, in the morning."

"Thank you so much."

"It's my pleasure. By the way, have you been to the
Night Market? There's lots of food there, and it's very
good. Have you eaten already?" she asks, taking my
empty plate away.

Have I eaten already? What's that got to do with it? I about-face and head straight there.

It's down the main road, past Mama Cleaver's Soggy Pork Fat Palace, and about a twenty-minute walk. It's worth every step, too. Not a whitey in sight and very little English spoken. Children point and stare. A few bravely shrill, "Hello!" before they collapse giggling into the laps of proud parents. This is more like it. If I'm going to be a freak, let's do it in style.

I get a pair of flip-flops, some hair slides, a pre-cut guava and some dipping sugar with a little salt and chilli powder, roasted mystery meats on skewers, a bag of nuts, and a bag of blood oranges for the boat trip tomorrow. I am relocating to Tainee Island.

No Problem

"Please get me to that island today – somehow!" That's my first waking thought. Soon I am ready and waiting for Honourable Younger Brother, who is relaxed and optimistic about it only being a fifteen-minute journey. He suggests an absurdly overpriced taxi and I decline, saying that I'd prefer a song-taew. He honours my request, dragging my case up the lane.

He explains to the driver where I am going, pointing to his watch. I distinctly hear the phrase "nine o'clock" more than once. He waves me off with a nice sweet smile. Then plans take another turn, of course.

The driver trawls for more trade, meandering at an annoyingly low speed all over the city, calling out to shoppers and other customers who clearly aren't going to materialise. I catch his eye in the rear view mirror, point to my watch, call out what I can, but this does no good whatever. If I miss this boat, there isn't another for seven hours. It's nearly nine o'clock and already broiling, so that's not a healthy prospect. I just want to get there, somehow. Please get me to that island.

We get to the dock at nine on the dot – and therefore the boat is full and the ticket office closed. I nearly weep. In fact I do weep a tiny bit, after taking myself into a private corner once I know I can't prevent it. This doesn't take long. At least I am efficient.

Dad used to travel. What would he do? He wouldn't cry, I promise you that. I can see him now, as I think "Please get me on that boat!"

Instantly I find myself making a very uncharacteristic move, against all reason and habit. I slowly yet deliberately leave my diplomatic, face-saving corner and return to the steps leading down to the boat. I stand there quietly and calmly, eyes down, in front of them all, right near the fellow who told me it was full. He told me three times. It's not full at all. It is overladen with cargo.

Perhaps I do look like I will soon break down sobbing. In this part of the world, this is exactly the way to be ignored completely. I order my face to appear neutral. I look at my feet and I hold quite still. No one says anything. The water laps. The boatman gestures for some cargo to be taken off and for me to get on, and we cast off seconds later.

I sit next to Swiss Peter, who has a theory. He tells me that earlier, as passengers accumulated, there was a minor fracas concerning the number of people in relation to the number of life jackets, as well as about the ridiculous amount of cargo piled dangerously high. Insurance requirements are very strict about people and life preservers, but you can carry as much cargo as you like. It's to do with the insurance pay outs, in the event of sinking. These boats do sink from time to time. This is accepted. It's not all that deep here, as seas go, Swiss Peter informs me with authority. If they lose cargo and luggage, a lot of it gets hauled back up. You might lose and damage some, but not all, and the insurance pays the difference. They'd rather not pay the astronomical sums which are required when you lose people.

"So in this case," he concludes, "we are carrying extra cargo but very few people, and thus they have solved the problem so that now we can sink legally."

Peter turns out to be one of the most hilarious people I have ever met, and if he reads this and knows his real name is not Peter, then I want him to email me and tell me he is happy and healthy and enjoying life back in Zurich.

It's a two hour boat ride with plenty of spray, just enough canopy, and loads of stories. He tells me how the Brazilian rubber industry was destroyed by wily English people posing as academic researchers, but who were in reality seed-thieves. They created plantations in Malaysia and destroyed their rivals. Apparently the banana trade went the other way, from south-east Asia to South America, in much the same fashion.

Here, the priority cargo is ice, beer, and rice, followed by lesser amounts of cigarettes, vegetables, and eggs. New Year's Eve is in two days, after all.

When we arrive, the boat circles the entire island, dropping things off at each "resort" – and here that word means a cluster of crude huts with a café hut in the middle. The boatman manoeuvres the boat vaguely nearby, as family plus their staff of Burmese workers wade into the surf to ferry to shore blocks of ice, and carry on their heads sacks of rice, and suitcases. Meanwhile, stunned European passengers are shoved over a ladder to land up to their waists in choppy waves, in which they swim or stagger to shore wondering how they'll dry out their passports. One charming, fey gentleman holds his special Italian shoes over his head.

These boats come and go only once or twice a day, so it's a big event. In one case, the right provisions do not materialise, and a hostile Big Mama With Clipboard climbs aboard and will not leave until the shortfall is sorted out. I hate to think what she will say, once we are out of earshot.

We proceed from place to place, throwing sacks of vegetables and tourists into the water. Peter and I note which things go where, and draw conclusions about which resorts accommodate, respectively, the alcoholics, the traditional types, the healthy vegetarians, and the chain smokers.

I am dropped at the second to last place, and Peter at the last. I tie my passport belt around my neck, and only get soaked up to my chest. My boat departs with Big Mama Clipboard. I have already shown my little note to the young boatman, who points to his mother's pal Ahm, the owner. She is screaming merrily at all her helpers to grab the food and the ice and the beer, and then she grabs me heartily by the upper arm.

"Welcome!" she yells over the crashing surf. She yells other things too that I cannot hear or understand, but I love her big smile and exuberance.

"You go there," she says, pointing down the beach. I don't get it. She motions to wait while she yells at young people hauling provisions out of the surf, and into a hand-pulled cart they drag over the soft white sand to the kitchen. Then she grabs me again by the arm, happily yelling, "You go there!" Finally she drags me and my bag to a large rock, four times my height. I stand there confused.

She grabs my arm again, and shows me steps carved into the rock leading up to the bungalow perched on, around, and carved out of a great boulder. I'm not sure I've got this right, but eventually it sinks in. I have a booked a bungalow in a rock.

It's about as beachfront as you can get. At high tide, the waves splash well over my balcony, and the din at night is extraordinary when the waves pound the walls. A storm would drown me, no question, but this only keeps me awake the first night. Low tide is splendid, with a hammock view of endless naturally dramatic gorgeousness. I am living in a rock, next to a blue, blue sea. This is worth risking drowning in my sleep.

In the morning, I awake and stagger over to the bathroom where I reach automatically for the light switch that does not exist. There is no electricity whatsoever. Instead there is a stack of candles, and a large ball of wax where former inhabitants appear to have read by candlelight. These wax marks verify the information that with three candles one can read. There is a large mosquito net, lots of mosquito coils on sale, and I douse myself daily in bug juice. Much of this is unnecessary, because the ocean breeze is so sturdy the bugs don't dare venture into it.

The bathroom floor has been carefully concreted so that all water collects in the middle of the room and has to be aggressively swept towards the drain, which is uphill at the end. The showerhead is an old plastic water bottle with holes crudely stabbed into the bottom. This is attached to a tank on the roof, and there is either on or off, no other gradations. It is warm for about three seconds. From then on it's very, very cold.

There is no mirror, but that's just as well. This is the prize bungalow, I learn, because it is the only one with a sink. The other guests tell me it's a little weird to brush your teeth and spit the remains into the toilet, but you get used to it.

It is fantastically quiet, with nothing but the sound of the waves. There is even more privacy at the moment, because hardly anyone speaks English. There are a few Germans and Austrians who are multi-lingual and very generous about switching into English for the benefit of a limited linguist like myself. But also, there are only two tables in the café, so there is some social juggling.

I ask about the village, but there isn't one really. There is a place inland with four houses. The residents come here for the tourist season and close the island down again when the tourists leave. It's a sort of all-island camping adventure park for Europeans to escape the comforts of things like electricity – comforts which a lot of the world longs for. For us materially spoiled types, it's not just totally beautiful, it is also a lesson in what we think we can't live without. It is heavenly, the peace and quiet. It's a joy.

I want to take a long walk down Long Beach, but our little cove is separated from this by some tall craggy rocks, a scary bridge, and the high wall of a reservoir. If it's low tide you can clamber along dangerously slimy rocks while worried onlookers cringe. If it's high tide, you can walk along a dangerously slimy high wall, and then they can't even look.

Then there is the river, and another "bridge", which is a series of very shaky, narrow planks balanced on three upright, asymmetrical logs and no hand rail. It's a bit like a tightrope walk, or a very long balance beam, over a river that at the moment looks deep in the middle, but it's hard to tell.

Across sits a Thai man in traditional fisherman's trousers and no shirt, mending a net. I look at the river, hesitantly. He sizes me up, glances at the water, and mimes a clear gesture that the water will come up to my chin. Then he points to the planks, i.e. the "bridge" and goes back to his nets. It takes me several nervous minutes to shunt my way across this thing, and of course several large Thai families have queued up behind me. Once I am done, they spring across like billy goats.

Long Beach is gorgeous. It is a perfect walking beach, long and straight and smooth and perfect. At the other end I discover the "Coconut Resort", which has an amazing view of the beach. It's the only one with an all-day generator, too. It even has lights, sometimes. It has internet at selected times of day. It's in the middle of a long perfect beach walk, without fording rivers or rope bridges. I cannot get these ideas out of my mind, particularly since I am tiring of scribbling by hand and retyping everything later. It becomes a quest to relocate to the Coconut. I've got the island, now I need the gaff. Onwards and upwards – or in this case, just further down the beach.

Meanwhile, back at the Rock, we all watch the guest known only as the French guy. He's always in Thai clothing, goes fishing all the time with a big net, and wears a huge knife in a holster. He normally works in a circus as a clown, acrobat, and magician, but is here for a few months to go extremely native and fishy. He spends his time sewing clever little weights around the edges of his fishing net and then practising how to fling them out wide, across the waves, in different formations – acrobatic and graceful and mesmerizing.

When I say "we", I mean a motley crew of people who do not speak much to each other, but today for some reason they're all at the table at once. Ahm joins the table. She mentions her "sister", Ohm, next door. Ohm is not literally a sister, but a close friend. Ahm seems a little jealous as Ohm is known as a great cook, and her place is always packed. She did some clever marketing in a German guidebook, learned to cook German food, and now it's always full of Germans. This of course is why we don't go there. Ahm is a fine cook for those who want to eat Thai, and deserves the business. Even out here, I can't believe how Thailand is so full of bratwurst and burgers. Still, business is business, I suppose.

To check out the competition, Peter and I go to Ohm's one day for dinner, and have a beautiful fish that is preposterously expensive, and we never go there again. However, Ohm does join us at the table, since we are new and all the other guffawing Germans seem happy amongst themselves and their beers and bratwursts.

Her English is very good. We hear about how her

husband died a year ago of stomach cancer, and how she has to run this place by herself now. She tells the story quite openly, yet full of quiet dignity. Now her seventeen-year-old daughter has a newborn baby. The father of this baby is not mentioned, but the daughter and granddaughter have just moved back in with her. Ohm seems a very decent lady, who is trying hard to hold up under all this.

Peter's incessant clowning stops during this story, but not for long. What was delightful hilarity at first is now becoming strident and relentless. Later when we leave, I wish Ohm good luck and I thank her for the delicious food. I also thank her for the talk, I add seriously. She touches my arm and says quietly, "Thank you, very much." She nods in Peter's direction, "Some talk good, some not so good." We both laugh. She has a wonderful smile.

This is the "mustard seed story" I needed to hear. I may be trying to mend a broken heart, a broken back, a broken business and a broken bank account, but nobody died. If my mother dies soon, she will die in her eighties. I am reminded of my good luck by comparison.

What's the mustard seed story? Long ago, a grieving lady who had to bury her dead little baby is so distraught that she goes to the Buddha and begs him to perform a miracle to bring the child back to life. He says this would be possible if she can bring him a mustard seed from any house where no one has grieved a loss. She searches, but of course finds not one. She sees the lesson: that none of us escapes loss, and that this can, in fact, become the seed of compassion – the very thing that links us all.

So, metaphorical mustard seeds were what seasoned Ohm's delicious barbecued fish.

Later, back at base camp, we all get drunk with Ahm and learn that her husband is a boatman. Their daughter is now in secondary school, but there isn't a secondary school on this island, so she moved to Ranong to live with her dad. Dad keeps a mistress in town, too, and makes no secret of it – routinely taunting Ahm in public. She is bitter. He turns up on the island now and then, yells at her, takes a load of money off her and buggers off back to Ranong, their daughter and the mistress, and his hard-to-finance heavy drinking. Ahm is trapped. She cannot sell the place without his agreement, and he also has their daughter living with him. He is not much of an earner as a boatman. No one can see a way out of this. We drink and drink as the sky grows darker. It's not such an idyllic life after all, on a desert island. Not if you can't leave.

The next day is New Year's Eve. "Tonight," she announces, "we make boom-boom." She shows us a great case of Chinese fireworks, and we all agree to come. Other than that, you'd hardly know it's New Year. This is exactly what I had in mind. I take another long walk down the beach and back, which more or less exhausts me. After some noodles (wonderful) and a coconut (perfect) and a short rest, it is late afternoon. Almost time for what I now call the Stampede.

Every evening, the generators whiz into action – but only for two hours. From every nook and cranny emerge pink Europeans running to the café, waving their phones and computers and other things to recharge. There are only so many sockets, so there is a race to get them. Those who lose out slink back to their lairs, growling and grumpy for another twenty-four hours without internet access. It's not as Robinson Crusoe as it first appears, this paradise.

Tonight, though, Ahm arranges tasty barbecued fish around a lovely campfire on the beach.

Peter thinks I mustn't move anywhere. "You cannot move to that Coconut place. It's not the right place. It's not our kind of spot."

"Our?"

"I mean…it's full of Germans!" he shudders.

"So is this place," I reply, but there's an eruption of objections from those who are Swiss or Austrian.

"It also has alcoholic English people," he adds darkly.

"So? The world is full of those."

"Ah," he pauses thoughtfully. "Yes that's true. You can't do anything about that."

"Anyway," I add, "are you staying here?"

"Of course not," he declares. "No one speaks English! I can't speak to anyone. Thai is too difficult, even for a

Swiss. I think I'll go to the Philippines. At least they all speak English. I can't travel without meeting people and talking to them." Fair enough, but I will try life on that end of the island, just to see.

Anyway, it's New Year's Eve. There are about six of us around the campfire, with a few drums. We pound them and sing, and some of us dance. Ahm is very happy to have some company. We are silly and we laugh. It's a raggle-taggle little group, which always has a certain magical charm. We eat very, very well, and the booze flows nicely too – not ridiculously or stupidly – just gently, like the breeze, like the waving palms, like the flickering fire.

"We only six people, but we make one thousand boom-boom!" declares Ahm. And we do. As the clock nears midnight, she leaps over to the long string of Chinese firecrackers she has somehow hung from an extremely tall palm tree. She lights them and, yes indeed, we make one thousand boom-boom. Then we applaud and wish each other a Happy New Year.

Later I retire to my rock while a couple of them keep drinking and singing and laughing and drumming, all of which blends like perfect music with the high tide's waves that beat against my rocky walls. There is something about this that is perfect. Happy New Year: boom-boom.

It's New Year's Day and a new couple arrive on the morning boat, along with more ice and beer. English speakers. Well, American, so that's close. We don't see much of the man because he is off photographing everything in sight. His wife, Lola, complains with a big warm smile that he loves the camera more than he loves her. She says it as one who is clearly very happy. She is very sweet and easy to talk to. She and I and Austrian Barbara soon make a threesome over a very long breakfast that turns into lunch without any trouble at all.

"Do you work?" Lola asks Barbara.

"Well, I do translating and teaching a bit. Mostly what I did was I raised two children."

"Ah!" chime Ahm and Lola and me. We are now full of questions: like how old and how many and so on. The men are instantly bored and turn elsewhere. Barbara has never travelled before, but started travelling like mad once her children were older and she could get divorced.

"I know it sounds funny," she says, "but after my divorce, life really became wonderful. I never really did anything until I was divorced, but now I'm doing everything I always wanted to do. I'm having a great time. I should have done this a lot sooner. Everything good in my life, other than my children, happened after I got divorced." She states all this matter-of-factly, and no one at the table is surprised in the least. It's just one of those facts of life.

Lola unwittingly provide a running joke when she meets Peter that will last for the rest of the week. She confuses Switzerland with Sweden. Apparently this happens a lot, he says, shaking his head sardonically, but mostly with Americans.

"It's the SW sound," she says, flustered.

"Of course," he retorts, "Like Swaziland, right?" She will never live this down.

I am still trying to contact the Coconut, but there is only one phone – in the kitchen – which we are allowed to use. I try ringing whenever Ahm isn't there because I feel like a traitor, but there is no answer. I'll try walking over there. I want that long straight beach walk on my doorstep. Also, I know that the Americans and Barbara are leaving soon, and this will leave me with nothing but the Germans who stare.

Yes, that does it. Tomorrow, I go get a room at the Coconut.

Finding Mai Island

I am determined to relocate to the other end of the island today. Rather than scale walls, walk a tightrope and risk drowning, I've learned I can jump on the morning boat to the mainland and get off at the other end of the island.

"Maybe fifty baht, tell boatman, easy," says Ahm.

Things are not easy, as it happens, the next morning. The sun is just barely up. I am having my usual noodle soup, when suddenly I have to abandon it. The early boat is earlier than usual. Ahm is disgruntled and looking hurt, perhaps suspecting I am shopping elsewhere when she really needs the business to support her philandering, alcoholic husband who is also the guardian of her daughter. I run for the boat and don't look back.

Some hermits have emerged that I've never spotted before, and we all stride through the surf and haul ourselves aboard. Their luggage is carried overhead by the Burmese helpers. I only have my little day pack.

The boatman snaps into action. "Where you go?"

"Ranong."

"OK. You?"

"Ranong."

"OK. You?"

"Coconut Resort."

"No."

"What?"

"We no stop Coconut."

"Ahm said yes."

"I say No. No stop."

Everyone is confused, even boatman number two. They always stop there. We all look at him quizzically. He mimes rough surf. More confused looks are exchanged, as we float on a placid clear sea.

"We go Ranong, only Ranong."

"OK." I get off the boat and wade to shore, backpack on my head. I walk through the rubber plantation, across the tall, dangerously slippery reservoir wall, over the scary bridge, all the way down Long Beach. All the way, every bloody step, I see this boat land stop at every single resort. When I arrive at the Coconut, there they are. The boatman can see me clearly, as he has at every other stop too. The boat arrives only half full, and no one gets off. There would have been plenty of room for me. Now about twenty people attempt to get on, and only half succeed.

The others are left, astonished, in the surf while their friends yell things like "Get tomorrow's boat and find us somehow!" Friends and loved ones putt-putt away to the mainland, while the abandoned are at first too stunned to wade back to shore, with their backpacks and their dangling boots and yoga mats. They will simply have to try again tomorrow. They will run to try to check right back into the rooms they just vacated. I sit and let them flood the staff before I do. I'm ready for several cool drinks by now, anyway.

The Coconut does a pretty good noodle soup, too, especially the fish balls. There's a big open-air café under shade, and its much less claustrophobic (or intimate) than where I am staying now. It is divided up socially, with areas taken up by old Germans, young Germans, and English speakers (assorted).

The extra space is welcome, especially as I spy two large and tattooed Germans crack beer after beer at eight in the morning. They seem to reign as double alpha males. One has the sort of loud, guttural laugh that makes my skin crawl. The other is sullen and menacing. To one side are two beautiful half Thai children with their Thai mother, who's exquisite but seems deeply unhappy. The kids are surrounded by expensive toys and prams and other familial detritus, and are shunted into a corner with the suicidal looking woman.

Is this where I am moving with such glee? What's odd about the other places is the claustrophobia. Here at least there's space. I am allowed to look at a few bungalows. They have electricity. There is internet. The beach is long, long, long and truly stunning. It's about the same price. I think it's worth a try, just to compare. I can write. There's the clincher.

I introduce myself to Mrs Mighty Coconut to pay for the room. She assures me I can relocate tomorrow, come on the morning boat. Will I have to lie to the boatman, and say I am going to Ranong, just to get on? I will cross that boat when I get to it.

There is a rare meeting of minds back at Ahm's place. It's possible everyone has given in, despite their natural cool reticence, to the warmth and friendliness of the American couple who have just landed. We're also hearing how German Angele is here to invest in agriculture. She decided that the economic downturn means she should invest in what people need most: food. She's just bought land in north-east Thailand and is starting a tree farm there. She wants to do the same in South America. "It's smart to spread out the risk, like in gold and agriculture and other things. It's for my security."

She is very positive and a good networker. She always gets to the electric plugs first, in that mad rush they have each night. She works hard on her laptop. She has all the faith, positivity, confidence, and IT skills that I lack. I can't even summon the courage to tell my feisty landlady I'm leaving. Where is the old Eileen, the one who had faith and energy? I want her back. She can't be gone with everything else, surely not?

American Lola and Kevin are showing us his wonderful new camera. He eagerly displays masses of lovely pictures of their three week trip, now nearly over. There are some of shots of me looking both troubled and weary. He captions one, "Thinking of my next book". Later he dubs another shot, "The writer considers". I have not said I was writing anything. This is wonderful. I keep my mouth shut and bask in suppressed smiling.

They then show us pictures of another island, which looks delightful: simple, but not as crude as this. There is electricity and reasonably priced bungalows, and not too many of the posh kind. They show us photo after photo, and this place looks better and better to me. They ask what I am looking for, and I describe my wish list. Instantly they look at each other, and turn to me simultaneously.

"You want Mai Island," they agree. I file this idea away for some future rainy day.

That night I cannot sleep. In my half-awake nightmares, my bags are too heavy, the boatman refuses to take me, and I have to walk all the way, with two heavy bags, over the death-defying waterfall and the rickety one-plank bridge, down the long, long sandy beach where a roller bag is no good, and my shoulder strap is broken, and there are no rucksack handles, and I am feeling faint… at which point I wake up, yet again bathed in panicky sweat. That's when one single word leaps into my mind.

"Leave."

When morning finally arrives, I have a leisurely bowl of breakfast soup, because the early boat is late. I pay Ahm and thank her, and wish her good luck. Neither of us is in a joking mood. I then say goodbye to the only other person awake that I know, the French circus guy.

"You go? Where do you go?" he asks.

"Ranong" pops out of my mouth. I'm as surprised as anybody. I paid for a room at the Coconut.

"For the day?"

"No," I answer, "for good," which surprises me even more. Sometimes an unexpected question is just the thing to pop out a simple, deep, true answer.

"Where you go?" asks the boatman's mate.

"Ranong," I say, and he helps me up the ladder. The nice Burmese helpers heap my luggage after me. I wave to Ahm and the French circus guy, and face the mainland. The Disney-style pseudo desert island adventure has concluded.

Back in Ranong, I check back into the spa place, shower, and take a walk through the streets of Ranong town. Only hours ago, I was on the most primitive beach I've ever known.. Now I am back amongst traffic fumes and chugging noises. I hail a song-taew and delight in getting it to work. I'm a little drunk on dehydration perhaps, but am somehow enjoying the swoons. I say numbers to Thais, they say them back, we confirm on fingers and calculators, and it all bloody works. I have learned enough Thai to not just go shopping, but to enjoy shopping.

I now know exactly where Ranong's Night Market is, and even have my preferred circuit around it (to the far corner, zigzag clockwise back to the entrance). I know my top five stalls. I get the cut guava with the dipping bag of sugar/pepper, and the spicy mystery meats on skewers. For the bus tomorrow, I skip the customary bag of oranges, and opt for some truly terrible crisps.

I know what this means. This is one of those days I allow maybe once a month. It must not become more. It is Junk Food Day. I buy deep fried doughnuts to prove it. Along the way, I also get a very nice sarong I really don't need at all. I just like the colours. Sea blues and orchid violets. Then I get my "combined ticket", meaning that for one price, this trip will involve buses, taxis, minibuses, local buses, boats where needed, and perhaps more. But it means I will get there – and I will have paid one simple fare for it all. The Thais are fantastically good at this. They put a little colour-coded sticker on your collar, and then a long chain of helpers steer you every step of the way. It's so much easier, sometimes, to revert to being blind cattle.

I get a ticket to Mai Island, which the American couple told me about. It was the way they turned to each other and grinned. It was their combined tone of voice when they said it was probably the place for me. They also said it's a great idea to hire a motorbike and zoom all over the island, but I don't fancy that. I have seen too many foreigners on crutches.

The next morning I am up at four, away at five, and on the minibus at six. The buses and taxis and song-taew trucks are fine and uneventful. The junk food en route is splendid in its shining hideousness, and I eat rubbish all day long. Nothing goes wrong. One rest stop is even labelled a "Happy Toilet", and it is.

A lovely big fat tub of a boat takes four hours to get to Mai Island – unlike the speedboat's two – but its ploppity-ploppity pace is comforting. These sorts of boat never slosh your guts out in bad weather, which the little boats do – all too effectively. I know. I've been on boats off which I have nearly crawled on my hands and knees. I am sure people have been carried off in stretchers. However, pay a bit less, take more time, and you get a nice slow tub – the proverbial slow boat.

It's been a very long but fine day. The ferry is not full, mostly carrying Thais either in families or in work clothes. There are very few tourists. Now it's getting towards late afternoon: that lovely cooling-down time when the breeze is so delicious and invigorating.

I'm not far from the junk food stall, honouring my pledge of the day. To be fair, there isn't a real food stall. I buy a sugary drink that I would normally never touch with a barge pole, because these are the rules of Junk Food Day. The stall is manned by a charmingly camp gay boy sporting a massive crucifix pendant and an overflowing – even hyperactive – eagerness to practise his English.

"You from Scotland? I know Scotland! I have been! I love Scotland!" He bubbles over about his trip there, the only time he's been outside of Thailand. He loves castles, which is why he chose Scotland. While he burbles on about his favourite Scottish castles, an island appears in the distance.

"Is that it?"

"That's it," he smiles.

"Are you from near here?"

"No! I am from Pattaya. Do you know Pattaya?"

I pause. Everybody knows about Pattaya, the biggest red light district in the nation. Of all the whorehouse-peepshow cities in Thailand, this is the queen mother of them all. This is the home of cabarets in which girls fire ping-ping balls out of their vaginas, sometime to music, sometimes into people's mouths, I really don't know. It goes far beyond ladyboy reviews, which can be excellent song and dance cabarets. Pattaya is known more for what you might call stage porn. What can I possibly say to this boy?

"I've never been there," I tell him.

"It's near Bangkok. I was born there, but I don't like it. Too noisy. Too crazy."

"I've heard that."

"Oh yes. Very noisy. I have sensitive ears. Cities have too much noise."

"Yes."

"It more nice here."

"Yes. Oh yes."

He is gorgeously, delicately camp; much better at being girlish than any girl could be, as is so often the case. He watches my bags as I find the loo. When I return, a lady sitting nearby seems to have taken over the next round of practising English on harmless-looking visitors. She's one of the local schoolteachers at the primary, near the main port town. I learn there's an English woman teaching there, whose husband teaches French.

Suddenly I desperately want to come here and teach English. A mere few days ago (and it feels like months), I was in the tsunami zone where I met a Burmese journalist who instantly made me want to go to Burma and be a journalist. This strongly suggests I'm a little too easily influenced these days, and that maybe I shouldn't sign any contracts just yet.

Our fat slow ferry is a charmer, but it does sort of roll. Four hours later, my queasy tummy's rolling too, and I regret the Junk Food Day idea. I still possess a large unopened bag of crisps that I knew the moment I paid hard-earned money for the idiotic thing that it was a waste of valuable plastic. I'll give it away, I decide, to the first people I see.

My victims soon appear at the junk food stall, dithering over what to buy. The bloke looks a bit distraught, counting up paltry change. He bought three tins of beer per hour, over the course of the trip, almost like clockwork. They're both ogling the many varieties of crisps, in every unnatural colour and flavour possible. They cannot decide. This is my moment to strike.

I give them my unopened crisps, and they're pleasantly surprised. They are both British. She's posh and he's not. The bloke is elaborately tattooed, and they sport identical bulky wooden jewellery. He has what I think is a Hare Krishna pigtail. We go our separate ways.

After the boat dumps everyone unceremoniously onto the pier, there is the usual organised mayhem of taxis dividing us up between them before racing away to various destinations. The Tattooed Crisps Couple are going to the village next to mine, and we decide to share a song-taew taxi truck.

This takes a while. We get an offer that sounds fine with me, but she disagrees about what constitutes the going rate. I am ready to hop in, but she bargains. She bargains and bargains and bargains. This gets us nowhere. We find ourselves in the strange position of having the cabbies walk away from us, and it's rarely that way around. There we are, stranded in a small port town, where she has alienated the entire vehicle-driving population.

"Let her handle this," the guy instructs me.

"I know," she says. "You two get drinks. I'll find one of my guys over there. I know him. It'll be fine. Wait here." She peels off some cash for the boyfriend to get the drinks, which means beer for them and a soft drink for me. She clippety-clops away in her high heels and middle-aged tan towards a café table of very unimpressed guys who all look like they own trucks.

"How many times you been here? I been here seventeen times. Seventeen! And her? Way more than that. She knows what she's doing. She'll get a good rate."

I don't care. It will be peanuts, and we could have been there by now. Meanwhile, we sip cold drinks, huddling under precious shade, and he offers me his life story. It's a terrible one. His drug addicted, prostitute mother committed suicide. His drug dealing, pimp father was murdered. He drifted off to the Hare Krishnas, which all went horribly wrong. Now he has been taken under wing by this very organised woman, twenty years his senior, who has an unnamed business in Malaysia. She may marry him so they can return there legally. She seems to have the role of his mother, nurse and social worker.

"She's a dyke," he informs me.

"Oh," I reply, with a pause. "Why are you telling me that?"

"I don't know," he shrugs, "Maybe you're a dyke too."

"Is this relevant?"

He babbles on about being unwanted and abandoned. This new guardian of his, however capable, cannot possibly be the entire hospital and support network it will take to establish any equilibrium in this whirlwind mind of his. I offer noises of positivity, but can see a horrendously rocky road ahead. He has multiple abuse problems. He is sweet and awfully confused. He wants me to come and stay with them. He says this repeatedly, and appears a bit obsessive. She comes back just in time.

She is annoyed. We are paying exactly what they asked for, half a broiling hour ago.

"It shouldn't be that high," she insists. "We've been here plenty of times off-season."

"This isn't off-season," I point out. "It's New Year's week. This is their busiest time."

"No," she snaps, "it should still be considered off-season, I'm sorry. Monsoon is barely over. Never mind. Finish your drink. Take your time. They can wait."

I don't want to wait. I want to go. I bolt the drink, and their beers don't take them that long either. He thanks her for how good she is to him, and hugs her thoroughly while she recoils, gently telling him not to. She's like a mother patiently training a toddler.

"We are not sleeping together," he says.

"That's right," she emphasises. "We share a room with twin beds."

I don't know why they're telling me this. They are starting to scare me slightly. I want to go.

"So, you're coming to stay with us, right? Right? Right?" He says this like a nodding dog in the back of a family car, over and over, with no sign of stopping.She taps her cigarette. "He does this", she says. "He latches on to older women he thinks will mother him. He's latched on to you. I can see it. I know."

"Come live with us, come live with us, come live with us." It's becoming like a chant. Hare Krishna, Hare Krishna, Come live with us, Hare Hare.

"I have a place to stay," I explain. "I'll stay there."

This exchange repeats itself so many times that I stand up, put on my rucksack, and wait for them to take the hint. I have my own chant: Just get me there, Just get me there, Hurry hurry, Just get me there.

"Come on," she orders us, "time to go". We locate the truck, and she tries in vain to bargain one last time before we pile in and bounce through beautiful hills dotted with palms and jungle to a cute village where I feel I might never get the smile off my sweaty, grateful face. I kick out my bags and leap into the dust.

"Come visit us," he yells for the fiftieth time as they drive away. I hear it's nice, where they're headed: the next cove just down the road. I might visit, in a few weeks, when I'm sure they're back in Malaysia and whatever unique reality they have created for themselves.

I've booked a room at the Swim Inn, the cheapest in the area. My modest hut on stilts is a funny combination of styles. On the one hand, ruffled dresses adorn rubbish bins and toilet rolls, and there are gift soaps and shampoo – plus the towels are monogrammed and folded ingeniously. There's a classy pine drying rack. On the other hand, there's no basin. Above the bed is a large plastic poster of Pekinese dogs in fluorescent colours. The floor is stick-on plastic. The curtains are on a crude wire and do not cover the windows. But everything and everybody here is really very sweet. I am so relieved to be here.

The next day, I'm up with the light to search for new digs. A small fridge with an ice compartment is now a fully-fledged obsession and love object. I'd trade a basin for a fridge, in fact. This place has got me used to spitting and chucking all manner of fluids into the toilet, so that obstacle is no longer a problem.

My morning consists of walking from one extreme end of this long bay to the other. I stroll through every resort and look at several rooms in each of them, gathering prices and details. In between, I drink coconuts and mango lassis. The Cola Nut I already saw last night, where I had fried rice as fast as I could and ruled it out quickly, but I do not blame the establishment. It was populated by very loud (and I mean very, very loud) Australian students, each out-shouting the next in a drinking game that involved pounding the table, yelling at full volume, and making chicken sounds on cue. I finished my meal efficiently. A mellowing middle-aged biker couple exited just before I did, nodding towards me a wry, respectful sort of complicity. We fled. I won't be back either. The far side of the bay is lovely, and unaffordable. I read there might be some cheaper digs around here, but that is all wrong. By the time I get there, it is stiflingly hot. I find a cluster of lovely houses. I sigh and drool and pine for my own kitchen. Oh for ice cubes! Oh to simply make my morning coffee and breakfast in my sweaty pyjamas! These lovely kitchened houses are full, of course. They exemplify my dream home-away-from-home. Just one burner and a mini-fridge, that's all I'd like. To snag these, you arrive during or before monsoon in the autumn. I haven't timed this well at all, just after New Year.

Here I spy a beach bar and I know I need fluids. I buy ice cold drinks from the lovely Mr Pai, a kind, shy and laid-back fellow who appears to live on his lounger or behind the bar. "Pai" means "to go" but he isn't going anywhere. I ask about houses. He struggles with English, but tries sincerely to answer my many questions. He even gets up, motions for me to follow, and tours me around to speak to some of his neighbours. Everything is full. Their mimes are unmistakable, as is his sweetly shrugging apology.

I buy another drink while he thinks about this. His face lights up with an idea.

"My friend, he falang…" he starts. "Falang", the infamous Thai word for "white and/or European person". Maybe it's just non-Asian? I think it can be "whitey", or even "honky", depending on tone. He says it nicely, just meaning "white guy".

"My friend," says Mr Pai, "he speak English. He have bungalow. Not here, but not far. I telephone." The trusty mobile is whipped out, and a call is made. Whoever this is, this foreigner of unknown Caucasian origin, he speaks fluent Thai.

"He come. One minute, maybe two minute. OK?"

"Thank you!" This is wonderfully OK. I'm gulping the icy drink, and Mr Pai, happy to have done his good deed, sinks back into his lounger. Soon a motorcycle pulls up, bringing a stocky, sun-tanned man in a rock band tee shirt and combat trousers with pockets stuffed and jangling. I can't tell what nationality he might be, approaching in his flip-flops. He's in his middle thirties, with short sandy hair, blue eyes, a friendly handshake and an extremely relaxed attitude.

"Ciao," he smiles.

Welcome to Mai Bay

Nic is Italian and has lived in Thailand for fifteen years. He's a sturdy guy, likes his beer, and can drive a motorcycle while smoking a cigarette. He speaks mostly comprehensible English with a strong Italian accent, a wide and colourful vocabulary, and a creative, mixed salad approach to grammar.

"I have bungalow. But, is simple. Is no hot water."

"That's OK."

"OK. Also, is no near sea. For swim, maybe five, ten minute walk."

"OK."

"OK, also, is up hill, very big hill. Some people do not like…"

"That's OK too."

"OK, so, you want to see?"

"Yes, I want to see."

"OK, let's go." He gets back on the motorcycle and waves for me to climb on.

I hesitate. I'm scared of these things. To be honest, I'm scared of the whole motorbike scene down here. Nobody wears helmets or much clothing, they drive like nuts, and there's always someone on acid. That's before you count the drunks and the stoners, who are everywhere at all times of day – during busy season anyway. Every other person has a broken leg or swathes of skin scraped off. There is no helmet anywhere near Nic's motorbike, and I am a wimp. He smiles.

"Please," he says, "I have family, three children. I take every day, on motorbike. I think you do not like, but is OK. I go slow, OK?"

He's an Italian dad. I decide to trust this.

"OK."

I climb on, nod thanks to Mr Pai – who's already back on his lounger – and grab hold of the side loops on Nic's trousers. I'm not usually so physical on first meeting, but needs must. He does indeed go nice and slowly through the village and to the foot of the aforementioned Big Hill. It's a whopper all right, more or less straight up.

"OK!" he calls. "Now, we need the power!" He revs so suddenly that I grab him like I love him dearly. Eventually I exhale and regain consciousness after we land on the cliff-top with a thump and a cloud of dust, and he hasn't lost the ash on his cigarette.

"Bella Vista" is daubed simply across a large grey rock. At its base sleeps a large black battle-scarred dog. A massive canopied wooden deck opens as wide as the spectacular bay, with its many boats and jungled mountains beyond. There's a scruffy, uneven, leaf-covered snooker table in the centre. To the right is a raised deck with a couple of hammocks, some floor cushions around low tables, and sunburned pink couples slurping soup.

Beyond the snooker table is the central feature: a handsome long table with facing benches, all of beautiful roughly hewn wood. Another pink couple dig at coconuts. Beyond that is another raised deck with rough wooden railings and full-length laying down cushions facing the best view of the bay, strewn with bodies, arms outstretched clutching beer bottles.

I really hope this is it.

To the left clatters the kitchen, in which an energetic Thai lady jogs an infant in her arms as she explains something to the cook, a stout Thai lady who is throwing ingredients into a sizzling stove while a small boy clings to her leg.

"My wife busy now. I show you bungalow." He pads across the deck and down some very steep stone steps, treacherously cut into the hillside, then down a grassy path to seven little huts on stilts, all overlooking the blue, blue bay.

I really hope this is it.

Unlike on the shore, these huts are not shoved right

next to each other. There's enough space for residents to sing in the shower and get away with it. Yet the café is just up the hill, so there's privacy yet companionship. This is a dreamed-of combination. This one even has a hammock already. The inside is simple and acceptable. The clincher? Back up those steps, the menu is half Thai and half Italian. I have, after all, seen every other bungalow within a three mile radius, and my head is still numb with dehydration. I've got to park it somewhere and this feels right. I pay right then and there: a whole four hundred baht (seven pounds or ten dollars), so that this cannot slip away from me.

"Naturally," Nic mentions casually, "price goes lower if you stay one week. Go down more for one month." He can see this possibility is written all over my face.

"Can I bring my things now?" I ask.

"Sure. I take you back."

Riding straight down the Hill out-thrills zipping up it. The girl at the Swim Inn is sweet about it only being one night. After a shower, a reshuffle and more cool drinks, I drag my stuff – too much for a motorcycle – slowly through soft hot sand to a corner with the word "Taxi" dribbled in paint on a plank nailed to a weathered coconut tree. The taxi, a typical two-bencher truck that's nicely worse for wear, rests near a souvenir shack, its owners snoozing inside on a mat amidst the sarongs and the frisbees.

Mrs Truck wakes up first, and shoves Mr Truck

upright. He's a tall, lanky gentleman with a big, sleepy, toothy smile. She's short and peppery.

"Where you go?" she calls eagerly, as he yawns and re-ties his drawstring trousers.

I try several pronunciations of "Bella Vista", and get blank stares. I hand over the business card in Thai and Italian, which doesn't help a bit.

"Nic? Italiano? It-a-ly?"

Blank stares. It's time to mime.

"Big guy, this tall, short hair, kind of a beer belly? Up that Big Bastard Hill over there?"

I mime all of the above, and it appears to ring a bell.

"Neek?"

"Yes, Neek!" By George we've got it. Mr Truck joins in.

"Neek!" they sing out in unison. Up the hill, they mime in unison. Come on, let's go, they mime in unison, herding me to the truck. Mrs Truck even offers me the honoured front, but I go with the cargo and the strong breeze.

When we get to the Big Bastard Hill, Mr Truck really guns it and I hang on tight. Again I'm breathless on landing. There is a wonderfully fresh breeze up here, with completely different smells than on the shore. Across the road is a steep incline of pure thick jungle and an almost syrupy sweet perfume. The foliage is totally tangled and there are no paths into it. It surges uphill.

Nic greets Mr Truck happily, the way you salute an old pal you haven't seen in a while. They gab in Thai. They start laughing, and Nic turns to me.

"We laugh about the business card no work. It never works in Thai, to write in our alphabet. No one can read this and say it so Thai people understand."

I've heard this. There seems to be no standardised or easy way to write down how to sing Thai. You'd almost need musical notation.

A lump buried in the larger hammock turns out to be a Thai granddad stretching sleepily. Grandpa quietly slides out of his hammock like a fish poured out of a bucket. He has salt and pepper hair and gently fading blue tattoos that might have been home-made in his youth. He wears shorts and nothing else. Collecting a key, he takes my bags and glides noiselessly down the stairs. Sounds of kitchen clatter and baby gurgling waft out of the kitchen. Around the café, abandoned plates and coconut shells await collection. The gang are gone, and so are all their motorbikes.

I follow Grandpa down the dizzying steps to my new home, Bungalow Six. On second viewing, I decide it's just what I've been dreaming of. It's simple and minimalist, all wood and thatch. It's high on stilts, with more of a ladder than steps. He leaves his flip-flops at the bottom, but waves that I don't have to. There's a narrow balcony with a chair, a clothesline, and a rickety, padlocked door. He unlocks the door, hands me the padlock and key, places my bag gently inside, and silently disappears down the ladder again. Soon my second bag appears at the top of the steps. I take it and thank him but he's already gone.

Home is now one plain room, one plain bed, a light bulb and a fan. To the left is a tiny counter with a basin and a mirror, and beyond that is the shower (cold) and toilet (European sit-down, not Asian squat type). There is no flushing mechanism but instead a large bucket by a spigot.

I am very pleased to see their traditional and fabulously practical water squirt gun, plumbed in right next to the toilet. I wish those were international. There is no loo roll, and nowhere to put one, but with the squirter plus soap and towel, there really is no need. In many ways, this alone separates the Tourists from the Travellers, or perhaps the Greenhorns from Anyone Who's Been to Asia Before. This is one of many tourist vs. traveller pecking order games.

Near the front window is a corner counter over a sadly empty space exactly the right size for the fridge which ought to be there. I long for in-house ice cubes, cold water, and fruit. Snacks! My kitchen dreams are drooling once more.

There are no hooks, nails, or anywhere to hang up anything at all. Tomorrow I'll go to the village and buy cup hooks, string, and hangers to create laundry lines and rope ladders. It's not just a practical task. It's a sort of travelling puzzle and an ongoing game. The more eccentric the contraptions, the better I like it. A few weeks play can evolve a complex jungle-gym or, maybe someday, hanging gardens Babylon-style.

For now, the clothes get released from their wrinkly, steaming prison of a suitcase, so they can fling their arms and legs across the four corners of the bed. I do too, after a nice freezing shower. As often can happen, the first twenty seconds of water is hot, having sat in the overground pipe in the searing midday sun. Then suddenly water gushes straight from the underground spring, icy and shouting brisk.

I am smugly aware that I have been to low-budget Asian places before, and I know the score: most casual places give you one sheet only, never two. A top sheet, if you actually use one in this climate, you cold, bloodless white weirdo, you yourself are expected to provide. Newcomers are seen wandering into the nearest junk stall late in the evening, stunned they must purchase some overpriced gaudy tie-dyed bedspread before they can go to sleep. I already have my overpriced gaudy bedspread from before. Others actually employ pyjamas.

I can hear tiny scratching noises. Please let it not be mice, or baby rats, or any other rodent? Or snakes, come to think of it – ah wait, they don't scratch, or do they? Giant roaches? No, it's a charming alternate. Dozens of tiny geckos, nearly transparent, are shooting all over the walls and ceiling, mosquito hunting.

The fan chugs lightly to and fro. Outside, a breeze scratches through the palms high above. Melodious birds are chirping, percussive geckos are pitter-pattering all over, and there is nothing in this moment but perfect peace and quiet. Bones settle. Muscles sigh. Lungs fill. Heart swells. An old spiritual song comes to mind. "Free at last, free at last, great god almighty, we are free at last." I can rest my weary head. Mission accomplished. Convalescence may now begin. Please be healthy by next month at the latest. That was the last order on that list, wasn't it? Get better.

I can see a little plot of land, divided into different lots for fruit and vegetables. One lot has clover. This field that has to rest a year, before one can plant there again. There's always a field like this. It's just not planting time. It needs feeding and building up. Forget about planting for now. Not here. Not this year.

Later I awake as if from one dream to another, and set up my new house. I select my least wrinkled shirt, which is still absurdly crumpled. I splash on "bug juice", evil chemicals which drive bugs away and possibly shorten my life. The mental shopping list adds mosquito coils, or maybe a proper mosquito net, though I find them claustrophobic. Anything is better than swooning around half-demented on anti-malaria pills, especially when they don't entirely prevent malaria anyway. The bug issue is a real one. Most things are better than malaria.

I am now slung in a hammock, gazing upon blue water, feeling warm and grateful. Somehow, with house-moving, I did not have lunch. That's like forgetting to breathe. I'm ready for an early supper and a beer or two. Even as hungry as I am, it's uncomfortable walking into a new place on my own. If the trip so far is anything to go by, it'll be more people speaking languages I don't understand. In that sense it's straightforward. I put a book in my bag.

On the long slow climb up the cliff face, while I wonder what to eat, I daydreamily drag my hand up the knotty wooden handrail, and meet red ants coming the other way. Their infamous bite is piercing and the itching is fierce. Thailand is where I learned why people leap when anyone cries, "Red ants! Red ants!" and everyone immediately starts dancing.

I wonder who else is staying here. Socially, a worst case scenario is that I'm the only older single amongst six pairs of demonstrative honeymooners. The second worst could be a gang of loud students doing chicken impersonations in drinking games. There are so many more.

I can't imagine it was planned, but the steps get taller and taller, until it feels like mountaineering. I need to squirt out an "oof" sound on the last three steps, and arrive breathless, clutching my side, panting and looking around. There's no one here.

Wonderful smells from the kitchen suggest garlic, onion, possibly beef, and maybe oregano or basil. The kitchen door is open wide. Nic stirs and sniffs and adds things to a large pot. A girl about seven clings to his leg, which is about as tall as she is. She is clamped to his leg like a splint. He tilts to divert cigarette ash away from the food, as the girl yells directions in Thai at him, pointing at the saucepan and jumping excitedly. He answers with gentle explanations of what he intends to do instead.

"Hello," I call. "That smells wonderful."

"Good evening, thank you. Is for my friends, Italians, big group, they come tonight. They want spaghetti. OK, is simple, I try. If is just cook for friends, like home, is OK."

It smells way better than a mere OK, so this is modesty. He stirs in something else, which the girl questions and then accepts. He lets her stir while he takes a drag on the cigarette.

"Everything OK, with the bungalow?"

"Everything is perfect with the bungalow!"

"Good! Would you like to see a menu?"

"Is there any coconut juice?"

"Sure." He speaks in Thai to the little girl, who brings a large coconut to the cook. After three impressive, violent whacks of her cleaver, she slips a straw inside, while the girl gets a plate and spoon.

"Can I also have chicken and garlic, any way she wants to cook it, on rice, and some fried vegetables, anything, any way she wants?"

He explains this to the cook, who smiles at me and proceeds to her wok. From the back room, Noo emerges jogging a small baby.

"Ah, now you can meet my wife, Noo. Also the baby, Beatrice, but we call Bee. Three month old, birthday last week."

Bee has huge dark eyes and seems interested in having a good stare at me from over her mother's shoulder.

"Bungalow OK?" asks Noo.

"The bungalow is perfect". The seven-year-old shouts instructions to Nic, who saunters over while she points and barks orders.

"And this one, this is the boss of the whole place, the middle daughter, Mia. Over there, older daughter, Tia." At a central table, salad greens for the Italian meal are getting chopped by Tia, a girl of about fourteen.

"You have three?"

"Three. Tia, Mia, Bee. They have long name too, but Thai people all have short nickname, for every day. You remember like this: Tia – teenager, Mia – middle, Bee – baby. You have nickname?"

"No, I don't think so."

"OK. Maybe we find one later."

The girls and women buzz around the kitchen, and set the big long table for the group. Mia carries my coconut to a little square table to one side, where I decide, OK, in this scenario I am happy to be the little square lady at the little square table to one little square side of the social galaxy. I sip my coconut and gaze at the bay and the warm pink glow of a setting sun. Soon my deliciously garlicky chicken arrives, and so do twenty Italian men.

Little Italy, Thai Style

The roar of their motorbikes heralds them. They are all fountains of energy, backslapping and deep heavy laughter. Some are impossibly good-looking, and even at my age this is unnerving. I have my book and wish I could be invisible, but I'm the only one in the whole place. Every single one of them greets me, one after the other as, I am to learn, is their daily custom.

"Buona sera" (good evening).

"Ciao bella." (Hey beautiful? I look behind me.)

Most Italians here act like it's incredibly bad manners to walk into a room and not warmly greet and spend time speaking with every single person there, touching them wherever possible. This certainly takes most Brits by surprise.

"Buona sera. Parla Italiano?" (Do you speak Italian?)

"Er, sorry, no. Well, 'un poco'?"

"Un poco, a little, this is good!" Nic announces. "Please, meet my friends."

"That's OK," I protest, "I'll only forget. You don't have to, really." I go all British.

He presents them all, one after the next, in a flurry of hand-shaking, cheek-kissing, shoulder-patting, and even some hand-kissing. It all happens rather quickly. I think there's Alfredo, Alfonzo, Vincenzo, Roberto, Guido, Stefano, a few Francos and some Marcos. There are plenty of tattoos, more chest hair than usual, and robust decibel levels. With gusto they snap off bottle tops with their cigarette lighters. Soon, forty hairy arms are gesticulating up and down the long table like an exuberant centipede.

"Ah," says Nic, "so sorry, I forget, we only speak Italian. My English very bad. And my friends, nothing. Nobody speak English here."

There is a guilty pause.

"OK," he admits. "They all know English, but they do not like." This starts me giggling.

"Is true," shrugs Guido. "At school, we study, many year. We no like. No remember nothing." They all nod, to a man, obviously understanding everything, which further fuels my giggling.

"Please, prego," I insist, "speak Italian. Buon' appetito!" They applaud this with toasts and cries of "Brava! Grazie! Buon' appetito!"

The pasta, sauce, salad, bread and trimmings pour out of the kitchen on the arms of Thai women: first the cook (her son hiding behind a pillar), then teenager Tia and middle girl Mia, followed by Noo with Bee, the babe in arms. She greets her husband's pals, with "Ciao, ciao" in her strong Thai accent. She understands their Italian but answers in single words, all in between jogging the baby continually.

"Baby is little bit sick, so they stay inside now," explains Nic. The men blow kisses and coo to the whisked-away child as the women vanish into the kitchen to organise their own dinner, which looks and smells entirely different to anyone else's. Soon it's just distant girl talk between intermittent baby coughs and shrieks.

The men pass things to and fro, making appreciative food noises, while I wade through my garlic chicken, which is juicy, fragrant and very garlicky. The guys examine, appreciate, and discuss every single thing they eat. They enthuse on and on. I wish I understood more.

"Sorry, we speak only Italian," says Nic. "I explain if it become interesting, but for now, everybody talk only about food. Normally is food, maybe football, maybe women – but mainly the food. First the fish, then the ice cream, now—"

"Now cheese?"

"Yes," he smiles. "This man, Alfredo, he have café. He find good place for buy buffalo mozzarella." Alfredo sculpts the details with his hands, and the men are rapt.

"Alfredo, he has fine restaurant, beautiful food. Here more like home kitchen."

"I like a home kitchen," I say, wiping my chin. Meanwhile Mia climbs into Nic's lap, grabs his fork and helps herself to his plate. He sighs and looks for another fork.

"I never eat my food, in this place," he complains, grinning. "Always somebody take my food. I live with four women. I never eat alone. I never have time in the bathroom. Look, look at this!" Mia eats merrily, as Nic smiles contentedly.

My juicy garlic chicken is thus accompanied by a discussion of Italian cheeses, pastas, vegetables, and wine, with a special section on bread flours and how to blend them. Some of this I get from the articulate gesticulations of Chef Alfredo. It's wonderful to listen to a language musically when you don't know what it means. Italian is more like music than any other language. It's just an odd accompaniment to a Thai meal. Words start jumping out.

Subito (suddenly).

Ma non troppo (not too much).

Some new topic is afoot. The tone and pace has changed altogether. Nic leans over again, with his loud stage whisper.

"Now we talk about the army. In Italy, all men must go to the army. But, we do not want to go. So, sometimes, we act crazy, shouting, 'No! Don't give me the gun. I kill you. I kill everybody!' Say terrible, crazy things, then you go home. Everybody do this."

"Everybody?" I ask. They all nod as one, like it's a national routine.

"Plenty people go to army," shrugs Nic. "Why everyone must go?" Could Rumpole of the Bailey have argued this any more effectively?

Tutti (every one).

Poco un poco (little by little).

Suddenly I remember where these Italian words are coming from. When I studied music, long ago, the instructions were often in Italian. It was literally decades ago, but I might know a hundred words. I eavesdrop in earnest now as the men drink, smoke, and slurp what the Brits call Spag-Bol. They enjoy stories, jokes, gossip, passionate political argument, and beer after beer, until their speech is slurred, loud and jolly, and the moon is high in the sky.

Piano (softly).

Lento (slowly).

This is hilarious. I am full, satisfied, immensely sleepy, and almost wish I were capable of ordering another beer and staying awake. After all, I was up with the light to find this place. I've come a long way since sun-up. I try to catch Nic's eye.

"Can I pay, please?"

He doesn't seem rushed. "If you like. But, is more easy if we do tomorrow. Is OK?"

"Sure, it's OK."

A sleepy Noo emerges from the kitchen, and I realise some of the shrieking has stopped.

"Baby sleep," she murmurs, staggering past the men with a "Ciao". The girls start clearing things away. Noo is as tall as Nic but half the width – sinewy and muscular – with pale golden skin and the weary look of the mother of a three month old and two older kids, plus with a café to run and a husband on his second or third large beer. She joins me on the raised deck.

"Everything OK?"

"Everything is perfect! Meal, bungalow, everything. Perfect."

"OK!" she beams, however tired and aching. "You want something, you say me. OK?"

"OK" I agree, smiling back.

Clattering noises eventually cease in the kitchen. Tia joins her mother, Mia follows and, finally, so does the cook, after laying her sleeping child to one side.

"This Taa," says Noo, introducing me to the cook who nods warmly. "Son, name Boo."

Taa looks a bit older, a bit fleshier, and that much more tired. But her smile is sweet. She knows much less English. She sits nearby, and the girls join the cluster, creating a funny choreography of two long lines of Italian men, next to a circle of Thai women around a single white female. Noo turns to me.

"Sorry, I forget. You name – how you say?"

"Eileen."

"A-i-din? Airin?"

Mine is not a great name for most Asians to pronounce, frankly. I've ended up in a land where I am unpronounceable. The girls test it out, tentatively, and get my thumbs-up.

"Baby OK?" I ask Noo.

"Baby OK. Baby sleep." Pause. "You have baby?"

"Me? No."

This gets communicated to the others, who seem puzzled. She battles on, much less sure of her English than her husband is. She gropes for the right words.

"You…you have…" She struggles, and finally points to her wedding band. "You have?"

"No," I answer.

They're surprised and a little thoughtful. "No have?"

"No have."

It's hard to explain in a few words. There's an odd pause, so I add, "Before, yes. Now, no."

They stare. Finally, I do the mime that has become a standard issue reply throughout this whole trip. I take an imaginary ring off my left hand's second smallest finger, and mime hurling it far away. Now they get it.

"You travel alone?"

"Yes."

They all consider this, as if for the first time ever. I have had this experience over and over, in many places the world over, where women tell me it's the first time it even crossed their minds that they might travel on their own, some day. It just didn't seem possible, let alone likely, for a thousand different reasons – many of them having to do with children, of course. Noo seriously mulls on this idea, and it doesn't take long to spill forth her thoughts.

"This good. You free. You want to go? You go. You want something? You do. You lucky. You very lucky!"

She explains to the others. Taa nods with feeling, and the girls are fascinated. There's some consultation and they prod her to ask me a question.

"Sometime, you afraid?"

"Yes, sometimes. Also, sometimes it's lonely."

They don't know this word. I leaf through my guidebook to find the nearest thing. "Sometimes… it's boring."

They agree instantly.

Noo thinks. "Here, family. I stay. But if no family, if no Nic, I go see all Thailand. I see Asia. Maybe after I see Europe. Maybe when children big."

Taa says something jokey and taunting. They all collapse laughing. Noo screams and pretends to beat Taa. They giggle and play fight until Noo is prodded to tell me. She refuses at first, in a mock huff.

"OK. She say, maybe I stay. Maybe I make baby number four."

They all shriek with laughter.

"I say, No! Three enough. No more baby!" Now we are all laughing and poor Nic is squirming, half in the men's conversation and half in ours. Taa shoves Noo to tell me more.

"OK. I explain you. Nic and me, we have three girl. He want boy, for baby number four. But I say no! Baby finish! Bambino finito!"

The girls are in full flow now, laughing and rolling about. Nic keeps his composure as all the women in his life announce his family planning to the new guest. The Italian men do not notice any of this. They are still talking about food.

"OK, I need to say goodnight." I get up and take my bag – and really mean it this time.

"Wait," calls Noo. She speaks to Taa, who disappears, returning shortly to bestow upon me a water glass, soap and toilet paper. I "wai" – the all-purpose bow plus respectful prayerlike gesture – bowing overly deeply as if for royalty, and this is hilarious to them. It's possibly my first in-joke here.

Noo shakes a smiling forefinger and mock scolds, "You remember. You need something? You say me. OK?"

"OK."

"Nic, he OK, but sometime he forget. You say me."

"OK. Thank you."

There is something so pure and delightful about any language in its simplest, most pidgin-y form. What could be sweeter and clearer than, "You say me"?

"I have a question. When do you open for breakfast?"

"Er, I no capito. Momento please."

What was that? Was that Italian and English mashed together with a Thai accent? She calls Nic.

"Yes, can I help you?"

"When are you open for breakfast?"

"Nine. About nine. Maybe something like that."

"Is ten better?"

"Ten for sure. Ten-thirty definitely for sure."

"OK. Thank you. See you tomorrow." Sounds like we're on for eleven, then.

Finally, after consultation and rehearsal, I say goodnight in Thai to the Thais, and in Italian to the Italians. The really sleepy ones just wave, and a few generous souls say goodnight in English. Torch in hand, I climb back down the stony cliff side to spend my first night in my new home: Bungalow Six, Bella Vista, Mai Island Bay, Little Italy, Thailand

Bella Vista: Day One and the Breakfast Menu

A soft breeze delivers sounds of distant fishing boats, vaguely barking dogs, and countless birds and cicadas. After seven years in the Scottish climate, any day that is non-raining, non-freezing, and non-grey is be savoured. Simple, plain warmth is never taken for granted. Oddly enough, it's uncharacteristically cool for this time of year in these parts. I pull up a few more covers (spare clothing, that is), thanking my lucky stars there is no alarm clock and I am near blue water.

Eventually I roll out of bed in the direction of the toilet. En route past the mirror, I get my customary morning shock at what my hair gets up to during the night. It's a raggedy mop-top, nested in a jungle.

Something in there is tickling my head. A tiny rubbery gecko leaps out of my hair, plops to the floor, spins like a confused compass needle, and shoots across the room and up the wall. Oh do I laugh! Deep belly laughter explodes forth, surges and rolls like ocean waves, one after the next, finally fading. What a gorgeous sensation. When did I last laugh like that? I can't even recall. Now there's a symptom. Even a couple of silly tears trickle down. The only prospect better than this, at the moment, is a breakfast of Italian coffee and Thai soup, which motors me into alertness and a seriously bracing shower.

At "opening time" (somewhere between nine and ten-thirty – OK maybe eleven), I heave myself up the gargantuan steps towards the summit, again arriving unable to breathe. It's another perfectly clear blue day, if strangely cool. The café looks unpopulated, that is, until Nic and Grandpa emerge from the kitchen with trays and boxes, and the look of an event in progress.

"Good morning," calls Nic. "How are you? You sleep OK? Can I help you?"

"I'm very well thanks. Yes I slept well, and please can I have a strong coffee?"

"Sure. You can wait maybe one or two minute, please?" he asks, juggling dishes.

"Of course."

"Thank you. First we make New Year gift. Is late but, we make."

He explains these are ritual offerings to the land spirits, who are in a way their spiritual landlords. Grandpa supervises the prescribed list of chicken, duck, pork, squid, fish, five fruits, and whiskey. He puts these out in a display, lights the incense, and says the prayer. I wonder how long the meat will be in the sun, and Nic reads my mind.

"When the incense finish, we put back in the kitchen. The idea is, the prayer cannot be heard by the spirits if it is solid. So, you burn something to take the prayer up into the air, to where spirit lives. After all the smoke goes up, the message is delivered. We say, thank you for let us live here. We promise be good tenants." Around his neck is the sort of medallion many Buddhists wear, with the photo of a revered teacher in a frame.

Grandpa is now hanging up a very long string of Chinese firecrackers. Nic looks embarrassed. "We want to do on the New Year, but I forget. I don't know how this happen."

He repeats this in Thai to his father-in-law, who chortles and shrugs. The two men motion for me to stand back, while they light the fuse and retreat. Another thousand boom-booms crack like rifle fire. The two men look rather satisfied with themselves.

Nic dusts himself off. "So, uno caffè italiano?"

"Yes please, er…Sì, per favore?"

"Prego! OK!"

He motions that I can sit where I like, and I choose the end of the great long table, facing the wonderful view. It's cool and clear, and the bay is electric blue. I just wish I had a jacket.

On the wall is a crude map of the island, and also a large yellowing poster of their royal family. It's from way back when the King was a young man with a young wife and a young family. It is hung very high in the traditional area of respect. Also very high on the wall are photos of a revered Buddhist teacher, presumably the same one pictured in Nic's medallion. This is typical of most small businesses here. In fact, it would be conspicuously absent otherwise.

Nic brings two coffees and joins me at the long wooden table, telling me more about that morning's offering.

"So, New Year OK now. We tell land spirits, we take care of their place, and we ask for help and good luck from them too. Anyway, minimum," he laughs, "is that you give them things so they make no trouble." So at its highest level it's a prayer for divine help and the promise of one's best behaviour, and at the other end of the spectrum it's a kind of spiritual protection racket, perhaps.

Lots of households and small businesses start their day this way. Many an early coffee for tourists has been delayed thirty whole impatient seconds while café owners say their prayers for a better day, a better self, a better world, and more kindness in the overall human pool. Then they go make someone's impatient coffee. First things first.

"Is this Buddhism combined with older religions?"

"Yes," he nods, "exactly. The Bon religion is older, and always about the Nature, and the spirits in the Nature, the family before you, and people who live on this land before you come."

"Why wait over a week for your New Year fireworks?"

"We wait for…here, I show you." At the wall calendar, he peels off yesterday, pointing at today's cross-referenced European and Thai and Chinese holidays, holy days, moon cycles and – in this case – special "Buddha Days" too. Auspicious days. Extra good luck days. Days for things like asking for help and making promises or agreeing to protection rackets and other offers one cannot refuse.

"This is Buddha Day, lucky day. Only a few each year. Also, today is Wednesday, and I was born on a Wednesday."

Here I learn, for example, that since I was born on a Thursday, I can join all the other Born-on-a-Thursday people by wearing some item of either orange or brown – the two colours I like least, as it happens. On Mondays, Bangkok is predominantly dressed in yellow, since the King was born on a Monday and the royal crest is on yellow. It's a big thing here. Your daily commute in any major town or city will show you plenty of people wearing the colour of the day. Tuesday's pink, Wednesday's green or grey, Friday's pale blue, Saturday black or purple and Sunday's red.

I do hope Nic and company get a nice slice of the Good Luck action on this heavily cross-referenced lucky day. We sip our coffee thoughtfully.

"Is it possible," I drool out loud, "to get a Thai style chicken noodle soup, with extra garlic and vegetables?"

"Of course, but not from me. Taa, the cook, arrive soon. For now, you want Italian bread with the coffee?"

Did he say Italian bread? It must be the beautiful home-made loaves everyone raved about last night at dinner. Of course I want some. I may just sit here all day, eating things, one after the next. He brings the bread and we both chew away. Then I tell him about the gecko that got tangled in my hair this morning.

He scratches his head. "This very strange. This gecko not normal. Normally they go on the floor, on the wall, not on the people. This gecko, he have a problem."

"It's OK. I like geckos."

"Ah, OK. I like too. They eat the mosquitoes. My family, they OK with the small ones, but not the big ones. Taa, the cook, she hate. And the grandfather, he kill." He mimes a big spear and a sharp thrust.

I shudder. I no kill. I have to stop talking this way.

The vroom of a motorcycle arrives up the Hill, with Taa the cook and her small bewildered son, Boo. Her oldest son, a macho motorcycle mechanic who can swagger sitting down, nods coolly and roars away. Taa has her apron on in no time, and Boo tears into the kitchen to hide.

Nic says something about soup and Taa nods. Then he mimes my gecko in the hair story and she shudders, rushing inside.

Nic grins. "She no like lizard in the hair. But she make nice soup for you now."

Noo now appears in her pyjamas, jogging baby Bee over her shoulder. The jogging is continual. When jogging in one place doesn't do the trick, she goes round what amounts to a racetrack around the snooker table.

Nic gestures with his cigarette. "The baby, she like move, all the time. So the mother, she need move, all the time. If still, she cry. So the mother is tired, all the time. I try to take, but this OK only five minute. Then she needs the mother, only the mother."

On her rounds, Noo manages a fragment of a conversation each time she trots past me, like on the old merry-go-rounds, where once each turn you can grab at a gold ring.

"Bungalow OK?"

"Yes, very good."

Next round: "You eat?"

"Taa is making soup now."

Next round: "You eat soup morning? You eat Thai food?"

"I love Thai food!"

Next round: "Good, you like Thai food. You like spicy?"

"No, not so spicy."

"Three chillies? Four? Five?"

"One, maybe two."

And so on.

Boo sticks his head out of the kitchen, and Nic beckons him over. He almost comes out, sees me, and goes back in."Boo is the youngest son of Taa, the cook. Only four, too small for school, so he comes with her. Is very boring for him. He no see other children, he no see nobody. But he love Thai kickboxing. Look."

Nic calls out something in Thai, and Boo appears instantly in front of him, both tiny fists up and eager, boxer style. He is about the size of Nic's lower leg. Nic pretends to ring a bell, and Boo leaps into action: kicking, spinning, jumping all over the place, and squawking like a monkey. They dance all over the deck, until finally Boo gathers all his strength and aims one determined kick at Nic's genitalia. Nic deftly steps aside with confident grace.

"Is OK," Nic drawls casually. "He does this every time, but I'm too fast."

Nic holds the boy's head so his windmilling arms can't connect to anything. Boo's arms blur like propellers as Nic gently grips the grapefruit-sized head with one hand while smoking his cigarette with the other.

"Poor boy, he have no father, no man to play with, like this. OK, is problem for the little bastard, but is pain in the ass for me too."

Taa arrives with a huge steaming bowl of soup and returns to the kitchen with Boo close at her heels. It's a classic clear broth with hair-fine rice noodles, tender slices of chicken, bits of sweet cabbage and other vegetables, and a heady waft of garlic and ginger. It is simple and perfect, and the whole set-up at this place is starting to feel the same way.

While steam coats my face, Boo magically transports himself to a new location behind a pillar, cunningly spying on me. It is not difficult to turn this into a game of the time-honoured classic I Can See You, Oh No You Can't, and other variations on that theme. I do believe we established a common language, or maybe terms of engagement.

"Good", observes Nic, "now maybe the cook can work."

Cabbage chopping noises commence. The day has begun. Grandpa – who I now think of as Pa – who is so silent I forget he's there, now takes some tools in hand and slips downhill towards the bungalows. Taa tells Boo again to get out of her way. The soup is gorgeous, and I drink every drop.

Noo returns with a nappied-up Bee.

"Airin, today, where you go?"

"I go to village." (Why do I switch to Bad English, or Binglish?)

"Where your motorbike?"

"No motorbike. I'll walk."

"No walk! Too far, too hot. You get motorbike."

"I don't like them."

This amazes her. It amazes all of them. Everything stops and time stands still. There's a short conference. Nic disappears behind the house and reappears with a bicycle. "Is this OK for you?"

I almost want to cry. "This is better than OK. This is perfect!"

His silent shrug says, "Of course is perfect. You want perfect? We bring perfect. Is simple." He pats his pockets and locates his keys.

"OK, now I go to town to get the food for today. You need something?"

"No. I have everything." This is so much truer today than it was yesterday.

"OK. If sometime you need something, you say me, OK?"

The three magic words are: you – say – me.

"OK. Thank you."

"OK. See you later." There is a stream of Thai from all sides, which sounds like a collective shopping list being hurled at him. With that he revs and roars down the hill.

Noo has settled Bee into a perpetual motion chair that she can rock with her foot while she chops fruit and vegetables.

"You want coffee? Drink? Eat? Something?"

"No, I'm fine." I am in fact utterly fine and dandy, for the first time in an awfully long while. With a bike, and a big hill, and a seashore, I'll be fit in no time.

"OK. Later, you want something, you say me. OK?"

"I say you, OK." Actually I have two questions. I'd

like a writing table and a kitchen, but it's only day one and too soon to be asking.

She's telepathic too. "What? What you want?"

"Well, do you have a table? Like that one there?"

"Sure. How many chair?"

"One."

"OK, easy. Nic bring tomorrow, OK?"

"OK. Thank you."

"And? What?"

"Well, is there a bungalow here with a kitchen?"

"Sì. Sorry, yes. Bungalow One and Two have kitchen."

"Really?"

"Yes."

"Are they full?"

"Yes."

"For a long time?"

"Yes. Long time."

"Ah."

"Why? You want?"

"Yes, please. I want. I want a kitchen."

"OK, I remember. If they go, you get."

"Thank you!"

A girl can dream. If they go, I get. A mere room morphs into a home-away-from-home, with just a mini-fridge, a single gas burner, and a mess kit with a few of life's top ten utensils. I'm officially in the queue for a kitchen. Now, as they say, it's time to get on my bike and see the village. However, Noo is holding out a bowl of pomello segments.

"You like?"

"I like." We munch and squirt. She stares thoughtfully.

"First time you come Thailand?"

Ah. Now there's a question.

Five Years Earlier: First Time in Thailand

It was a twelve hour flight from London to Bangkok, and I arrived a seventy-year-old pale, dehydrated raisin. I was new to long haul travel. Once, as a young student, I went from California to Japan, That flight was so long it felt like going to the moon, with a first meal, a movie, another meal, a matinée movie, an early supper, another movie or two and follow-up documentaries, after movie snack or late dinner options, the late night movie, and so on, until I expected the young on the flight to start pairing up and creating the next generation of this commune in the air.

There is something distinctive, buttock-clenching, and nerve-twisting about that visceral moment you're confronted by a squiggly alphabet you cannot decipher, and when you realise with certainty that if anything went wrong you'd have tremendous obstacles. You cannot

communicate at all. This adds a certain frisson of risk.
My first arrival in Bangkok was a matter of handing a
scribbled address to a cab driver who politely pretended
he read English, and hoping for the best.

There were misunderstandings and wrong turns, but
we finally arrived at a quiet little nook. It was a bit
stranded from all public transport, but a good place to
recover for a night or two. It was near a lovely local
market and a temple, and walking distance from the
river. I did try a brief walk, weak-kneed and dizzy, and
soon also to be nauseated by so many blood-soaked
butchers' stalls, and fragments of old fish everywhere, all
held close in a thick, humid cloud under a low, stuffy
roof. I'd have to learn the hard way that alcohol is not the
answer to jetlag. Still, in the original journals, my first
impressions are ecstatic:

In Thailand for the first time! A dream come true
for me! First impressions of Bangkok? It's
amazingly tidy. I actually saw people taking litter
off the street to put into bins. I don't mean
cleaners, I mean everyone. They just did it.
It's huge, sprawling, crowded, smelly and noisy,
yet has nothing near the mayhem and chaos of
India or Nepal. It's like an extraordinarily
organised beehive, rather than just a wild,
hysterical swarm.
Street vendors of tender fruit and vegetables place

them carefully in a plastic bag, then inflate the bag
and knot it, to protect them from bruising. This kind
of clever, thoughtful practicality is everywhere.
I am blown away at every turn, it seems, by
bumping into orchids. Carpets of orchids, growing
like weeds? I can hardly believe it. That's the
ultimate symbol of rarity where I come from. Here,
there are pots of them, hanging baskets, shrubs,
everywhere like daisies. The flora is so beautiful,
and this is even before leaving the city. I saw a
hairdresser clearing out a decorative bowl, chucking
out old orchids like used soup vegetables, piling in
the fresh ones.
My dream, once on that island, is to buy an air-raft,
and float around the bay giggling like a giddy
kiddie. Would that life could always be this simple.

These gushings pause at this point, thank heaven. What
follows is a newcomer's list of Dos and Don'ts in
Thailand. This is only the starting point of a list which is
lifelong, complex, and endless in its detail. Meanwhile,
this gets to grips with basics:

No shoes inside. (Disgusting and filthy.)
Don't touch anyone's head. (Defiling, insulting,
    inconsiderate, oafish at best.)
No loo roll down the bog; that is, toilet paper down
    the toilet. (Practical point, re narrow pipes. Please

wash instead.)

Keep your left hand to yourself. (See above.)

Electricity and water are not 24/7.

Never, ever touch Buddhist art.

Never touch a monk or nun of the opposite gender.
(Whatever your sexuality and however ironic it
may seem.)

Never criticise their Monarchy. (Serious offence
that can mean deportation or detention.)

Never, ever point with your feet. (See shoes.)

Never assume they understand you, nor vice versa.

I landed here, also armed with contact details for Fair Trade organisations I'd researched and contacted, and whom I'd meet later, on my way through the city en route back home. The immediate agenda was rest and relaxation, recovery from another workaholic year, on a little hideaway place let's call Layzee Island, typical of the many vacation spots billed as beachy yet affordable, with enough mod-cons for a working person's holiday. For the first time ever, I had two months off. I had never dared do that before, and never could. This was a huge luxury.

Bangkok got just two cursory recovery overnights, followed by a long overnight train ride, getting up very early to be driven to a boat in a rather seedy port, getting loaded into something so rusty and so low in the water that I really was rather worried and sat near the exit. It was stormy. I managed to keep my stomach to myself. Others could not. Somehow this thing got us all to the main island, just late enough to miss the little boat to Layzee.

That night was spent in a place kindly recommended by the nice ladies at the pier with their flip-books. The New Babylon was mainly empty, dominated by its lead resident guest – a boney, leathery-skinned, seventy-year-old German woman who did not believe in wearing any clothing at all, ever. That night she cooked dinner for her three obese male friends who were clad only in three tiny thongs. She made her big entrance from the kitchen, totally naked except for two pot holders, in which she delivered a gigantic roast fish, dripping in grease and onions, to her ravenous and sweaty admirers. The men almost dived in headfirst. It was quickly devoured, and washed down with beer, while she officiated with haughty elegance and nipples nearly dipping into the lemon slices. I lost my appetite. Jetlag's funny that way.

The boat to the island the next day was straightforward, and soon I found myself loaded into a rough pickup truck, along with crates of beer, sacks of rice, and bags of frozen chickens, with local people balanced on top. Tourists were wedged between cargo to keep it snug. We bounced along wildly rutted dirt tracks, while a fellow traveller remarked it'd be a long but not so bumpy trip this time, seeing as we have the beer and no one ever drives so badly as to shake it up.

Nearly a jiggling hour later, on the other side of the island, I was deposited at a cheap but nice beach resort let's call Cheapy But Nicey Bungalows and Café. It even had screens on the windows, which was way above the call of duty at this price range. It was the typical low-budget hut on rough stilts with thinly woven bamboo screening for walls, if you want to call them walls. There was a shabby thatch roof, stairs more like a ladder, and a narrow, tiny balcony with a plastic chair and an ashtray.

Usually the bathroom tap will not be secured to the basin, so it goes around in circles when you turn it on or off, and you'll soon be trained to make this a two-handed task. Basin, shower, and laundry water all empty directly onto the bathroom floor, and run downhill out of a simple hole, sometimes with a pipe. If it doesn't drain, you go at it with a stick.

Inside the main room, barely enough for a bed, there might be a nail or two shoved into the walls. They may or may not be robust enough to hold a clothes hanger. If there's a nail, there's probably a hanger on the floor right below it. If there are screens on the windows, they will not fit these particular windows. If there are locks, they won't really lock.

Finally, there will be only one electrical socket, so you will forever be choosing whether to have the fan, or something else. If you buy an adapter and plug in two things at once, you will soon hear a "pfft" sound, smell something terrible, and will not have any electricity until someone comes and repairs what you just fried.

This hut was exactly in this mould. There was a toilet, but it didn't flush, and instead there was offered a tap and a bucket. There was no hot water, but there was a shower. There was only the one sheet on the bed. I loved it all. I embraced that one sheet. I collapsed onto it like a ton of bricks, with all the force of a whole year with no days off. Thud.

This! This moment right now! This face down on a hot foreign pillow moment! This is what I was working all year for. This was the point of all those seven day weeks and extra evenings and early mornings. The maths seemed simple, at the time. If I never took Sundays off, then later I could take them all in a row, which made about seven weeks in total. My reward was a hut. I could buy a top sheet another time. I slept deeply and soundly, the sleep of the tired but grateful.

Later, swimming through one of those transitional twilight zones, a half dream presented me a chaotic pile of bricks as all I had left at the end of that year. Each day I staggered along, step by step, breath by breath, and by sunset I managed to haul one brick back into its original place. After countless months, I finally got my house rebuilt from its shabby ruins. It stood once more, but it was teeter-tottery, and had no mortar holding the bricks still. "That house is almost fifty years old," said a neighbour. "What do you expect?"

Thanks so much. The waking answer was to go to the beachside café, order a banana lassi, and enjoy it in front of calm waters. Middle aged and falling apart or not, this was a childhood wish come true, and it is right next to a chalkboard advertising a fish barbecue that night. That sorted my first order of business.

Presiding over this little resort was an older Thai man, nicknamed Ten. He was thin and dark with a wispy goatee, and was the widowed granddad and great-uncle of the various young people running the kitchen, the bungalows, the grounds, the deck, and their stretch of beach. He wandered about, coaxed the mynah bird to show off what it could say, and – if prompted – would chat about the old days when he was a boy in one of the first families to settle these islands. There were only a few huts and no lights. You needed a torch to walk down the beach, where baby sharks swam right into shore and were harmless because there was so much for them to eat elsewhere, unlike now.

Some of my journals from this time aren't very detailed. What I can generally remember is a long hazy list of too much choice. Would you like your pancakes with sugar or honey or both? Choose from a string of eateries called Shangrila, Zazen Den, Mocha Yoga, Yogini Bikini, Magic this and Zanizbar that, none of it to do with south-east Asia. The rest presented used bookshops, hammocks, motorbikes for hire, and genuine wood oven pizza. It was typical of a tourist spot, all white folks served by brown folks, and not much else. It was easy to imagine the entire local populace leaving on the last boat of the season, closing down the entire island, and then opening it up again the following autumn, like a Thai franchise of a Disneyland theme park. At that time, I was very happy to try this out.

Getting back to the food theme, I honour Douglas Adams's idea that those Iron and Stone Age classifications don't sum up our species succinctly or truly enough. I agree with his suggestion to divide all human history into three food-related questions, to represent the What, How, and Where stages of human history. They are these:

What is edible?

How can we cook this?

Where shall we go for lunch today?

There was a lot of stage three around here. I was the only one within miles who wanted a kitchen. Eating out absolutely all the time, for all the others, was the entire idea of a holiday. If they so much as boiled water for tea, this was a disaster, an offence, grounds for whinging. I'd keep looking for my kitchen, but meanwhile I'd be eating all over the place, just like everybody else. Café war reigned.

I avoided our immediate neighbour, Mama Crab, because she frightened me. She was a huge woman who sat on her porch with a stout wooden slingshot and a heap of stones. If a dog so much as sniffed at a tree-shaped piss target, she walloped him and sent him sprawling and yelping. Her aim was remarkable. The other weapon at her elbow was a three metre pole with a thick, serrated dagger strapped to the end. Somehow I sensed coconut dog curry in her history.

It didn't take me long to find my favourite noodle soup place, and make it my "usual". I love having a usual. This wasn't on the main beach road, but the smaller parallel road. There were only two roads anyway. This B-road had the decrepit dwellings for those who worked at the beach places on the A-road, plus black oily garages and dusty builders' merchants. Somewhere in there was a shack with a few wooden lounging platforms and mats, three bubbling cauldrons, three ancient betel nut addicts, and the best soup ever in my life, before or since.

The betel nut addicts were two old women and one shrivelled man, all looking well over ninety. They were always snoozing on their mat, teeth blood red from the betel habit, and a huge spittoon nearby full of the outpourings. The cooking area was on the other side of the place, thank goodness. There were usually three pots of things simmering at any one time, but only one was ready for serving. The pots smelled different each day – always rich and enticing. I believe that was the result of weeks of meltdowns. I went nearly every single day. Lunch was sorted for the weeks ahead.

The rest of the time on Layzee Island was an indulgent merry-go-round of meals here or meals there, snacks here or snacks there, swimming, reading in hammocks, and wishing all life could be this way, forever. I got a raft specifically because I was too lazy to swim. I floated about looking at the clouds through sunglasses.

Obviously this was not to last.

Five Years Earlier: Highlights of the Lowlife

How to choose highlights, lowlights, novelties, and gifts from this time? Allow me to describe my most memorable collection of neighbours.

In the hut to the right was the simple tale of Killian from Ireland. Every few mornings I found him sleeping on his front porch, having lost or forgotten his key. I played big sister, got the spare from the front desk and un-padlocked him.

"Tanks."

"Good party?"

"Dunno. Musta been."

In the hut to the left were the guys I called the Tattoo Brothers. Big Brother Tattoo had across his entire back "Jesus United" on a globe of the world. On both his arms were hand grenades. On his calves were a hammer and sickle, a moon and star, a cross and pentagram. After seeing these, I stopped looking. He was overly muscled, skinheaded, and had a military swagger gone nasty. Younger Brother Tattoo had opted for a mixture of nautical and love themes, by contrast.

One evening Tattoo the Younger was heard knocking repeatedly at their door, calling "Hey! You in there? Open up!" This turned into banging and shouting. His tone escalated from worry to urgency. He left, returning with a Thai man who worked there, plus two female workers trailing behind. He tried more of the same, to no avail.

There finally arrived an archetypal moment with its internationally famous virile gesture: our Thai hero waved for the women to stand back, and lifted his sledgehammer. In fewer than ten blows, the padlock flew off, and the door was wrenched open.

I couldn't see inside, but I could see their reactions. The Thai man peered cautiously and went wide-eyed. The two women looked in and recoiled. The brother looked, sighed deeply, and reluctantly entered. Myriad murmuring ensued. The Thais waited outside, one on the phone in low, serious tones. I groaned. So much for these neighbours.

Would this someday turn into a funny story, for any of those concerned? This didn't look lethal. It looked stupid, messy, and possibly requiring hospitalisation. I got the feeling he'd live but would be a big pain in the backside.

From the two huts opposite sprang another saga altogether, one I'd never witnessed at close range before. They arrived as a foursome: two French men who spoke nothing but French, and two Thai girls who spoke nothing but Thai. The two couples assumed side by side shacks. At no point could either gender speak to the other. Every moment looked awkward. All bloody weekend was awkward.

Girly A was sewing something with a needle and thread as Monsieur A teasingly pushed his face within inches of her nose, clownishly impeding her progress. She was tolerant but unsmiling. The girls chatted. The men muttered. Later that evening they arrived with a plan and two large bottles of whiskey. The newly sewn, sequined party dresses were now on the girls, on display. They twirled and danced, the guys leered and grabbed, the girls wriggled away, clumsily and repeatedly.

Later on, when loud grunting animal noises ensued, I assumed they were having sex on the balcony. Not so. The guys were literally doing animal impersonations. They were at one end of the porch, facing the girls on the other. They were attempting vocal communication through grunts, snorts and growls. The girls occasionally managed a giggle, but it was clearly a big effort, and they looked confused. Eventually they all retired and there was quiet.

The next morning, Girly A emerged first, looking miserable, head in hands. Her life must be awful, if this is what she does. That's all I could think, other than being glad beyond gratitude that I always had more options. She could only call out plaintively to her buddy, who finally stuck a towelled head out the window, said something curt, and went back in.

Girly A, in her "No Money, No Honey" nightie, paced, pottered, and looked lost. She asked something of a Thai man walking past, which sounded defensive. He appeared to answer sarcastically, even scathingly.

Later, the cave men evolved some form of speech – almost. Three grunts with gestures indicated "You – me – swim?"

One unison glare from both girls said, "No way."

The two guys left in swimming trunks and snorkels. The girls waited for them to be out of earshot, then exploded into a frenzy of excited chatter, derisive mockery, and vicious impersonations of the men, filled with scornful guffaws. They only had an hour or two to get this out of their systems.

Can they please have a better future? All of them?

By contrast, I went to the pharmacy and ended up with a date. It wasn't a real date, of course. It was much better than that. I needed mosquito repellent, but was ten bhat short of the cost. The nice girl at the counter said I could bring the rest the next day. This was now My Pharmacy. There was a lot of competition, too. There were big signs advertising their services: motorcycle accidents, birth control, Viagra, stomach bugs, malaria, cosmetic surgery, etc. This assistant pharmacist informed me that her friends gathered there every day, around six in the evening. Did I want to come help them practise English? Of course I did.

I think each week they just collected whatever foreigners would talk to them. This was fine. I'd be their pet of the month. One's name was Gan (meaning "dutiful daughter") and the other, Em (meaning "Em", just a name, or maybe the letter). They were students respectively of hotel management/tourism, and law. They were from Pattani, down south, near Malaysia. They'd been working here two years, and were eager to save up and get back to their studies. All of this was explained in excellent English.

They were Good Girls, i.e. they covered their shoulders, always wore bras, did not wear much make-up, and did not act slaggy. They were surprised but pleased to hear of my interest in Buddhism, and especially impressed that I agreed with the idea of cremation, although I had no idea why they asked about that specifically. Meditation was another common link, but not reincarnation. Food was heavily and continually discussed. Topics wandered about in long, noodle-shaped patterns, day by day.

I asked if they liked tattoos, and they were both against them. It wasn't a moral matter. They wrinkled their noses and said, "Too pain." They pointed to the Thong Café, and asked if I like that music. I said no, and it was also too loud. They were baffled.

"You don't like that?"

"No."

"Why?"

"I'm old."

They didn't argue. I learned that Em wanted to be a barrister, not a solicitor, and therefore wouldn't have to specialise. She wanted variety. I learned that, on this island, there was only one primary school, and kids wanting more education had to board on the mainland to attend secondary school. Loads of people were illiterate, but didn't want to admit that to outsiders. It was also said that, in a big extended family business, not everyone needs or wants to be able to read.

One day I went over to the pharmacy and the nice girls were gone. I hoped they were back down south, and back in college, where they wanted to be.

I went for a walk on the beach. Every night they turned it into a fairyland. Bonfires were lit, baby coconut trees in pots were arranged in formations, and scores of lamps and flaming bottles created a washaway theatre, recreated afresh each new tide.

Our best sand artist sculpted another naked lady. He'd done many, and I'd seen how lovingly he worked on their thighs. This one started with a flat belly and pert breasts, but fattened up later – parting chubby thighs ever so slightly. She was never given a head or hands. The next day her limbless torso looked like a toad.There were many imitators. People built other things too: dragons, elephants, ships, castles and Buddhas. Mostly, though, there were nude headless women with bodies like toads with tits.

It started to rain. I got back in time to see both banks of the stream collapse, and dog gangs fall into mad barking confusion. It occurred to me then that after so much doing nothing, and amidst a load of snarling dogs, I might be ready to do something for a change. It was time to book a ticket back to the Big Mango. Within the day, it was done.

Back in that dusty old oven, Bangkok, I was here either to do business or to pretend that I could. I was already involved with the Fair Trading network, previously as a volunteer and as a long-standing consumer supporter. The scene here was at least thirty years old, and many producer groups were on board.

I had been helping NGO-sponsored textile and paper craft groups to sell their goods in the UK. The goods were produced Fair Trade style, but it was all done on a charitable basis and not on a business model. I saw those relatively small amounts of income make a huge difference to some people. I was here to expand all that, wherever I could. It was looking to me like business models tended to work far better than charitable ones, and for longer. I wanted to explore that idea in practice. I was testing a switch from Aid to Trade.

I tracked down an export agent who represented dozens of groups, and organised sales events. The latest of these I'd just missed, of course. There was a very good range of producers. Thai silver and other crafts weren't around much on the UK market. I was hoping to get some samples. I was inconveniently persistent and allowed a brief visit to a cramped office.

I tried to make it as quick as possible, but my main obstacle was the great pleasure to be had ogling jewellery. I selected many silver earrings, some bangles and necklaces. I also got a few baskets, quite a few cards (personal favourite), scarves, and some shoulder bags. I grabbed a few pretty mango wood bowls, mainly for me. At the last moment, on a whim, I topped it up with two funny little gecko-shaped fridge magnets, woven from old newspapers. Cute, I thought. Great idea. Who knows? I certainly did not think I'd sell thousands of them later on.

I think I spent about a hundred pounds that time. I figured if the business idea flopped, I still had lovely things to give as presents. When I got back home to Scotland, I planned a series of one-day trips. I loaded my vehicle with samples and trundled over to whichever nearby gift shops didn't hang up the phone on me. They viewed and handled the samples. They saw the price list. They placed orders. In between my other work that year (four part time jobs cobbled together) I made these trips over and over. Then they became overnights, with the help of the spare rooms of generous friends (thank you again and you know who you are). I only covered some of Scotland and England, but that hundred pounds' worth of samples turned into over a thousand pounds' worth of orders. That may not be huge to you and me, but it was a huge amount where it was going. This was more than worthwhile.

With an arts background, I was new to trade, but not to common sense, diligence, and honouring a plain agreement. I ordered the stuff, distributed it as agreed, got a smidgeon of a minimum wage, and mainly got the wherewithal to order even more and go back again, same time next year. It looked like I could go year after year.

I was in business.

NOODLE TRAILS

Back at the Bella Vista: Has It Been a Week Already?

My first week at the Bella Vista involves getting to grips with certain pre-dawn, pre-breakfast, pre-historic survival options. I want to evolve into a routine. One of the many differences between a traveller and a tourist is that the traveller is more likely to look unnaturally happy when forming some kind of routine. I now have a wonderful routine. Every morning, I start with total amnesia.

In the early morning, as pale light considers how to slide into my consciousness, from the innermost fog emerges a faint voice asking simply, "Where am I?" At first nothing much answers. Later, still swimming in this pleasant Neolithic murk, a hope forms that I'm on a tropical island. It might be a dream, but it feels real. I'll go with the You're in Thailand theory, eyes still shut. Then again, perhaps it's time to remember the body attached to all this. Eyes open. Thatched hut in Thailand is confirmed. Waves of gratitude pour forth, but I pull some covers over me. It is still uncharacteristically cool at the first crack of dawn.

So, paradise too has its little pranks to play. It's a freaky January for this part of the equator. It's unseasonably cool and grey. Every day, people commiserate and long to go swimming. "It's been cool for months," long-termers sigh to us newcomers. Everyone has a jacket on and no one laughs at my down vest. All nationalities are shaking their heads and rubbing cold hands together.

It's still two or three times as warm as Scotland was a few weeks ago, which is still covered in thick ice, so I am over the moon by comparison. Half my aches and pains are gone just by being here.

I'm awake and happy. Now I can contend with the classical elements of air, water, fire, earth and doughnuts. Here's today's version.

Air? Cold.

Water? Undrinkable.

Fire? No.

Earth? I'm hungry.

Doughnuts? A bike ride into town.

As for drinkable water, one's first thought is that of being spoiled back in Europe and the Americas by having allegedly safe drinking water on tap, although reports differ. Here, only locals drink tap water. The rest create mountains of plastic water bottles. Some are recyclable but most are not.

I like starting the day with plenty of water, but there is no drinkable water in this hut. I have to lug large bottles from the café to the hut last thing at night, every night. If I forget, this means the next morning I must stagger forth, clutching at my throat, gasping all the way to town. I get up early, but this café does not.

My idea of water meeting fire means caffeine. My sunrise watering is ideally followed by a short, but mind-blasting cup of high quality coffee. Then I eagerly jump on almost any day. Food, the earth element, can wait for now. Instead, I swallow a dose of artificially coffee-flavoured granules, swished around the bathroom glass with long-life, overly sweetened, almost-milk soya-surprise drinkette. It's hideous and I shudder; but it's a drug and I'm awake.

The next round is ablutions and "putting on the water heater" for tonight. This means filling six large empty plastic water bottles with undrinkably poisonous tap water, putting them outside to bake in the sun all day (if there is any), and returning at dusk to rinse off the day's dust with warm water. Sometimes it's almost hot water. I learned this from the father of a four-year-old who refused to take cold showers. I know how he feels. The morning shower here is bracing beyond words. This alternative works well.

The next few hours recycle this sequence: water, stretching, writing, water with juice, more stretching, writing, and repeat and repeat. Eventually, pain departs to some distance to echo as mere aches. Hunger surfaces, usually two or three hours before the café is open for coffee – and even longer to get anything resembling food. It's either waiting, or a bike ride into town.

Today, at the moment, I am not prepared to bike anywhere. I am not ready for food. I am not ready for thought. I am distracted by the stretching process. Bones and everything attached to them shrink in the night, apparently, and now need to be coaxed out of their shells. As anyone can tell you, this is time-consuming, painful, and boring, which is no one's favourite trio. Perhaps this represents the classical earth element – or better yet metal, because it feels like trying to melt steel girders with your breath. It takes time, especially in cool air.

This lack of warmth is strengthening my wish for the warmth of a cooking area too. I enter my hammock to consider intelligence I've gathered concerning my place in the competitive kitchen queue. This has been twice upgraded from game to search to serious mission. It is now an official part of the routine. It includes longing for those twenty litre, recyclable water barrels delivered to one's door. I particularly like the cartoon nurse who's on the label to reassure you that because she is pretty, this must be clean water.

There are two precious huts here with kitchens. One is directly uphill from me, and one is directly downhill. Whichever way the wind blows, I can smell what's cooking. Mr Uphill is Italian and a good cook, with every waft painfully delicious. Mr Downhill's emanations alternate between fried eggs and bleach. No one knows his name. No one has seen him in weeks. They can't even describe him. They think he's German, stays alone, and gets up early to go scuba diving. Not much else is known.

Both men reportedly love their kitchens and have talked about staying here forever. However, I am next in line to that throne. Meanwhile, I depend on bananas and leftovers hanging on the laundry line, which doubles as my pantry.

A note on food and fauna, and this will have to do for my earthy element. The laws of the jungle, the laws of tropical health, and the laws of camping all converge here. I've never camped with bears, in any sense of that phrase, but have heard from veterans that food is kept far from where you sleep, in bags hung high in trees. This is why my bananas and nuts hang on the laundry line. Allegedly even ants and insects take longer to locate it. If rodents find it, at least they're outside. The same goes triple for fruit bats, more still for snakes, and even more for things I hate to remember. With that thought, I can wait no longer. Into town we go. Like all epic journeys, it will involve feats and monsters, especially the first time around.

"Biking into town" sounds a simple practical matter, but it isn't. It's a feat worthy of the legendary Sisyphus who forever pushed boulders uphill only to watch them roll back down again, over and over. I did say I wanted to build up my strength, so it's just another warning to take care what you wish for.

Leaving by the main gate means facing the vertical concrete Big Bastard Hill, down which one can only slide without recourse to brakes. The back road to the village is less steep. It is also gravelly and weedy, which provides some traction. This is Big Bastard Hill's Sister, who's less of a bastard.

I went on foot only once, over the lagoon bridge. I had this fairy tale idea of crossing from there to walk along the bay beach to the village. As with many fairy tales, a monster had to be confronted first. This was the Danger Bridge, which delivers one over a small lagoon. The lagoon is not deep, but filled with a muddy quicksand and surrounded by locals who shout sharply and wave you away with alarm.

The Danger Bridge is disproportionately high, with two tall ladders reminiscent of trapeze artists in a circus. It is feather-light aluminium, is flimsily shoved into two haphazard piles of building waste, has jangling chain handrails, and sways wildly in any light breeze. Looking at it brings to mind rickety rope ladders spanning deadly gorges in cheap adventure movies. It is terrifying even to muscular, tattooed young men. I tried it once, and changed my route forever.

Now I bike down the back road and stick to this side of the lagoon, which is the boat yard road. This yields its own marvellous gems. Every day, sometimes several times a day, I stop at the boatyard. I stop for longer and longer each time. The boats are so pretty and pleasantly strange to my eye.

The yard has room for half a dozen small vessels, a dozen people, and a crane between the lagoon and the waiting cradles. There are many styles of boat, all languid, lyrical, and graceful. Some have an upper deck, some have a canopy, some are long and sleek, and others are stout and chubby. They are all made of pure wood in traditional designs in which southern Thai people have sailed and fished for centuries. They are here being lovingly and exactingly repaired and painted. The colours are strong and vivid, varied and perfectly harmonious. I find the scene mesmerising.

The bows are often tied with a cluster of multi-coloured ribbons and scarves, plus sometimes a bouquet of flowers or a garland of marigolds. This is the heart of the boat. Ideally, this will never, ever be destroyed as it is thought to be the home of the spirit of the boat. Destroying it would be like vandalising a temple or someone's home. Sometimes, if the rest of the boat has come to the end of its useful life, this piece of wood is saved and reincorporated into the main spine of a house, or better still a temple, school or another community building. If it cannot be used, it must be burned with ritual and respect, and the spirits inside somehow re-housed, at least metaphorically.

At first, the boat workers turn their backs to me and keep doing their job. By the end of the week they stop turning their backs. One of them even nods acknowledgement. A woman in a nearby shack starts to say hello to me each day. She gestures to my clothes and says I am OK. Later it is explained by Noo and Nic that, because I always cover shoulders and thighs, I am a step above the usual sweaty, semi-nude barbarian, and therefore I can be tolerated and even spoken to. This is high praise.

When I have sighed and ogled enough, I continue my bike ride into town, through the coconut grove with its smouldering bonfire of husks, past the huge-horned chocolate brown buffalo with the stark white birds on its back, past the gently chugging water pump, past the wild orchids and the rampant morning glories, on to the village and my mission of the moment: breakfast and snacks for later – for all day if possible.

This is round one on the Noodle Trail of Mai Village. Morning snacks in town are part of a bicycling circuit that has become a charming part of my routine, especially at this end-of-week milestone. A clockwise loop includes certain regular landmarks and personalities, many foods, and anywhere from five to ten kilometres of exercise, plus that Big Bastard Hill later. None of this was possible at the beginning of this week, however slowly I tried.

First there is the European convenience store, which I try to avoid if possible.

Next is the fried banana lady who sometimes is also the fried sweet potato lady. She seems open-minded about serving foreigners. If she holds up three fingers, it's thirty baht, and the rest is done by smelling, pointing, nodding and smiling. This is not a café. It's a card table next to a tripod precariously supporting a large wok full of ominous-looking, very hot, sizzling deep fat. I stand well back and she stands capably close. Her manner is quiet and calm.

Next is the fresh fruit stand, where the lady is bubbly and eager. She points out all kinds of nice things, and I must smile and be clear that I do not wish to buy everything she has. Usually I get a bunch of bananas plus one other fruit I've never seen before and cannot pronounce, no matter how many enthusiastic, giggling times she repeats it. Her manner is perky and helpful.

Next is the cool-faced, plump lady who makes batches of banana-rice goodies wrapped and steamed in banana leaves. Sometimes she shapes them like pyramids, other times like logs. Sometimes there's sweetened coconut with peanuts inside. Other times there is spicy ground pork. She never says which. She hasn't once been keen to communicate on any level. She relents if you persist in holding out money. Her manner is glum and petulant.

Next come a series of people in quick succession. There is the pancake guy, who believes in lots of fat and lots of sugar. His manner is straightforward and, perhaps, overtired. He refuses to do the spinning, clowning performances of his pancake selling colleagues on other islands.

There is the sausage grill girl, serving either feathery light vermicelli rice and pork sausages or extra rich, greasy garlicky pork sausages. These are both excellent and very burpy for hours afterwards. They're sold with a little bag of chopped cabbage and chillies. Her manner is sweet and shy.

Then at last is the matron of barbecued fish balls and suspiciously reddened fried chicken. She has an authoritative style that suggests she owns a lot more than one mobile grill.

Whether or not the savoury lunch vendors set up late morning is anybody's guess. They get there when they get there. Every morning there is also an unpredictable number of doughnut people, and I never know when or where they will spring up. These doughnuts are "of the moment": soft and gorgeous with your morning coffee, but more akin to rifle pellets if you leave them till nightfall. There are also fried balls of potato, coconut and spices that are unlike anything I've ever eaten. I don't really want to know what's in them. They're beautiful enough unquestioned.

These things do not appear on a regular basis. I

suspect their appearance follows local agricultural cycles. One morning you may see a pickup truck loaded with sweet potatoes, pineapples or other mystery fruits, or vegetables and herbs. It makes drops at a selection of houses, and within hours card tables are set up along the road, each spread with different home-made delicacies interpreted from the same basic ingredients. There will be added waves at school lunchtime, after school in the afternoon, and after work in the evening. Whatever it is, it will all have disappeared down the collective village throat within hours, until the next cycle.

True, up the hill I know people's names, and down here I know none. We do most of this wordlessly. But these are my rounds and they recognise me, and even know what I'm likely to buy. I often get the usual, as it happens.

As is the local custom, I am handed my goodies in small plastic bags, either flipped closed or rubber-banded, to hang from the handlebars. I eat some immediately, and pack the rest into my basket. Then I huff my way laboriously back up that hill. I'm amazed that I can. I stop every twenty huffs. I can't believe how long this takes. Once back, I crash into the hut, drink and drink, shower away a bucket of sweat, cool down, change into a crisp shirt, drink some more, remember to go hang the snacks from a tree, and drink some more while the liquid is still cool. That's never for long. Then, when ready, I commence the long slow climb up the cliff face to the café.

I even arrive at the summit with a milder "oof" than

that first night. This is after a week of doing this climb a few times a day. Now it's mid-morning. There's a fifty–fifty chance someone is awake, or soon will be. Then it's the usual: Italian coffee, Thai soup, mixed family gossip.

Has It Been Two Weeks Already?

It's been such a good two weeks that I decide to stay for a month, and have already paid ahead, happily. I'm told no one does this. I'm doing it for the statement. It's to pitch my flag. It's also for the sheer pleasure of it. I also get a small discount, of course.

I've been and gone to the village. It's well after ten, as usual. It may or may not be time for breakfast and The Usual. I now know to approach quietly. Grandpa's generally up first. He nods towards the kitchen. This is Nic's cue to shuffle out in pyjama trousers, dishevelled hair, and nothing else but sleepy eyes and an assortment of religious medals glued to his chest. He holds up his beloved special Italian coffee maker, points to it as I nod, and shuffles back in.

Soon there is fine Italian style coffee and nice Italian

leftovers, quietly brought to my table in one continuous motion in which he emerges, delivers and, without missing a beat, glides straight back inside again, usually in the vain hope he can return to sleep – or indeed get any sleep, ever again, now that there is a new baby in the house. She is awake now, appearing instantly before him. In fact, she is shoved into his face as Noo zooms towards the toilet. He glances at the time.

"OK, we have one minute, but Mama can use toilet very fast, yes? Now you dance with Papa, OK?" He dances her around, singing something sweet and Italian into her deep brown eyes. She likes it, but with reservations. It doesn't last long. She begins searching all corners of the room, increasingly agitated.

"Two minute maximum. Then she want mother, only the mother. If she no see the mother, the noise is incredible."

He plants exhausted kisses on her as she squirms, making anxious sounds. Noo races back and grabs her in the nick of time. All exhale as if watching a bomb disposal expert.

Just then a motorbike roars to a halt. Pa climbs off it, his two school runs completed. A flurry of arms snatch away milk, fruit, and other bags, leaving him windswept with the last thing in the bag: Nic's cigarettes. Soon Nic is at his computer, which he has hauled out of the bedroom window to set on a table. Noo glances at the goods before they disappear into the kitchen.

She starts playing one of Bee's favourite games, which is to have her feet dangled over the pool table, on the pool balls. She can't get enough of it. It's even a solution to her bad moods, sometimes.

The second major motorbike screech is Taa's oldest son, the cool bike mechanic. In one motion he deposits her and the tiny, bewildered Boo. He always runs into the kitchen and hides under something.

Taa beams, "Hello. Noodle soup, vegetable?" I nod. She proceeds to her tasks, sometimes flinging a small boy out of her way. She knows it's The Usual. She knows this means no tomato, extra carrot, loads of extra garlic. I don't have to say. It's so nice being a regular. I fondly recall a waitressing job at age eighteen where we all fussed over an old postman who ate there every single night. He always had the daily special where you got seconds for free. If we saw his car approach, we got his double Manhattan ready on his table, and his special of the day ordered up. If you did as little as that, he tipped really well.

Noo agrees a task with Pa, who disappears with a tool kit. She then starts walking baby Bee in circles. The pool ball thing only works for so long. We now know how to talk one line at a time, each round of the table. We have a routine. I just wish I knew more Thai. She just wishes she knew more English.

Somehow, as I eat, the birds seem noisier and noisier, building to a screechy hysteria. Then I realise it's not birds. It's Boo, hidden under a table, doing bird calls. They're good enough to fool both cats and the dog, who are all staring intently. If I act surprised and applaud Boo, he beams and rubs his stomach, which I assume is a happy sign.

Over the last two weeks we have established his skills in a number of monkey-based games, chasing games, tickling games, hidden surprise basics, and hammock-related games. He used to like Swing Me In Circles By Any Limbs You Like, but this was vetoed on staff hangover mornings. Most people prefer the silent version of Peekaboo Around The Pillar, which stays in one place.

Animal noises are his main language. He doesn't even speak much of his own native Thai. He tries only rarely to speak to me, shyly, and cannot understand why I just stare at him or speak nonsense in return. He is so tiny and perplexed. It makes more sense to him to run around doing animal impersonations, especially since they are superb by any standards.

"He doesn't say much," I muse, "but I don't get a single word of what he says, not at all."

"Is no Thai anyway," explains Nic. "Is island dialect, totally different. Old-style dialect too, not like today. He learn from the grandfather. Is strange, little boy talk like eighty-year-old man. He need go school. He need friend. Him and me, we both go crazy, like this." No one looks like they are longing for friends more than little Boo himself. Noo just shrugs. That's how it is.

Taa drags Boo away, his feet scraping the floor. I enjoy my soup in peace, listen to the wind, drain every drop, and thoughtfully crunch every shred of onion and cabbage and carrot and all that extra garlic. They say it's too much, but it's never too much. I never leave anything in the bowl, not a scrap.

Nic stands up from the computer and stretches. "The computer is free now, please take. I go shower. Today I have more time. New people come yesterday. They go to Jungle Party, all night. Maybe we see, maybe no. I like these Jungle Parties."

"Good music?"

"No, this music always shit. I mean, they make big parties far away in the jungle, and nobody hear nothing. Nobody bother nobody. Is good idea. Good business."

He thoughtfully stubs out the cigarette, sets up at my side a tray with a second cup of coffee, water, juice, more tasty bread, fruit or whatever's easily negotiable. Then, towel over his shoulder, he disappears. There are distant kitchen noises, and baby noises, which all recede inside their living quarters behind the kitchen. I have the place to myself. I am surrounded by sounds of the wind, faraway dogs, and small fishing boats.

The email news from Scotland is that it's still covered in thick ice. All manner of well-wishers send their love, and I am strongly encouraged to stay right where I am. Fine.

News from elsewhere in Asia comes in the form of New Year greetings from suppliers, and Christmas cards from producers who think I am still in business. There are lovely hand-stitched cards that are signed by all the staff addressed to me, someone who can purchase nothing from them this year, unlike the seven or eight years previously. This is rather painful.

According to one end of year report, of the Hope Cards group, I was their main customer in February, usually a desperately slow month. My order of nearly a thousand pounds kept them all afloat that month, give or take a few families. From my point of view, a quarter of those cards sold for cost plus a small mark-up, and the rest are still sitting in my loft. I can't buy new stuff until I sell the old stuff. I'm stuck and useless, and they're wishing me a good New Year.

First I need to go back home . This isn't home, however pretty the holiday fantasy. The UK is home. A house full of unsold stuff is home. I need to find a way to sell it off. It takes up three rooms of a four room house, and almost none of it sold this year. Most of it only sells at the end of the year anyway, so when people ask me how it's going I have to say I won't be sure until next December.

Other thoughts from back home suggest I need a new job altogether. There are employment pages in some of the English language newspapers in Thailand and more on their websites. I surprise myself by scanning what's available. You never know. I do this secretly. Changes are ahead, one way or another. There are enough questions floating around to drown a minnow like me.

And so, uphill and upstairs: this is the morning routine for a couple of weeks. On the other hand, there has been a complete shift in personnel, anthropologically speaking. One by one, most of the grizzled, sloppy old Italian fishermen left, and their emptied bungalows fill up with young, groovily dressed Italian couples.

I meet the first couple one afternoon, after my second or third brunch. I'm at my beloved perch, checking the view, the emails from home, and the latest snacks delivered to my elbow by Noo on her baby-track rounds.

Suddenly a figure appears over the parapet, followed by a second. They are fragrant, un-showered, bed-headed figures, clad in what they slept in. It's also possible they haven't slept at all and came straight from a party.

They crawl back onto the same cushions they vacated last night. The impressions of their bodies are still there. One's job is to wordlessly roll cigarettes for both. The other shuffles to the kitchen to order drinks in the tone of desperate begging.

Soon, green teas arrive with large bottles of water. Later come turbo-coffee and the return of the power of speech, and a breakfast that's always sugar-based. Soon a similar couple appear and stagger over to the next set of cushions, where they enact this same sequence of events. By the time I am ready to go, all ten of them are assembled, having slithered in as pale as refugees and brought back to life by green tea and chocolate croissants.

They then accumulate around the huge long table, usually women at one end and men at the other. They do everything in a pack. Their conversation is in very rapid Italian, and they are kind enough to provide me occasional summaries. They cover many topics, including where to get more intoxicants, which parties are where, what you pay the police if you get caught, where and how much the cheapest bungalows are, and where to get the best, most authentic and yet reasonably priced food. Of course they do not mean Thai food, but Italian food.

They also collectively wonder about the couple known as the skinny arguing people. She arrived home but he didn't. There is bound to be argument about that. She has his flip-flops, and will go back to find the barefooted fellow. Meanwhile, everyone agrees that at these parties, the drugs and the music are both crap.

At some point the women will coo at Boo, and he will usually get a good dose of his favourite game: being chucked in the air and swung about by large fit men who know exactly how to turn him into a happy, squealing aeroplane.

I assumed this gang already knew each other, but they all met recently, here. They come from every corner of their country, and insist that if each person went into their local dialect none of the others would understand a thing. Still, they are known here as The Italians. This is how they explain lots of things. They say it's Italian, or, it's what we Italians do.

"Is Italian. We do at home too. We do everything together."

Here, they favour a double shift system. They meet at lunch to revive from the night before. Then they set about getting inebriated again. Or ill. Or both. The point is to render oneself comatose for the rest of the daylight hours and some of the early evening ones too. Then, after sundown, like vampires they arise, re-paint, and re-emerge into the night, looking for ways to poison themselves afresh. They are very devoted to their daily routines.

For now, they are riding a crest of caffeine and sugar. Conversations and friendly arguments percolate up to a high bubbly fizz.

I've finished my lunch and the emails, and deliver the dishes to the kitchen. The resident gang poke their heads out, surprised to see the place has livened up this much. The party people are frisky and are pointing at menus. Discussions of what they may or may not order are getting louder and livelier. I am now used to every meal being preceded by either a fulsome analysis of the menu, or a major debate or drama about the best way to cook something.

Later I stick my head into the kitchen, and finally see why nicknames are such an everyday thing around here. Nic is organising. "It's chicken for Big Hair Lady and pork for Ponytail Man. Spaghetti for the No Shirts, with bread, no salad. In the corner, Fatty gets noodles, and the

Heavy Drunks don't mind waiting...oh hello Eileen, ah, sorry – we need these stupid names to remember."

"Can I help?"

Nic and Noo answer simultaneously, with opposite answers. Nic waves me away confidently, "No, we are fine," he calls from amidst a whirling chaos of people juggling things.

Noo, however, answers bluntly, "Yes, you can help. You want something? You take. You want glass, water, ice? You take. You want anything, you take. You write down. You pay later. More easy for us. OK?"

Are kitchen privileges OK? They are the best. I deliver all sorts of replenishment drinks to the hordes, by way of thanking my hosts for the new house policy.

Pa is tending baby Bee in the baby hammock, which is right next to his. It's only continuous, uninterrupted rocking that keeps her asleep, normally. Now that he's needed in the kitchen he tries slowly to reduce the rocking speed to a standstill. He gets only two steps away and she starts to thrash and writhe. The entire family stops as if he's stepped on a landmine and they all heard the deadly click. He steps back and rocks the cradle. She goes still. He tries to leave again and she gets upset again. He's stuck. He's leaning towards the kitchen but is trapped with a baby who is a ticking noise-bomb.

"I can help," I hear myself say. "You go."

He speaks no English but he gets it. He steps out and I step in, and we don't lose a beat. The rocking rhythm is unbroken and the baby is snoozing. We wait a little. She doesn't stir. It's working. Everybody exhales. Pa trots over to the kitchen and joins in. Everybody goes back to work, and so do I. I assume the position: which is flat out in the hammock, rocking me with one hand and her with the other. Later, I am rewarded with a coconut.

"Now you work here, you need nickname for sure," jokes Nic, grinning.

A customer hears this. "Really? You work here now?"

"Sort of, yes. It's good, isn't it?"

"Sure! Your first work in Thailand."

Ah. Not exactly.

Four Years Earlier: That Second Trip Meant Business

The following year, probably to the day if not sooner, I went back to Thailand. This second trip was entirely different to the first one in a myriad of ways. This time I went entirely on business. This time it was serious. This time I also went via India, which turned up some noticeable contrasts.

Why was this trip so different? What happened between then and now? Reading these journals later, even I am surprised at this change. The year before, I haphazardly grabbed an armful of samples for over a hundred pounds, which later turned into over a thousand pounds' worth of orders. I could go back for more. This time my budget for samples was nearly five hundred pounds and I was planning more selling trips around the UK. The shops that bought stuff last time said to come back, especially with new designs – doubly so if they're for men.

Also, between that first and second trip to Thailand, I'd been to Zimbabwe to work with producers there. It was a short and intense week, hard work, a tough education, and yet some good came from it. They were desperate for cash and I bought their stuff, so how much more direct does it get? This gave me masses more motivation to pour into this fledgling Fair Trade importing business, however small it was.

Coming home from that life-changing trip, I was presented with a marvellous gift from a man at Heathrow airport whose name I never learned. I wish I could find him and thank him now. Returning from Zimbabwe, more than a little tired and emotional, I faced an awfully long immigration queue to get back into the UK – which had been home for years getting into decades. My American passport was stamped properly with a permanent resident's right to live there. I could live there, work there, pay taxes there, receive healthcare there; but I had no right to go through the fast queue.

I was rewarded manifold for this wait. I was handed a sterling idea on a metaphorical platter by a customs official with a charming African accent and a debonair way, professional with a hint of warmth. He scrutinised my passport thoroughly and the looked at me directly.

"May I please explain to you something?"

"Yes of course."

"May I encourage you to apply for a British passport?"

"Really?"

"Yes. May I tell you why?"

"Sure."

"I see you have been living and working here legally for over twenty years."

"Yes."

"I see you travel a lot."

"Yes."

"Perhaps you have friends and family, far from here?"

"Yes."

"Perhaps you worry, if ever you need to go there suddenly."

"That's right."

"Perhaps you worry that if you put in this application it could take a long time, and might be difficult to get back suddenly, in a case like that."

"Exactly."

"That used to be true."

"Oh?"

"It is not true now. Now there are new regulations which say every application must be processed in full within a maximum of two months."

"I didn't know that. I heard it took nearly a year."

"It used to, at times. Not now. Now is a good time to apply."

"Thank you for this information!"

"You are more than welcome, and the very best of luck to you too, young lady."

What a sterling man. I did, in fact, know one pal who got her British passport for a fiver somewhere in Peckham, south London, but let's not go into that. Mr Nice Accent gave me this valuable nudge on October 17, 2005. Two years later to the day, on October 17, 2007, I'd be sworn in as a proud British citizen – and that is quite a coincidence, if you ask me.

Meanwhile, I was very keen to get to Thailand. I'd already tried and failed to do business in India. There was little point going down that trail. The UK was full of Indian stuff. The styles I saw in Thailand were minimal, subtle and elegant. They'd be something different. I thought they'd fit in well in the Fair Trade niche back home.

I also just loved Thailand in general and wanted to go back. The then partner persuaded me instead to go to an old haunt of his in Goa, and it was indeed a lovely place. Later he wanted to continue his own magical mystery tour by precisely retracing the stoned footsteps of his youth across all of India, bottom to top. By contrast, I needed my own journey and a different sort of route. I got a ticket to Thailand.

To go from India to Thailand or vice versa is a striking study in contrasts. I flew from Delhi to Bangkok, and here's what I had to say on arrival:

What a total and absolute contrast. After Delhi and Mumbai and the rip-off taxis, the airport bullshit, the non-answers, the chaos and the lateness, and the whole fake grinning We Hate Memsahib thing, finally I land in a world of smiling people who are organised, tidy, considerate, polite and lovely, whatever they may be thinking about white folks. It's just business. It's so much simpler.

Sales people simply display their wares and aren't aggressive. No one is grabbing at my elbow, screaming at me that she can't pay her rent and her kids will starve if I don't buy this pink chiffon sari ensemble, complete with real slave's hand-beading on the sequined gold lamé slippers. There's been none of that.

Even most beggars seem realistic and not given to loud hysteria. For the last few weeks in India, I spent a lot of time removing little hands from my body, my pockets, my bags, my everywhere. Very touchy place. This didn't happen once here, whereas there it can happen all day long in India. For the untouchy, India probably is not the place for them.

From my fussy visitor's point of view, most of Thailand doesn't shout at me and also keeps their hands off me. I am so relieved to be here.

In Thailand's climate, an Indian cotton dress plus baggy trousers is a great option, but I soon tired of explaining to people that while my dress was Indian, I was not. I was a temporarily tanned white lady. That's when some Thais said terrible things about how Indian behaviour is so different to their own. That's a nice way of putting it. I had just spent a few weeks listening to Goans say much the same awful things about the Indians. I stopped wearing those dresses, cool and pretty though they were. They just brought out the worst in some people.

The most stupid thing of all was my thinking that I'd recovered from malaria for good. I don't mean real malaria, I mean an obsession that takes over some people. If the India-phile bug bites you, it's similar to malaria, in that it can always come back. It has an amnesiac quality, like childbirth. You block out the hardest parts, and it's only amnesia that gets you to do it again and again.

There are endless tales of people going through extraordinary traumas, psychic misadventures, spiritual torments etc., often combined with destitution and dysentery, and yet they go back for more, like amnesiacs. It's a kind of cultural malaria some Europeans succumb to. The suffering brings a badge of honour, or a proud battle scar.

I don't seem to have caught this bug. I think there's a particular breed of it that struck and flourished in the 1960s, but I wasn't there then. This led to an entirely false sense of security on my part. I really thought once I'd left India, I'd leave behind all its jolly chaos too. This was to be a classic case of the kharmic pendulum swinging extra high before giving me a bop on the butt.

First, I settled into a hotel I'd pulled off the internet, which I'll call Bangkok Boring Big Hotel. It was near the big trade event I wanted to attend in a few days' time, which I'd missed the previous year. A huge room is filled with stalls of Fair Trade producers, as many as eighty of them under one roof. I'd collect masses of samples, and arrange orders for wholesale export later through a central agent.

At the hotel, I indulged my perversion for reading those rule books hotels leave on your desk. My favourite section: "A lady joiner is not allowed to stay overnight with an in-house guest unless she registers at the front reception. For security reasons, the lady joiner has to deposit her ID card at the security department. The room rate for the lady joiner is 650 baht net (without breakfast). She would collect her ID card the following a.m. upon checking out. Payment is by cash only. The lady joiner will not be entitled to use the hotel's facilities, such as the swimming pool, etc. The hotel is not liable for any losses of the guest's personal effects. Thank you for your cooperation and understanding."

What if it's a boy joiner? Can he go in for free, but not if dressed as a ladyboy? What if I had a man joiner? Had this not occurred to them? I wonder about these technicalities.

This trip gave me other glimpses into life in Bangkok. I enjoyed Lumphini park, where mornings are well known for their armies of Tai Chi practitioners. Late afternoon is more for aerobics and leotards, or groups with vivacious pop music. The muscle men have their own area.

Everybody everywhere halts when they hear the national anthem, played every day at six in the evening. This includes the dog-walkers, the necking couples, and even most of the drunks. The city stops dead in its tracks and no one moves until the anthem is over. In train stations, for example, tourists wander into this frozen scene, unable to comprehend why suddenly, absolutely everyone as one, on the last chord, instantly resumes whatever it was that they were doing.

The city's air pollution stings the eyes and gives a metallic, chemical irritation to the throat, thickens the coating on the tongue, and makes the lungs wheeze. I spent two or three days going around in a surgical mask. More and more people do the same, and you can buy them in packs of five from any chemist. The white masks are disgustingly grey by the end of one day, which is worrying.

My favourite surreal item of the week involved a good Samaritan who almost killed me. At a busy pedestrian crossing was an elderly Thai bag lady with oversized army fatigues. She pushed the button to cross, and grabbed my arm with surprising strength.

As the light turned yellow – and cars accelerated enthusiastically, trying to race through – she launched us into the fray, dragging me into vehicles dodging us by millimetres. She was laughing her head off as vans and motorcycles screeched. If we'd died, I'd have gone first. She was ingenious at keeping me in harm's way.

We arrived at the other side of the street – not the eternal other side, I'm pleased to say. The light then went red. Cars stopped and their drivers glared at me. I thanked her politely. She waved cheerfully and left, pleased with her good deed for the day – or perhaps her latest prank. It was genuinely hard to know which.

At the Fair Trade event, I met all the groups I'd later come to know better. I saw thousands of new samples and bought dozens. Those cute little geckos woven from recycled newspaper had sold very well, and I went for more creatures, plus more baskets. There was also basketry woven from the pesky water hyacinth that chokes their canals and needs clearing continually.

I loved this group's green cause and many of the gorgeous textiles and baskets I saw, but bemoaned my lack of storage space. I headed for the silver jewellery and other smaller things.

I spent my budget, arranged for it all to be sent home, and then was free to trot about the city, with no one to talk to. Evenings were usually spent in the comfort of the hotel's air-con, away from the country-and-western music blaring from the concrete Palm Court downstairs. I became extremely tired of having no one to talk to and was more than ready to go home. It was all I wanted, at that point.

I was very foolish not to have packed my ruby slippers. Where are they, when you need them most? I'd finished all my business in Thailand and was on my way back home to the UK. En route I'd stop over to see a supplier in Delhi, just for a day, in a last ditch effort to do business in India. I'd also see an old pal there too, which tipped the balance. The next day was my flight back to London. Much of this plan was not to be.

This is because I'd never dealt with Air Sari before. I'd forgotten I was not yet out of the malaria zone. My journals at the time are a bit stressed: "I am exhausted and confused and really not sure what blender I was just put through. At least I'm not crying now. But, my plans exploded, and had to be put back together from scratch. I am weak at the knees as a result, and was very wobbly to start with. I was so eager to go, so ready, so desperate, so tired, but the answer was No. They gave my seat away. Yes, I reconfirmed and reconfirmed, over and over, but this doesn't seem to matter. When they suggested I buy a new ticket, I think that's what did it."

In showing emotion I had committed a major faux pas. In Europe, if you get weepy in public, people might get embarrassed but they will probably feel sorry for you. Not here. Here it's a sign of immaturity and lack of discipline. The two women at Air Sari's ticket desk stared at me with contempt and shame. They addressed each other as if I were not there at all. I became invisible. I knew this happened in much of Asia if you got angry. I had no idea it happened if you got upset and frightened. That confused me at first, as the tears receded.

I stayed and stayed. I sat and sat. Finally one of them spoke, as if she were sick of playing nursery school teacher to the less than intelligent.

"Perhaps you do not need to buy a new ticket."

"Thank you."

"Would you like to go tomorrow instead?"

"Yes. Thank you."

"Would you like me to arrange that now?"

"Yes. Thank you." I did everything but kiss her beaded lamé slippers.

Back at the ranch, I re-arranged a mountain of details and cancelled all business in Delhi. I prayed to somehow make my connection to London, though I could see there were excellent chances for everything turning into shit. I really wanted the comforts of home and just about anything familiar.

From the original journals: "What a complete atmospheric change. It hasn't rained in three months, and yesterday the humid heat almost made my head explode. Today's rain is heavy and cool, and the pressure is off, in so many ways. Yesterday's catastrophes were a pain and an upset, yes. But now it's all cancelled. The India trip is not going to happen. I will not be doing business in India at all. Ever…Oh my heavens, is it possible I am now finally cured of Indian malaria? Hallelujah, let this be true!"

Compass, let's chart another course. I'm no longer worried about having the kind of Indian malaria which you forget every time. I sense I am going to remember every damned step of the way.

My hotel was now filled with a huge unruly group of Indian businessmen. To see Indians and Thais side by side all week, trying to deal with each other, showed me the vastness of their cultural differences. These businessmen loved loud arguing. They had lots of energetic dramas, passions and ordeals, while Thais glided around, graciously smiling. It was as if there had been two different tunes playing in this lobby, all week. Now the louder band was checking out en masse.

They were shouting for taxis, pushing and shoving, grabbing trolleys out of the hands of shocked bellboys, opening their over-stuffed suitcases in the middle of the lobby floor, throwing their belongings all over the floor before re-stuffing them into a case full to bursting. Most of them, whatever the activity, were standing directly in the way of everyone else, in doorways, in thresholds, blocking traffic. The poor staff were patient, but some looked obviously pained. My journals at this point are hopeful yet desperate:

Phase 1 of 4 is completed. I am on my way to Delhi, this flight being phase 2. Phase 3 is the crap ten hour wait once I get there. Phase 4 is the overnight flight to London. There's another day after that to get back to Scotland, and then I shall sleep and sleep.

Two ladies sitting nearby are cheerfully comparing shopping. They've both got padded neckbraces. Our flight attendants are astonishingly haughty, covered in gold jewellery, pushy and brusque. They clearly despise their work, or maybe having to work at all. They look like angry aristocrats who lost their fortunes and consider work an insult. They are beautifully stylish at flinging their sari scarves over their shoulders and into people's faces.

There is terrible cheap distortedly loud music blaring out – oh please let it not be for the entire five hour flight! Well of course it is.

That long wait at Delhi airport, when I am on the verge of tears and exhaustion most of the time, is described thus:

IT IS A TEST FROM THE BEYOND! AGH!

I am only a few hours into phase 3, which is a ten hour stretch. I went to the only hotel in the area, and stretched one snack over most of those ten hours. But now, oh dear, the music has started. I thought I'd heard enough elevator-style ABBA to last a lifetime, but no, the beat goes on.

Girlie lounge-lizards are everywhere, of various nationalities, many in halter tops, with grotesquely mediocre voices, murdering a series of pop songs, one after the next, in a sort of karaoke war. What's worse is making bad country and western even worse than it already is. Right now we have a Greek treatment of ABBA, with bazukis. We just had 'Yesterday' with sitars, which kind of almost worked."

Sleep deprivation is such a very basic thing, isn't it? I could easily have hallucinated that I had also just heard sitar arrangements of "Take Me Home Country Roads", "Sealed With a Kiss" and "Down on the Bayou". Surely that's the fever talking? There is one bright point, however, when someone chose the song "Simple Simon". Not the nursery rhyme, but the pop tune recorded by the 1910 Fruit Gum Company (I had to look that up). The real lyrics are:

Put your hands on your head
Put them down by your side
Shake them to your left
Shake them to your right.

Instead, the girly sang the following from the magic screen:

"Put your hand on your heart,
"Put it down by your seed,
"Shake it to the laugh,
"Shake it to the read."

This poetry was almost worth the whole trip, especially to see her sing it with a straight, trusting face.

Nearing the end of phase 3: "I am actually back at Delhi airport now, after an eternity of squatting in a hotel lobby. It's only three or four hours until boarding, all going well." That's really a silly thing to say, isn't it? I'm chanting: "Nearly there, nearly there, holy-moley, nearly there". All of this is tempting fate. Then comes another test: another bout of malaria.

The strong-willed looking lady who opened up the counter informed me there were not enough seats for everyone.

"But I have a confirmed ticket," I whined. She waved this detail away, and got right to the point.

"Can you wait one more day?"

"No. I want to go home."

"Even if we pay you?"

"No. I want to go home."

"We will pay you two hundred and fifty pounds, and send you to an allegedly five-star hotel, for tonight, but not tomorrow of course. Tomorrow you must then come to the airport first thing in the morning and wait twelve hours before getting on the next flight." (This is paraphrasing.)

"No thank you. Please can I go home today?"

"Are you sure you don't want the two hundred and fifty pounds?"

"I'm sure!"

"Really sure?"

"YES! 100% sure! You couldn't pay me enough to stay

here one more HOUR!"

We were both surprised to hear that come out of my mouth like rifle fire, but it certainly stopped her from trying any further. "Treat this one nastily," she typed into her computer, "Bitchy attitude problem. Hates Indians. Don't feed her."

It turned out her twin sister was the flight attendant, who wanted me to take a chicken meal. This was back in the days I gagged on meat.

"Can I have vegetarian meal, please?"

"No, there's chicken." (She was holding two vegetarian meals in her hand.)

"Can I have vegetarian?"

"No, there's chicken."

"What's that?"

"That's not for you. You can have chicken."

Finally she gave the two vegetarian meals to the two Indian women sitting next to me. She never came back.

"Aren't you eating?" one of them asked me.

"I'm waiting for a vegetarian meal. Are you vegetarian?"

"No."

"And your friend?" She shook her head.

They finished their irrelevant vegetarian meals and later tried to talk to the staff on my behalf, but no food appeared. Did I need any further hints? India did not need me back. It had made this clear. It was south-east Asia for me, next year, and every year, from now on.

That second trip settled it. Thailand was officially now my number one trading partner.

Back at the Bella Vista; One Month Already?

Nic sweeps forward ushering in a new visitor who gapes at the view, because everyone does the first time they come here.

"Here, English-speaking lady can help you."

I am at my station, the courtesy desk of the Bella Vista We Speak English Travel Agency, situated at the north end of the big wooden table, just past the ashtrays. I'm on the phone with an airline, on behalf of one of our residents.

"Yes, I can spell it. M-a-r-c-o…" I re-route Marco's flight, play Follow The Feet under the table with Boo, and keep an eye on Pa who is rocking Bee in the hammocks. When the time is right, he steps out while rocking and I step in, like two musicians trading phrases.

We now do this as a matter of routine. He does a certain nod, which is my cue.

I know I can't stay here forever, but in a way I wish I could. We're all going to pretend for a little while more, just for fun. Noo emerges from the kitchen looking genuinely grumpy and exhausted.

"Airin, sorry, I tired, no English, cannot – Nic say you, OK?" She staggers back inside.

"She want you come with us to temple festival, this evening," Nic tells me.

"Temple festival?"

"Is every year. Big community thing. The older girl, Tia, her class do a dance, so we go. You can come too. One seat left."

"OK. Thank you."

That I have been personally invited is an extra honour. This is real honorary aunty stuff. Getting there is where the adventure starts. Our convoy demands a two motorcycle team. Nic is on the first bike with Mia and me. Noo is on the second bike, with Pa holding baby Bee in one arm. Tia is already there, they tell me, getting dolled up.

The plunge down Big Bastard Hill always takes my breath away. Nic zigzags niftily around numerous deep new potholes, which change daily. Last night's mineshafts may now be full of stones. Whole new caverns may have opened afresh. We bounce along. I close my eyes. When I open them I see Noo driving one-handed while turning around to talk to her dad.

I have never ventured far into the local temple's

grounds. Once I followed the path in, and was soon surrounded by over twenty awful, snarling dogs. I haven't been back since. I'm not sure where they are tonight. The temple grounds are far larger than I ever knew, encompassing all the land behind the main street of the village. Within these grounds are the main temple, primary school and sports grounds, various monks' buildings, the crematorium, and more.

The festival fills this space, so it's huge for a village of this size. Every parish on the island takes turns to host it, and everybody goes to all of them, each after the next. There are enough food stalls to feed the entire island, and plenty of shopping, games arcades, and beer tents. There are three different sized sound stages, for all the various musical and dance events. There are roadies who loiter, leer, and wear black T-shirts. There are all kinds of cheap plastic souvenirs for sale, even joke dog turds. It's a proper carnival.

Nic finds us a filthy table, because there are only filthy tables, and gets a rag to mop up old syrupy beer. Bee is writhing and not enjoying the din, and Noo is doing her best with the increasing squirming. Mia and I wait for anything to happen.

"It's not like Rome," he remarks, "where the Church pays priests a salary. Here, every little village has to find money for their own temple, for everything." After Nic delivers us cold drinks, he gets his beer and joins the other

Italian men clustered around the bar. They, too, are married to Thai women, who are together elsewhere. Everybody's happy to get back to their mother tongues.

We are slightly early for Tia's group. First there is a class of younger girls dressed like a cross between Wild West harlots and can-can girls. The choreography is somewhere between silly pop princess and pole dancer in training.

Every dance is followed by the traditional fund-raising practice of allowing people to rent bouquets of plastic flowers to present to the troupe lined up across the stage. Mountains of bouquets fill the arms of each panting ballerina or harem temptress, as the style may be. The flowers are immediately collected and returned to where they started, at the rental stall, ready for the next group. Age groups compete to raise the most donations. A team of mums is at the desk, counting, recounting, and recycling the plastic stems.

Nic returns. He sits with the family, of course, while his daughter is up there. He even stubs out his cigarette, mumbling, "So expensive, these dresses. Stupid. They wear one time. But, all the children do, so we do too." He looks like he wants another beer already.

Tia's group do a classical style dance. She is so made-up and wigged-up that I don't recognise her. The costumes are traditional, beautiful, chaste and elegant. The girls do a good job, folding and unfolding their lotus-petal wrists, gliding this way and that. They're graceful and lovely. Next year their teacher may choose the saloon floozy theme.

In all but the kindergarten age group, boys are not required to dance. Here, though, a quartet of teenagers offer a hip-hop number. This is refreshing. They're good too, and well-rehearsed.

Noo looks relieved and eager to go home. Mia is trying to see how far she can bend her fingers to the back of her hand. She's immensely pleased I do less than half her distance. Nic swallows his beer in one go, and Noo is ahead of everybody on her way back to the bikes.

At home, she heads straight for her bed with the baby, calling over her shoulder, "Sorry, cannot speak, go sleep, goodnight, see you tomorrow, bye-bye-ka."

I say to Nic, "Thank you for including me."

He shrugs. "You're family. Is too late. You must suffer this stupid shit like everyone else."

The next morning, things are much as usual. Then a familiar clumping signals someone trying to bump luggage up the cliff. It's Guido, hauling his battered old case and wrinkled old self onto the patio. He mops his brow. He looks forlorn. He's the last of the fishermen to go.

Noo brings him Bee, and he grins. He sweeps her up in his arms and sings something sentimental to her, nose to nose. They enjoy one last waltz before the taxi toots his horn. He kisses her. For weeks he's been the only stranger who could sing her to sleep. Of all of us who tried, only he charmed her with his rural Italian folk ballades.

This is the same man we saw on video, wildly dancing, nearly naked, high on acid at a full moon party, which his friend videoed all too thoroughly. This is the man who has a thousand such stories, each a line on his face. All the crude vulgarity, all the grabbing of his and others' genitalia, all this is gone. Nic loads his tattered bags. He doesn't want to go. He grabs Boo and twirls him like a plane.

Suddenly Guido-the-thug is a model of restraint and respect. He "wais" and bows to all of the Thais, and shakes hands with the Europeans. He almost looks tearful, and yells at the driver to hurry up. They roar away and we wave him towards whatever is next for him.

"Will he be back next year?" I wonder.

"I do not think so," says Nic thoughtfully. He says nothing more. Soon his phone rings. It's Guido. The message is short. Suddenly Nic looks panic-stricken. Immediately he tears down the hill. Minutes later he's back.

"Sorry. Is OK now. Guido left two tabs of acid in the bungalow." He pats his shirt pocket. "I don't want, but somebody want. OK, who needs something from the village?" Everyone in the café jumps on him, and he disappears underneath a sea of waving hands and tickling fingers.

Boo runs over to his mother, asking frantic questions, which she patiently answers one after another. Nic smiles to me.

"She explains to Boo, Guido not here tomorrow. Guido go home. Maybe Guido come back next year, but Boo doesn't understand when is next year. Then Boo asks does Kun Yai go home today too? Is Kun Yai here tomorrow? His mother answers, Yes, Kun Yai is here tomorrow. Kun Yai isn't going home now."

"Who's 'Kun Yai'?"

Nic grins. "You are. Little Boo, he gave you a nickname."

Boo's mother is smiling and so is everybody else. They're all nodding, saying Kun Yai and smiling at me.

"Kun Yai is big respect, from the very young to much older people. It's very good, from a Thai child."

"Is that like 'grandma'?"

"Sometimes, yes. Other times, like Great Aunt? Not exactly. 'Kun' is Mrs. 'Yai' is big, or grand."

"Mrs Big?"

"If you like."

"Thank you," I say, adding it in Thai to Boo, who does a "wai" and a bow, which he's never done to me before.

The next day, I pay ahead for a second month. My visa lasts sixty days and I shall spend them here, in my new home-away-from-home, where small, animal-like children call me Mrs Big. I will need to extend my visa, but I can arrange that at work.

NOODLE TRAILS

New Villains, New Heroes

Staggeringly hot weather arrives with my second month here. It's like someone opened an oven door. Even the locals are surprised at its suddenness. The warmth everyone craved for weeks is here, all at once, with one sudden red hot sledgehammer.

I'm at the office at my computer. Actually it's Nic's computer yanked out the window again and placed on a picnic table next to some papayas. Smiling Taa places my usual soup in its usual place, as I enjoy my usual tasks of the day. Everyone else is inside.

A very British voice asks, "Hello? Excuse me? Can we have a menu please?" A pale pink, older couple in matching shorts approaches politely, assuming I work here – and in a way I do.

"Sure, have a seat. Need something cool?"

"Please! Large bottle of water, two glasses, extra ice?"

"Lemon?"

"Yes please."

The drinks get delivered, and their order goes to the kitchen. Back at the computer, Stefano the Silent shows up for his appointment. He's the latest in the line of Nic's pals who need their scrambled, basic and painful English translated into intelligible, smooth English. It's a funny sort of niche, in which I decipher obscure phrases, play charades a lot, and seem to have a knack for it. Sometimes it does need a group effort, and all café customers become consultants.

I have met Stefano already, last month, at what I call the twenty fishermen's dinner. He was the only quiet one. He also excelled in swinging Boo up to the ceiling, to the boy's shrill and whooping delight. He does seem to do everything silently.

Stefano has a house nearby (with a kitchen!) but usually eats here. In fact, he never cooks at all, and this boils me in envy, but I say nothing. For years it's the same. He comes to Thailand for a few months to avoid the cold in Italy. He goes from fishing island to fishing island, a few silent weeks in each place.

Today, he needs help to change his air ticket. As happens with many people, he found he just could not go home. He wants – we all want – to extend this stay as far as it can go. We want to pretend we live here, and we really want to pretend we can retire here, forever, into immortality.

It's a Saturday, and all three of Nic and Noo's girls are at the pool table. Tia is playing dangle the baby's feet, which means that Mia cannot play death ball hurling. It's an ongoing disagreement that hovers at an altitude of fierce murmurs. Only last night, Nic and Noo were telling the girls they shouldn't always win at pool against their guests, especially when they cheat so blatantly. They are both enthralled with cheating and do not want to give it up.

I wait for the nice lady on the phone to do her clickety tasks. On the deck opposite are more Italians who have found this haven of their language. The upper deck is dressed in "Scandies", meaning miscellaneous blond Scandinavians and other honey skinned couples and their pals, with no cares and no kids. They wear the signature tie-dyed Indian groovy festival clothing worn by non-Indians worldwide. There are drinks and snacks and semi-dressed people draped all over the place. The British, of course, are fully dressed, except for white legs.

A man walks in with no shirt and swathes of colourful, violent tattoos. His eyes are rolling around in a nasty cocktail of edgy pharmaceuticals. He's sweaty and jittery. The atmosphere turns to ice within a minute. The girls stop their bickering and disappear into the kitchen.

"Hello, how is everyone today?" He has a strange accent I can't place. Maybe it's chemically induced. "My name is David, how do you do?" He goes from table to table repeating this so psychotically that no one dares answer. "Maybe you can spare a cigarette?" he says to one man, who hands it over without eye contact, sliding the lighter across the table as well. David uses it, pretends to steal it, grins, plays cat-and-mouse instead of returning it, then flings it onto the table.

He gestures as if to stroke a woman's arm, then instead jerks his hand away, grinning around the room. The women recoil. The men bristle and watch closely. Nic appears at the kitchen door, also watching.

The woman he did not touch now looks tense and nervous as he looms in close and breathes on her.

"Hey, you like this place? It's OK, huh? Maybe me and my girlfriend move here. She's having my baby, yeah? Nice place. Maybe I come back. Maybe I come live here." Then he touches her arm, she snaps it away and several men leap to their feet.

He smiles. "Yeah, hahaha, nice place. See you again." He saunters away, revs his motor viciously, and departs.

"Bastardo."

"Piece of shit."

"Where was he from? Poland? Finland? Russia?"

"Crazy-land. I hope he goes back."

"My word."

I can't help but shudder. "Lisette, yech, he touched your arm. I'd have smacked him!"

Stefano clears his throat. He is about to speak, and the room listens, because this does not happen often. He makes his statement simply and persuasively, adding emphasis with his pointed fork.

"No," he says. "This no happen. Nobody touch nobody. If he come back, he do nothing. Finito." He punctuates this policy with the fork, drawing a circle to include most of his cohorts who are now nodding as one. I do believe if more than five Italian men nod as one, they really mean it.

It would appear that whether old or young, blond or dark, we are hereby enlisted under the protectorate of the brotherhood of Italian males. That's world-class protection, as anyone from New Jersey can attest. I nod thanks, which he acknowledges as the fork plunges back into its regular duties in his Fusilli Carbonara. I order another coconut.

I don't normally meet dangerous psychotic drugged-up nuts. I scarcely ever meet those who enjoy scaring people. I need an antidote. I ask myself to name one of the most positive times I ever had, working as a Fair Trade importer. The Hope Group was the first group to spring to mind.

Several Years Ago: Hope in Bangkok

I used to collect greeting cards and postcards for fun. I did it for years and had hundreds. I loved flipping through a huge box to select just the right one for each person on each occasion. In Fair Trade, I worked with many different card-makers, from many places, and in many styles. One of these was the Hope Group in Bangkok.

I first met them at a massive retail and wholesale trade event. These were frantic days where I'd quickly grab samples, speak with each group for just a few minutes, and move on to the next while my head spun.

These particular cards sold well the year before. My client shops wanted more, and new designs. I was happy to reorder, and this time I asked to visit.

Their rep, Taya, was hired by a sponsoring missionary group to manage the workshop. She said she'd collect me from my guesthouse from the opposite side of this sprawling metropolis. It sounded way above the call of duty, but she insisted.

She arrived eagerly an hour early, before I'd had breakfast. This turned into time to talk about her complicated journey – two trains and a boat – to get to my guesthouse. She agreed with my suggestion that it was cheaper to go back by taxi. We treated ourselves to "air" (air-conditioning) and more talking time. During the next four hours, we talked so much my jaws hurt. It was that kind of "good pain" that comes after a rigorous workout that stretches you further than ever before. She was so very sweet, and brimming over with keen sincerity and eagerness.

The Klong Toey area was a soggy, boggy maze of tiny alleys, full of open sewers and smelly swamps. The workshop was in a converted block of flats that were modern, concrete, and hot. There were a couple of long tables with women making cards and pre-school children playing underneath. A few small fans moved the muggy air around thickly. It was a small, but very tidy and organised workplace.

After greetings, introductions, and cold water, I saw my order, ready and waiting to be packed, with cartons and the cursed string at the ready. I say "cursed" because this was the source of a problem last time when each group of twenty cards was tied with string, but some were tied too tightly and were damaged. Maybe this information didn't get passed on, or followed up? This is why I wanted to see them directly. I was glad this wasn't our first topic.

The design meeting was particularly useful, and unexpectedly funny too. I asked where they got a steady supply of new ideas for designs. As with so many such groups, this is a constant challenge. They certainly can't pay designers, but sometimes art students enjoy contributing for the practice and another item for their portfolios.

Many of their designs are classy and simple, but are mainly in pastels or earth tones. Once they added the manly shades of burgundy, navy blue and evergreen, I ordered more, and so did others. They added motifs like leaves, trees, mountains and rivers, fishing and boating, bike riding, and playing with dogs.

They asked which animals are best for Father's Day or a father's birthday. We agreed on horses, elephants, birds (if strong and large), cats (if butch or wild), dogs (if handsome), and bulls (if noble). Father and son animal pairs had extra value.

We agreed to avoid donkeys, snakes, reptiles, weasels, insects, and most cattle, especially oxen (dumb) and buffalo (stupid and slow). Probably it's best to avoid monkeys too, unless there's a clearly affectionate joke. Magnificently horned or antlered things like elk, reindeer, yak, and moose might be better.

What's best for women? Avoid cows, dogs, all fish (especially trout for the UK), rodents, and most insects, except perhaps for cute busy bees, pretty butterflies or elegant dragonflies. No reptiles or monkeys unless very, very cute and anthropomorphised.

Good choices include most cats, pretty dogs like poodles and collies (but no pitbulls), horses (not too muscular, ponies are better), chipmunks and squirrels, birds – but not eagles or any bird of prey. Owls are fine, but no vultures. Anything with mother and baby is terrific.

This went on and on, and it was all very entertaining. "Our ladies…think like ladies!" they laughed. They were excited to start drawing new designs. To find new designs for men is going to help them hugely.

Our general meeting was also very happy and productive. They had a new idea, to approach Oxfam, and were about to research their website. The Canadian branch of the Fair Trade organisation Ten Thousand Villages had ordered recently, for example. That's very, very good. If they were anything as huge as their USA chain, this was great news.

As for details, they'd ever only used posh cream envelopes, but I requested natural unbleached recycled brown. It's cheaper, greener, and looks better. We were pleased with that.

Stick-on tags are better than loose ones which are slid into the sealed plastic bag. We want tags to be read twice or more: first by the buyer of the card, second by the recipient of the card, and third by others who see the card. So I asked them to stick them on. This may sound dull, but it can make the difference between selling or not.

One of their agents used to take 27% of their takings at a retail market stall event. This has gone up to 32%. One has to sell spectacularly well to make selling at these events worthwhile. I understood all too well. They were surprised when I explained that I was a small, one-woman company. I sometimes did market stalls too, often on my own. If you rent a stall and sell very little, you go home even worse off. This is an awful feeling. At least with these events, they pay nothing if they sell nothing. These women didn't realise I was small too.

At this point, as for packing, it was easiest to show them, without too many words. String tied too tight can cut creases into the products, while items packed loosely will shift around and get damaged. I wished I could explain why European shoppers are so damned spoiled and picky that the tiniest crease means I couldn't sell these things.

Still, they were wide-eyed and open-minded. Now they could see the problem. There was discussion. There was also scrap paper all around us. We tried wrapping a flat strip of paper around each bundle, and glued or taped it shut, with extra care about not pulling things too taut. It worked. Future parcels arrived with absolutely nothing damaged, whereas previously I lost 10–20%. All it took was some direct communication. This was very satisfying.

About delivery: they liked courier services, but didn't realise that for small parcels it's better and cheaper to use Thai post, by sea. We decided to do a recce to the post office later.

As usual, the really good stuff came after the official meeting. As things were winding down, the choicest story rolled forth. Taya revealed that they all knew I had complained about the string packaging and they thought I was coming to tell them off. They were dreading this terrible lady and were greatly relieved that I was not a punishing ogress. Everyone was taken aback when I helped wrap and pack, showing alternative ways of doing things. I'm just practical. We sealed all the boxes. I tested for shaking, and we heard the beautiful silence of everything packed snugly.

Our trundle to the post office gave me the chance to see other parts of the area, like "klongs" (canals), sub-klongs, open sewers, and algae covered lakes with narrow concrete paths between them and barely enough room for two small kids to pass, let alone grown-ups toting cargo. It was a wonder we and our rolling freight didn't tip straight into the gunk. Yes, it stank too. I'm not being ironic when I say I'm glad she showed me the neighbourhood. It put me in the bigger picture.

It was bloody hot, and Taya said this is why they like the courier, who comes to their door. But when we got to the post office she saw how much cheaper it was. Comprehension and pleasure spread across her face, and then mine. A kindly postal worker talked her through the pamphlet of prices, and she couldn't believe it. She armed herself with forms and a web address, and bought the off-white recycled paper envelopes too.

As we left, suddenly I remembered another card-making group, in Zimbabwe, of about thirty or forty families combined. They started every day by getting into a circle and having a prayer, a song, and a dance. I have often wondered what this world would be like if every workplace started the day like this. I think we might start with the banks.

I also once dreamed that Sir Alan Sugar met these Zimbabwean women, and said about them that "a team that can dance together is a team worth being part of." I quite agree.

My new young trading partner walked me to the train station, mulling over how they sell twenty thousand cards per year, and my order was about one thousand. I'm 5% of their year. They sell next to nothing in January and February, and every year they get nervous. So this was a very well-timed 5% too.

She said solemnly, "This is good. We need this, after Christmas. This is very good sale!"

I feared they hoped I'd be back in a year to take the same again, or even more. I suspected this would last me two or three years.

On the walk to the station I saw even more of Taya's neighbourhood, which has a name for poverty, drug trafficking, related violence, and gang warfare. It also has a reputation for being a thriving community that intends to be positive and healthy, nonetheless.

It looked and felt that way, from my one-day visit. Here, at least in one house, there was income and less stress for the next few weeks. There was hope.

The Risks, the Raid, the Party's Over

I am at present avoiding meals at the Bella Vista. I am exploring every conceivable sort of takeaway meal baked on a motorcycle sidecar. I drag these things to my lair and eat like a savage with my hands. Then I bag up the rubbish and hang it from a high tree. I wait until early in the morning to take it to the communal bin when no one's there. They keep asking me where I am and why I don't eat there anymore. I'm vague and sad.

The routine at the café has definitely changed. There are two alterations to the menu which do not agree with me. One is a very argumentative and domineering alcoholic regular guest. The rest of the mess started one late dinner session.

Dinner went so far past most bedtimes that all the Thai females went to sleep. Out came the papers and the

crumbled hashish, and the spliffs poured forth. Then it
was assumed this would be done every night, then every
lunch, and then basically all day long, until you couldn't
get a cup of coffee without leaving the place smelling of
thick, oily hash smoke.

In my opinion it's stupid to do illegal things in broad
daylight – or in public at any time. Therefore, for a
while, I either eat out or buy things to bring back to the
hut. Also, it's fun exploring different places to eat. In any
case, I do not go up to the café any more. I don't want to
be there when the shit hits the fan. But it turns out I have
uncannily good timing for being there exactly when the
shit does hit the fan.

It all starts the morning I snag a lift back from town
on the back of the motorbike of the terrifyingly swift
maestro chef and compulsive dare-devil, Alfredo the
Great. I had no idea he had a death wish. It appears he
wants to die in flip-flops, without a helmet or long
trousers, at speeds I seldom experience even on the
motorway in my van.

I shut my eyes, glue myself to him, and sincerely pray.
I also vow to take taxis from now on. He does the
journey in record time. Our electrifying entrance sends
me, desperate for my life and some cold water, sprawling
into an armchair. Mia and Boo come and sit on the
armrests, reassuringly.

The partying couples are at the long table. All are
grumpy. Nobody slept because of the noisy skinny

couple arguing and screaming all night. Maestro Alfredo is not to be deterred. He has a great story for them, and starts with arms outstretched and plenty of excitement, "Ciao, ragazzi!" He doesn't get far.

Suddenly, a truck bangs to a halt. Two stone-faced police blackshirts stride in, followed by a supervisor in dark suit and shades. They are intimidating and scary, but businesslike and extremely controlled. Mia and Boo both jump into my lap. The men bark orders in Thai, which Nic quickly translates, first into Italian and then into English.

"Stay still. Do not move."

The Thai women huddle with Pa in the kitchen doorway. Nic is the first one they search. He spreads his arms and legs, and leans against the pool table. He is not intimidated. He cooperates with tall posture, a mild hint of disdain, and cynical acceptance. It's a game. It can be a serious and expensive game, but it is still essentially a game.

One million thoughts in a nanosecond later, I wonder what's at stake for so many guests who probably have something illegal in their pockets right now. They all look seriously miserable.

Mia doesn't understand this is real. She makes a toy gun out of her fingers, and shoots everybody, including the cops, "Bang, bang!" I gently lower her weapon, saying, "No. Stop." She calls something to her dad. Her mother barks back what must be "Shut your mouth and keep it shut!"

As the blackshirts search each European male in turn, little Boo becomes increasingly agitated. He clings to me and starts to whimper. Mr Chief of Police approaches him discreetly and whispers in his ear. The boy calms instantly. Meanwhile, the last male search is done.

They do not touch any of the white women, but they search all their purses except mine. My bag is at my feet, and the two Thai kids are on my lap, and maybe that's what does it. They walk right past me.

Absolutely nothing is found. I am amazed. These people have been rolling up their joints all week, all day every day. I'd expected to be the only European not dragged to the police station, but now I remember they just take everybody in these cases. Suddenly the police leave as quickly as they came, and everybody starts breathing again. Many ask for beer.

"You see? We complain we have nothing to smoke."

"Is good luck."

"Is no good luck. Is miracle."

They explain. Only moments ago, they were all livid there was nothing to smoke. "Is problem when group share everything," moans one of them. "If everybody has, everybody has. But, if nobody has, nobody has." They all nod glumly.

Noo looks like she wants to kill Nic. Instead she yells at Mia, who is fairly defiant. Noo mimics Mia harshly, showing how stupid she was to say, "Papa, you have ganga in your pocket?" Noo yells again at Mia, who now gets that it's no joke. She herds the girl into the kitchen, saying things that make Nic wince. It's good I don't understand.

"What happens if they find something?"

Nic shrugs. "It's only a matter of money. Is more every year."

"Fines go up that fast?"

Again, he chuckles good-naturedly. "This is no fine. Is just money in the pocket. They don't want to stop people smoking. They only want their percentage. Is just business."

"Can the policemen not touch the women?"

"No, cannot. There is one police lady on the whole island. She only comes if it's big. This different. This guy is the new police chief for the province. He visits every place. He walks in, looks strong, try to scare people, fucks off to the next place. It's all to say he is the new man, the new boss."

"But why did they search this place, and no place else?"

"Who knows? Often this is jealous neighbours. The resort down the hill has less business now we are open. They don't speak English, Italian, nothing, only Thai, and this is difficult for many tourists. So they come here. Some Thai people don't like it. Maybe one of them gets drunk one night, calls his friend on the police. This is how it is. They tell the police you have drugs."

"But you do. Everyone here does. Nobody had to tell

the police. Anyone driving by could smell it. This is why I stopped eating here."

"OK, OK. Anyway, now we wait and see. It's only a question of how much. Is business, this is all, just business."

Noo does not like this tone at all. She doesn't need this shit. This is written all over her.

That night I eat out, just for a change, in a nice seafood place near the pier. I am in the middle of a delicious kingfish steak when the two blackshirts and their boss come striding in. This time they don't search anyone. They strut militarily up and down the aisle until all the guests are distracted. Then they move on to the next place. They work every door from one end of the village to the other, while I work through the kingfish and a spontaneously needed second beer.

Back at Nic's that night, no one sleeps much. It's our very own all-night soap opera. The skinny arguing couple come home late from a party, and wander the grounds for the rest of the night, screaming at each other. They are natural performers, it has to be said. It was different before, when their shrieking was the hilarious merriment of drunken song as they thumped their heads on trees. Now their decibels have no joy.

I think for this crew, the party may soon be over. The next day I help some of them change their plans and relocations. New personnel with fresher rucksacks are already buzzing around the freshly emptied bungalows, sniffing out possible new digs.

"So you work here?" one asks.

"Not really. Just helping."

"Where are you from?"

Despite not being sure in the least, I give the next best recent answer. "The UK. Scotland."

"Oh. Scotland. That's near England, right?"

"Yes."

"So, what do you do there? I mean, when you're not here?"

Ah. Now that's a very good question. I used to do things. What were they again?

"What Do You Do in the UK?"

In those years, I was living in rural Scotland and doing about half a dozen part time jobs. This included piano teacher, academic tutor, assistant librarian, massage therapist, and housekeeper. The import business started as another small thing, but it grew the fastest and held the deepest satisfactions – certainly once I started meeting its main beneficiaries.

That several hundred pounds of samples, the second time around, turned into many thousands of pounds of orders. The snag was I didn't have that sum to hand, but I did have a stack of orders promising payment on delivery. Back in those days, you could get a loan for such a reasonable proposition. It worked and the loan was paid back, twice as fast as agreed.

In my stack of journals there were no longer occasional

thoughtful jottings about whether or not I might try this or that in business. All of a sudden, there were whole box files dedicated to order forms, spreadsheets, product lists, labels, invoices, and so on.

My spare room became a packing room, and everywhere else became storage areas. My personal belongings were too numerous anyway, and I'd always thought I should strip down. This forced me to. Every few import shipments, I'd clear a shelf of my books and clothes to make way for more gecko magnets or coconut spoons, or whatever was rolling in.

At first, I was clueless at marketing. Later I remained that way. There was much wasted time in that department. In the early stages, for example, I'd pass a shop that was closed, wonder if they might buy my things, and jot their name and number down. Many of these were dead ends. I was trying anywhere remotely pretending to be ethnic or ethical, green or groovy, new agey or arty, because these places can sometimes cross over into the sale of Fair Trade goods too. They had names like Pagan Celtic Wonderland, Valley of Mystery, The Golden High, Pretty Mysteries, The Natural Charmer, Menopausal Munchkin. You get the idea. They came and went.

What worked was focusing on the shops that were dedicated to the idea of Fair Trade or environmentalism, or both – of which there was a national network. What worked was staying in the niche I knew best and believed in most, and sticking with those who were similarly focused.

It took what seemed like countless phone calls to organise enough appointments to make a trip worthwhile. I only usually had to visit a shop once. After that we could operate via email and the website, when I finally had one. In between my other jobs, I was always planning trips. I'd grab a few days here and there, always trying to cover more each time.

I spent a lot of time on motorways wishing there was time to take A-roads. B-roads would have been ideal. That's British code for back roads. When you work on the road, some people think there's time for sightseeing. It's so frantic, there's barely time for work plus hours of driving. In fact there's barely time to get to a toilet.

I'd be up well before dawn, drive a few hours, have breakfast, meet Shop A at their opening time, eat lunch on the way to Shop B, get to Shop C before they close, drive another few hours to a B&B near tomorrow's sites if I was lucky, grab a lousy takeaway meal, eat it while typing up orders and emails, arrange routes and maps for the next day, all while hoping for at least four hours of sleep. Sightseeing? Excuse me?

Every thirty or forty towns or so, I'd hit one that made me want to move in and start a life right there and then. I even sometimes got a local paper to see what jobs were going or if there was a cheap big old farmhouse, good for an expanding mail order business. You never know.

Random favourite moments included:

- One Indian takeaway was in a thatched, mock-Tudor cottage. Nearby was a house I wanted to buy.
- Marlborough is twinned with a town in the Gambia. It looked old, rich and grand.
- Pucklechurch won that week's favourite name contest.
- One year, the best image was of two Japanese tourists in a field photographing bored sheep.
- There were lists and lists, towns and shops, and more. What could I fit in a short round trip?
- Edinburgh. North Berwick, Berwick, Alnick.
- Carlisle, Durham, Whitby.
- Birmingham, Leicester, Rugby.
- Finsbury Park, Crouch End, Berwick Street.
- Colchester, Ipswich, Norwich.

"Back home in Scotland by Sunday, yippee!" My notebooks were now filled with this sort of thing. I visited, showed samples, answered questions, got orders, and it all snowballed. I knew so little then about this business, about any of it. And yet one learns. And yet it grew.

The journals also contained reminders to keep an eye out for things I could only buy in cities, like ingredients for Thai cooking. A selling trip to Edinburgh also meant a quick stopover in a good Asian grocery for a year's supply of decent sesame oil and fish sauce. Back then, little Lockerbie's supermarket did not carry Thai fish sauce. Ten years later it would.

There was a warning about the strictness of the parking attendants in Edinburgh. Friends reported cases of a hearse and even an ambulance being clamped by traffic wardens.

There were things to be named, products to be given tags like etched crescent or coffee bean danglers. That note about a jungle bell must have meant a jingle bell.

I also become a van person. I can't say van man, but I was very close to it. I knew true van love. This I say in truth. One day a large package arrived. I'd no idea what it was. These things get ordered way in advance when shipping by sea, and one forgets what's coming when. Of course, it was the elephant dung paper stationery. This sort of thing had become normal by then. Meanwhile the nice delivery driver wasn't listening. He was distracted by my van.

"I like your van," he said.

"Thanks," I said, "but I wish I could upgrade."

"This one is OK," he countered firmly. "That is a fine old workhorse."

"It is. I agree. I just yearn for a Mercedes Sprinter. But, they're that bit more expensive."

He waved an authoritative forefinger at my vehicle. "That is a good van," he insisted. "That's a very, very good van." We are van people. We are family.

These rare delights were set amongst long tedious days of paperwork, internet research, and phone calls; trying to arrange more trips, more markets stalls, and more festivals that involved rigging rope ladders all over a small circus tent and festooning it with everything I had.

Of all the events I did, I loved best doing slide show talks about my foreign trips and the groups I met. These were to women's clubs, church groups, Rotary branches, Girl Guides, students, and single mums' groups. One of the best parts of this life was telling people on this side of the planet what and who I met on the other side. That was magic. That was pure love.

Every year, I'd work frantically in the autumn run-up to Christmas, recover from that, travel to where all my stock was made, and order more for the following year. Then too, every single year, I'd return to the UK and see the latest retail casualties on Lockerbie high street. The high turnover of shops was continually demoralising.

One year I wrote, "Back home in Lockerbie, there's a second chippy? Is that going to work? There's a sign in the first chippy, looking for help." They both survived, last I heard. One had loyal regulars and later evenings. The other did a wider menu, sit-down lunches and, to my palate, a much nicer batter recipe.

There was one bizarre year of bad luck or bad information when three Indian restaurants opened in the same summer, in a very small town that eventually found it only needed one. One died quickly (and six years later would still sit derelict), one served sit-down meals for a while in the old cinema, but the takeaway on the main street was the one that lasted.

"There's only a few ways to make money in this town:

alcohol, fish and chips, and sweets." This was from Andy, owner of a fine wine shop known for one hundred fine Scotch whiskies and excellent mead as well. It, too, sadly came and went. A small hand-written note appeared, "Closed now. Bye." It isn't necessarily easier to make a living just because we're not in Asia.

My local bank branch might not at first have been familiar with sending money to Peru, Vietnam or Kenya, but they acclimatised very quickly.

Finally, my nomination for outstanding anecdote from those road trips across Great Britain is the following. "The flowery shrubs in the centre of the roundabout leading me from the motorway into Bolton were clearly meant to spell out 'Bolton in Bloom', but somehow it had been mangled into saying instead 'Bolton in Gloom'." This was very much how I found it. I can only wish it luck. Of all my noodle-shaped wanderings, this was the only time I got lost in an ugly, angry part of town, where lots of windows were smashed and boarded up and hysterically hostile young men glared at me for having a vehicle at all. I locked my doors, hid my purse and, at traffic lights, I remembered to leave some space between me and the car in front to get away from any sudden attempt at a mugging or hijacking while sitting trapped at a red light.

I learned that in Zimbabwe. I can't believe I applied it to Bolton.

The Bella Vista, Tea and Indecision

Somewhere mid-month, it crossed my mind I need a visa run. I can't avoid it much longer. It must be arranged soon. In this sense, I am my own worst customer. The Travel Desk is today situated on the other end of the table from the ashtrays, near the plate of dried fish and the ginger being chopped one-handedly by Noo as Bee drools down her back. Boo is under the desk perfecting reptile impersonations. Tia and Mia are at school.

I'm on the phone, on hold, helping an Angelo change his air ticket. He keeps changing his mind, about both dates and locations, but swears that once they answer the phone he'll decide then and there, spontaneously and melodramatically.

"But why," he groans, "why I have to go after only one month?" He pleads like a hero condemned to death in a Puccini opera.

"It's because you got the visa on arrival. Then you get thirty days. If you get a visa before arrival, you get sixty days."

"So, now I must leave Thailand, in order for to stay in Thailand?"

"Exactly."

"Agh, no, is crazy."

"You can also go to the Immigration office and pay nearly as much. You may as well take a nice little trip and see something interesting." This is true for me too. I feel much the same as poor snivelling Angelo. I am equally indecisive, and yes, of course, childish. Vacations, treats and privileges do not always bring out the best in people, strangely enough. However, to spare me further thought on this conundrum, an assortment of the café customers spring into action. It's very community spirited.

"Take bus Malaysia, most cheap way. Only one day. Very very long day, but only one day."

"No, go Burma. Is better. At least is interesting to see Burma. Malaysian crossing is joke. Is shopping centre, and not even good shopping."

"Burma same!"

"All no good. You go by land? Two weeks more only. Go by air? Get thirty days more. Get cheap air ticket, maybe Kuala Lumpur. Stay a night, come back. We do this last month."

These are only some of our helpful consultants at the

We Speak Broken English Travel Agency. Can we call it Binglish please, by the way? It's not really bad or broken at all. It's international flexi-English, and I like it because it's often clearer than real English. It's certainly more streamlined.

Angelo is still in agony and cannot make up his mind. He says to wait until tomorrow. This doesn't stop him from droning on, repeating himself over and over, finally agreeing that he is not addressing me at all. That's considerate. Now I can think about my own visa run. Why am I being so spineless about this? Just go anywhere and get a stamp. What's the problem?

I hear Laos is very beautiful, and has a sweet and slow pace. There are loads of websites. So I don't look at any of them, declare my work shift over and return home to the bungalow. That afternoon I go in circles inside my head. How long can I stay here? How can I move here forever? In the meantime, where do I go to get that extra month?

Where would I like to go? I'd like to go back to Cambodia, where I visited and also traded before. But now there is no trading to do, and I'm back to square one on that question again. The bags and jewellery I got last time were all lovely, but I ordered far too many and there's plenty left to try to sell. I feel like a drowning person clinging to a small craft only strong enough to hold me and no one else, as much as I'd like to share, somehow. I'm sinking from unsold stock.

There is embarrassingly superstitious behaviour sprinkled across these weeks, in terms of getting advice from any damned place. I don't know where to go. I don't know on which auspicious day to go or not go. I gaze at the multi-cultural calendar, wondering if I should consider my father's birthday or my mother's, or the precise midway point between them, or the upcoming good luck day for Chinese roosters. Anyway, do they mean metal roosters, water roosters, or Chinese or Thai or which? How do I decide? I get more and more superstitious, the more I don't know what I'm doing.

There's an old Chinese saying that when you make an important decision when drunk, reconsider when sober. By the same token, if you make a big decision when sober, reconsider when drunk. If it works both ways, it's a good decision. I try that too, but with unconvincing results.

I do know that staying here longer is a good thing, and that is all I need to know right now. Now, before I secretly spend a week with an I Ching, let me say that eventually Angelo opts for a simple and bold one-way ticket to India. Best of luck to him.

This is rather like looking for your glasses when you can't see them...guess what, without your glasses. I also need a compass. Once I find my glasses, I'll look for the map that leads me to a compass, which will find the radar to locate the gyroscope, to navigate to...what?

Someone to ask? I want to do this without Dad's help, whether metaphorical or any other way.

My daydreams trawl top stories of getting lost and getting found:

- I once asked directions in Dublin and was told, "You go straight down there, keep going, and then ask somebody else."
- I also once asked directions to exit Tel Aviv airport. The policewoman was very confident of her heavily accented English. "You go strange, strange, strange, and then you left."

Now whose life story is that?

My favourite story of getting lost and found was about Big Al from Australia, a disarming retired tram driver from Sydney. I have him to thank for talking about Hanoi in such a way that I put it firmly on my list of places I intended to see. Al's wife was Vietnamese, and he had family all over Vietnam.

"Yep, the Viets saw off the Japs, the Chinese, the French, the Yanks. Yeah they've said goodbye to quite a few, and they're still there. You got to hand that to them."

His wife had escaped from the north to the south as a baby in 1954, and was separated from her brother and other family for decades. Finally she could travel to the north again and, on one of these return trips, she asked her husband to come with her on an errand. She led him to an obscure part of the city, wandering about, looking lost but continuing to wander with him in tow and without explanation. Finally they got to a small apartment building. He assumed she was lost and would finally ask directions.

"It's here!" she announced with satisfaction. "This is it."

"This is what?" he asked.

"It's my aunt and uncle's house."

"What! Why didn't you tell me?"

"I didn't think it would still be here."

"Here's me looking like a slob."

"Never mind that," she said, as the door opened, "get in there." There was shock, and then screaming hugs and an unimaginably beautiful reunion.

Retelling the story to me, he said, "They fed me to within an inch of my life. They brought me warm clothes because Hanoi is much cooler than you might think. I was suddenly in the bosom of that family. My wife never told me these people existed."

"I didn't know if they existed," his wife had said. "I didn't want to say."

"You just can't assume anything," he concluded, with a thoughtful look.

I quite agree. One cannot assume anything, but that idea is not making me more decisive. I've had enough of "Yes, no, maybe. Yes, no, maybe." How does one make big decisions? Finally, I've got it! The Needle Story!

This is a great answer to that question. The Needle Story is one of those turning point stories we all have in our lives. There are points you can look back at, decades later, and see how that fork in your path brought you here, years later, to such different terrain.

Some forks are bigger than others. Everybody knows this. I was in my early twenties, fresh out of graduate school in Japan for music education, temporarily living in a cheap room in San Francisco, wondering where to go, where to live, where to find work. A job had recently fallen through and I was suddenly up in the air with two suitcases in a grotty room, greasy from the Chinese takeaway downstairs.

There were a few possibilities in different corners of the globe, all equally hazy, so it was difficult to choose. One night I was doubled up in extraordinary gut pain and high fever, and was rushed to the nearest hospital with suspected appendicitis. The diagnosis wasn't clear at at first, so they did blood tests – lots and lots of tests.

This meant taking lots and lots of blood. As the nice medical fellow lined up the many vials, I asked him to distract me with conversation because of my extreme cowardice. He was excellent at this, quizzing me about where I might move and so on. As he labelled all his bottles and papers, I had plenty of time to run down my list of pros and cons, reasons and counter-arguments, in exactly the kind of swirling eddy that stays in one place.

"Do you want a second opinion?" he asked, patting affectionately the seventeenth vial ready for action.

"Sure."

"OK. You've done enough reasoning. You're repeating.

You need one good strong gut instinct. So, put everything else away. Do you need to shut your eyes? OK, do that now. I'll ask one question: spit out the first thing you think, as fast as you can. Instant gut instinct: no pausing, no thinking. Want to try?"

"OK."

"Answer me this. Where would you rather live next, in your life – the Canadian Rockies or Israel?" Jab! The needle went in.

"Israel!" yelped my mouth before I knew it. That was a surprise. My technician didn't look surprised at all.

"Well then," he said matter-of-factly, "if I were you, that's where I'd go."

That settled that. I went, and spent a fascinating two years there. What's the moral of the story for me? When I'm looking for a needle in a compass in the dark and in the fog, what helps is one kindly yet unexpected question. If the answer pops out swift and sure, you can never really ignore it. I'd trust it.

Therefore, this game needs a trusted second player, to ask the question you were not expecting. This is what friends are for, and also some hairdressers and bartenders.

Finally, I'd like to pay tribute to a concept brought to me by the fine folks behind the *Rocky and Bullwinkle Show*. Genius scientist dog Dr Peabody, with his boy Sherman, proves that if you want to find a needle in a haystack, then sit in the haystack. Chances are you'll find it painfully quickly.

These reveries dissolve at the sight of a coconut carried by Nic playing comedy butler.

"Here is your coconut, Madam. Tell me, please, where will Madam be travelling for the visa run this time?"

"I don't know. It's hard to decide. I don't know." I writhe a bit and he looks sympathetic. He has only seen this trillions of times.

"Everybody tell you many things, yes?"

"Yes."

"Too many different things, yes?"

"Yes."

"You want maybe one week?"

"Yes."

"Forget that shit. OK, is not shit, but you understand. Just say, now, where you want to go?"

"Well. I'd like to see Cambodia. One last time."

"So."

"It's just a feeling."

"OK," he shrugs and considers it settled.

Noo sticks her head out of the kitchen and startles me when she yells, "So? You visa run? Where you go – where?"

"Cambodia," I spit out.

Nic leaves. I get on the computer. It's arranged in no time. One coconut curry with chicken and extra carrots later, the café has refilled with the post-swimming crowd.

"You're going where there's no beach? Why?"

"I know people there. I'd like to see them."

They take this in and dismiss it entirely.

"Luang Prabang – better architecture. Might be a pool somewhere. Great beer."

These are all tempting points, but it's been decided. There is a plan. I've been missing them lately, so now there is one, I am guarding it carefully.

Bombshells into Ploughshares in Phnom Penh

"Hello Madam, you need taxi?"

"No."

"My tuk-tuk very good. Tonight you go out?"

"No. Tonight I go in." I am trying to get into my guesthouse.

"You go out tomorrow?"

"Maybe. OK, yes."

"You go temple?"

"No."

"You go Palace?"

"No."

"You go Museum of Genocide?"

"No!" I bark, with more vehemence and disgust than I'd intended. We're both embarrassed, and there's an awkward silence. "Sorry," I add. We both soften. He looks genuinely contrite. "Maybe you go shopping?"

Near enough. I sigh miserably, "Yes, shopping."

"Shopping!" he rejoices. "Shopping good."

"Yes!" I go along with it. "Shopping very good. I buy one thousand things."

"Very good," he approves. "You need very big suitcase."

In truth, I will buy about one thousand things. I am a small wholesaler, but a wholesaler nevertheless, and by the end of this visit I will order a few hundred bags and a few hundred pairs of earrings. He doesn't know this. He thinks I'm absurdly wealthy, and compared to him I am. He thinks these are all toys for one frivolous madam. I really don't like that this is what he thinks I am. However, I'm not exactly a big buyer for the likes of John Lewis either. I'll get one carton of stuff to shove in my loft and try to flog at market stalls and the like – using a somewhat softer sell than his, I might add. His patter isn't too bad. Like most Cambodians, he is persistent, but he has a soft voice, a gentle politeness and very good manners. Salespeople here do not grip your arm and scream threats in your face like in other unnamed parts of the world. It is, however, relentless.

"What time you need tuk-tuk tomorrow?"

"I have tuk-tuk." The hotel arranged it. He is crestfallen, momentarily. "After tomorrow?"

"I have tuk-tuk tomorrow, and next day, and then I go home." He is dignified in defeat, and smiles with puppy-dog eyes.

"Lee-high," I say, which means goodbye. I try to use his exact same soft tones. He beams, like they always do if you say even one word in Khmer, because no one ever bothers.

"Lee-high!" he coos. "Lee-high, lee-high!" His sweet birdcalls fade musically into the distance as I flee into the guesthouse lobby where I know the staff will not let him follow. I need to get ready for tomorrow. I have business meetings. I feel like a fraud – an ant in elephant's clothing – but these are business meetings all the same.

I will not have any time for tourist attractions. Even if I did, it wouldn't be the Genocide Museum, although I will be a few short blocks away from it. For one thing, it's not like post-war Germany when so many denied the Holocaust's existence that others had to insist Yes It Did Happen. Here, everyone knows it happened. There isn't a single family unaffected. Limbless landmine victims are everywhere you look. Most would rather bloody well forget about it and get on with life. So would I.

However, reminders are like oxygen. It's in the air – unavoidable. Can you go to Hiroshima and not remember the atom bomb? Can you pass through Auschwitz on the train and not think of the Nazis? And for heaven's sake, I live in Lockerbie. Can I mention that to anyone without them frowning as if the town still lives mournfully inside the crater? I moved there from London, partly for the cheap rent and pretty countryside. Mainly, though, I wanted to live near its neighbouring Buddhist monastery,

which is too surreal to explain to anybody, even
Cambodian Buddhists. The idea of Scottish Buddhists
would blow the wheels off their tuk-tuks.

For the rest of this chapter, then, I dare you to not
think of a pink elephant. I didn't think of one, even once,
all the way through my bobo. (That's a breakfast soup,
which is a great idea once you get used to it.) I was
similarly focussed throughout the elaborate introductions
to my tuk-tuk man for the next two days. These guys
love this sort of gig. It's the easiest money around. For
ten dollars a day (about six pounds), he'll go anywhere in
the city, take as many stops as you like, and wait in
between. He'll get several weeks wages in a very easy
day, so it's a hot ticket. It's also why some tourists try to
haggle them down to local rates, but not me. I think it's
great.

This fellow got good reviews from the guesthouse
staff. He was born and raised here, speaks good English,
is helpful, etc., but they all say that, don't they? In this
case it's true. He is nice, his English is impressive, and
he knows the city as well as anyone. That's saying a lot,
because it's a total maze even to many Cambodians.

After breakfast I am lead to his tuk-tuk and all his
colleagues who protectively surround it. This example is
a sort of covered cart pulled by a motorcycle. The guys
are neatly turned out, in dark plain trousers, white crisp
shirts and basic brown shoes, all of which look like

they're from 1950's Russia. They are very tidy, with their hair slicked nicely. First, we practise English:

"Good morning, Madam."

"Good morning."

"How are you?"

"I am fine. How are you?"

"I am fine, too. What is your name?"

And so on. This is repeated six times with each of his co-workers or cousins or whoever these smiling short men are. I am completely comfortable because they are polite and don't stand too close. Best of all we are all the same height. It may sound silly, but I'm fed up with standing on European trains where I face a world of armpits. I want a nation I can look in the eye. Asia is perfect. Back home, I am forced to look up to most people, and that can't possibly be healthy, either for your upper spine or your self-respect.

We shake hands, all of us, one by one, eyeball to eyeball. Then I hand the driver the slip of paper with the address on it. Now things get interesting.

Most streets in Phnom Penh are numbered, but don't be fooled. It's a labyrinth. People who have been resident for ten generations still double-check. My man and his pals confer. It's a frank and lively debate, and appears to arrive at an agreement. Then their leader phones the place I'm going, just to make sure.

It's near the Russian Market. Right around the corner from the Genocide Museum: the place I will not go, the place with the history I don't want to think about. Fine. I am helped into the spotless tuk-tuk after they all dust it down yet again. I'm shown how to hide my bag under the seat, and am encouraged to wear one of those surgical face masks that lots of people wear here because you'd be poisoned by the pollution if you didn't. I will have a hacking cough in twenty hours anyway, as most people do. Thus equipped, all six comrades wave us off, and we lurch into the fray.

Phnom Penh's wacky morning rush hour is a mish-mash of manic tuk-tuks, rickshaws, bicycles, mopeds, even the occasional car or truck, and a few converted lawn-mowers. I am not a tourist. I'm going to work like everyone else, so how fantastic is that? I am grinning underneath my face mask, despite having read that half the cars here have steering wheels on the left, the other half have them on the right, and horrendous accidents are frequent. Let's add that to the pink elephant list, shall we?

Here are some other things I am putting out of my mind. If you want to skip this historical summary of the worst, jump past the next three paragraphs. I quite understand.

In the Khmer Rouge's four-year reign in the late 1970s, they eliminated a quarter of their country's population, or nearly two million people. They targeted anyone with education, a trade or profession, an art or craft, those who could speak a foreign language, even those who wore glasses because it suggested they might like reading. When Pol Pot escaped into obscurity in

1979 there were allegedly only three hundred people in the entire country who had any form of higher education. The others had been killed, or had fled.

To save bullets, they beat people to death with hammers and shovels. They have preserved a rule hand-written on the wall, now translated as: "While getting lashes and electrification, you must not cry at all." The museum houses a map of Cambodia on the wall created completely from human skulls.

Today, millions of landmines remain undetected, forty thousand Cambodians are missing a limb, and half of all rural children are physically stunted in one way or another.

There are times in one's life to do the sort of pilgrimage where you will be deeply moved. There is Anne Frank's House in Amsterdam, and the Holocaust Museum in Jerusalem, or the Robben Island Museum in South Africa, and more. In a way I feel I should but… thank goodness, we're here.

We arrive at Rajana, an attractive gift shop filled with textiles, wood carvings, stationery, teas, candles, and all the things you find in gift shops. They are established Fair Traders. This is why I am here and not down in the main market, where things are so cheap you hate to think why.

I try to tell Mr Tuk-tuk how long my meeting will be, but it truly doesn't matter. He points to a corner where he will hang out with a load of other tuk-tuk men, and he will be there when I come out, whenever I come out. I go upstairs and greet Mr Sab, the manager.

It has to be said, Mr Sab smiles more than anyone I have ever met. He is in his thirties and is a devoted father of two, but acts like an eager young spaniel. He's full of energy and enthusiasm, loving every minute of everything, wagging his merry little tail and running all over the place. He pumps my hand vigorously and leads me into his office, passing through a work area where half a dozen women paint flowery motifs onto textiles. They allow me a peek, and later will even agree to photographs, but they are painfully shy.

One of them has a toddler daughter with her, who stares at me suspiciously. I smile. I wave. I say hello in Khmer. Her dead stare is immobile. Her mother takes her tiny hand and waves it for her, which she allows, or perhaps doesn't even notice because she is so hypnotised. Finally Mum succumbs to giggling, which ignites the others, and soon they're all giggling – all except the child, naturally.

"Doesn't she meet many white people?" I ask.

Mr Sab giggles and shrugs. He says something to the girl, who looks unconvinced by his words, by my face, perhaps by the entire world she's been born into. Who can blame her? Her mother leads her away while she continues staring over her shoulder.

It reminds me of a wonderfully bizarre encounter I had with a tiny child in a supermarket in a remote part of

Japan. After much staring, the child asked his mother, "O-kaa-san, nan dess-ka?" meaning, "Mum, what is it?" Not "Who is it?" but "What is it?"

His mother replied, "Gai-jin dess," meaning, "That's a foreigner."

I knew a few phrases of Japanese, so I did my party trick. "Hello, I'm a student, my name is…" but got no further. The kid started screaming.

"It speaks Japanese! What is it, Mummy, what is it?"

The mortified mum dragged away the hysterical child, bowing and murmuring, "I am so sorry. I am so sorry," keeping her head significantly lower than mine, and leaving long black marks on the floor where the shocked kid's heels were being dragged by force.

Of course, in terms of global history, it's important that as many rich and/or white people as possible have this experience, possibly on a regular basis.

Mr Sab and I settle into two tiny chairs by a tiny table in a tiny corner of a tiny room stuffed full with files and sketches and fabric samples and wonderful, rich, lovely colours and textures. High on the wall, above everything else, three immense photographs peer down. He sees my quizzical look, and suddenly becomes uncharacteristically serious.

"That is our King, and his father and wife. All offices have this. It is to show our respect."

This sounds like possible duress to me, but I say nothing. Meanwhile, a girl has gracefully placed a welcome glass of ice water before me, and has shimmered away before I can thank her.

"How were sales last year?" he asks.

"Good," I answer. Overall it was bad, but their stuff did well. I'd mainly bought cards from them, a few bags, and some bangles. This year I'm especially interested in their brass jewellery, made from melted down bullets and bomb casings. They call it their "Bombshell Jewellery" range, and it is a blatant pro-peace statement.

The "bombshell bangles" I got last year stopped everyone in their tracks. Whether they bought one or not, every person who noticed them stood there and held them and pondered and reflected, and were visibly moved and inspired by the very idea. This year I'll get earrings and necklaces too, but with my limited budget I need to choose carefully. I can try three designs, maybe four, so we start sifting through their photos and sketches. I settle on a seashell, a long dangle etched with flowers, and a leafy pattern in a teardrop.

"Where do you get your ideas?"

"Sometimes the customers have their own designs," he says, "and that's easy. But we must also offer our own designs too. We use traditional patterns, and then try to make a modern version from them."

By "traditional" he means the geometric and other abstract carvings that cover every inch of the one hundred and twenty Temples of Angkor Wat, which spreads over seventy square miles and spans six centuries of history and world-class artistry. Most contemporary teachers of these arts are gone now, so rebuilding the skills is painstaking. He hauls out an enormous tome filled with abstract shapes and swirls descended from the era of these temples. One of them catches my eye.

He lights up, delighted. "We like that one too! Look, this is what we want to make!" He shows me a sketch of an earring, a busy cluster of curlicues. "What do you think? Will English people like this?"

"I don't know. Maybe if it's a bit simpler?"

He's twinkling, intrigued, and hands me a pencil. I cross out a few extra curlicues, until it looks like an elongated infinity symbol, with swirls across. Nice and simple. He loves it. He lights up, all teeth.

"Nice! We will call it 'The Eileen'!"

Wow. I won't call it that – I couldn't possibly – but I certainly will enjoy a few moments of sheer, silly vanity. Then I grab a calculator and work out that I can afford maybe fifty pairs of earrings, plus matching necklaces. I decide also to sell them singly, for those individuals so groovy they'd never dream of buying two similar earrings, as in "Don't be absurd, darling, no one buys a *pair* of earrings anymore." And for men, of course.

"Would you like to see where they're made?"

We climb the narrow stairs to the top floor, which is open air. It has to be because of the chemicals they use to clean and work the metals. This floor is all blokes and noise and banging hammers and wooden benches. There's also a radio playing weird music that sounds half Asian romantic folk ballad and half European advertising jingle. There is one young woman amongst them who, he explains, really wanted to work with jewellery, so she joined the men, even though that's a little unusual in their culture. He shrugs happily, "It's OK, she wants to work here, OK, she works here." He just wants people working. That's all he wants. He says this over and over during my visit. If he could create employment for the entire nation, he would. That is his mission.

When I ask to take photographs, the men do not blush coyly like the women. They sit up a bit, puff out their chests a bit, and smile. They are subtle and not vain, but clearly enjoy displaying their wares and their skills.

On the windowsill is the base of a large bullet, with "1946" printed on it. This will be turned into a lovely bangle bracelet with intertwining arches in an ancient classical design, and will retail for perhaps twenty dollars or more.

I return to the sales floor and select more samples. I've spent most of my budget, but these are odds and ends I can show the shops I sell to. If there's enough interest, I'll add to the order later.

The young woman at the counter does the paperwork while we retire to the office for more ice water, passing by some vivid shoulder bags with Rajana's cute logo on them. Three elephants, large, medium and small, are walking in a row, each trunk holding the tail in front."It's a traditional image," he explains. "It means, in the elephant herd big one helps middle one, middle one helps little one, so the whole herd is better off if each helps another."

It reminds me of an old Buddhist idea that heaven and hell are two different banquets. The world is a huge banquet, with plenty of wonderful food for everybody, but at each place-setting are chopsticks a metre long. Try though you might, you can't get the food into your mouth, so the whole scene is one of starvation and anger and desperate frustration. In other words, it's hell. However, the solution is for everyone to feed the person opposite. Everybody gets fed, and everybody learns helpfulness and what's often translated as "interconnectedness", which they say is a prerequisite for a heavenly state of mind. You can't do it on your own. You need the connection. That is essential for a heaven.

As we sip ice water, we confirm that there are no other matters to settle, and there's a lull. With ebullient Sab there aren't many lulls, so this is noticeable. Then I remember something my customers requested. I'm no journalist, and hate intruding, but here goes:

"Can I ask you about your background?"

"Of course!"

"It does help, with our promotions and publicity." This is abundantly true. The more information that comes with a product, the more people like it. They want real stories, not sales slogans. They want information, not spin.

Anyway, I am torn between being nosey and being sensitive.

He leans forward attentively. "Please ask anything, anything at all!"

"How long have you worked here?"

"About ten years."

"And before that?"

"Before that I was in Thailand."

"Thailand?"

"Yes, for many years."

The slight pause almost induces me to say, "You don't have to tell me if you don't want to," but he's already telling me. I wouldn't say he needs to tell me, but he has obviously told this story before. Without any prompting at all, it pours forth like a river.

"I escaped over the Cambodian–Thai border in 1984, after the Pol Pot regime. It was about five years after that. I was eleven years old. My father died during the Pol Pot regime, when I was four or five, and my mother died when I was eight. I was living with my sister, but we were very poor.

"At that time, so many groups were fighting each other: mostly the Khmer Rouge, the Bara (Cambodian freedom soldiers), the Vietnamese, and other groups too. The Bara helped me escape. I lived with them in the jungle. I cooked rice for them, fetched water, and carried their rifles. I helped them, and they took care of me, for about one year. Not much food, very hard.

"They helped me to escape to Thailand. There, I was in the refugee camps, different ones, for twelve years, from 1984 to 1996. The first Cambodian camp I went to had about twenty thousand. A Vietnamese camp had between fifty thousand and sixty thousand people. There was a Lao camp too.

"The Thai government provided these camps, and tents – no, they did not 'provide' them. They rented them, to the UN High Commission for Refugees. They do not give, they rented."

This is the first time I see Sab register anything resembling suppressed anger. When referring to the Khmer Rouge, he seems fearful, crushed, head quietly bowed. But when mentioning the Thais, he looks me in the eye. He is incensed that they didn't help. It wasn't Thailand, far and away the richest nation in the area, that took action and rousted the Khmer Rouge. It was the Vietnamese who rescued the Cambodians that time, and they aren't likely to forget it.

"Then I went to a holding camp. Some refugees went to America or Europe, but I wanted to come back home. So, I stayed in the Thai holding camp. I find a place where they teach English, and I work there as a volunteer, looking after children. The nurses show me how to give vaccinations and take temperatures. I learn English.

"Then finally I get permission to go back home. We must wait for the day we can go." Now his voice really gets emotional, despite his efforts to remain calm. "The

Thai authorities, they have no place to keep us, so they keep us in a jail, for three months. They are not just using the jail building. They lock us in. We cannot write or contact anybody outside. We cannot leave. No one knows where we are, that we are in jail. Thai authorities do this.

"Then in 1997, there is a coup in Phnom Penh, and more fighting. Two groups fight over who will be prime minister, and there is war in the streets. We read this in Thai newspapers. It is too dangerous to go back now. We ask to wait, but they force us to go back, right at the start of this coup.

"In Phnom Penh, I go to a temple and the monks hide us. We eat their leftover food, when there is some, and sleep on the floor next to them, in their rooms. Everyone is afraid to go out. I don't go out, for three or four months.

"When things are quiet, I find a job as an English teacher, but it's only part time. Then I apply to Rajana. They teach me to make wood earrings, bamboo earrings, hair ornaments from coconuts. Now I have been here ten years.

"Now Rajana company has three shops, and soon number four. We employ more than one hundred and twenty-two small groups in villages, making these products. Some groups are ten people, some only two or three. So Rajana has come a long way.

"We want to expand more, make more and more jobs. In the beginning we have funding from the UK. But, in

2000, there is no more funding, so we are independent. Now we are self-supporting, no funding. Just business."

The girl enters the room with my paperwork, and I settle the invoice. I will pay ahead in full. This is not the usual way. Usually groups ask for half up front, half on delivery, but I'll take the risk. For one thing, I trust them. For another, this saves on bank charges. We all win. He can hardly contain his excitement. By my reckoning, this eight hundred pound order could represent several weeks' salary for everybody in the building. Twenty more clients like me and they're set for the year. In the UK I'm an ant, but here I'm a baby elephant. A thought catches me: I wonder if ants can walk safely under elephants, too small to be harmed? I must look into that. I like that idea. If only it had an economic equivalent, like me v. Tesco, for example.

I get out my face mask for the next journey.

"Yes," he nods, "you need this. Bad pollution, we must improve. Much work to do. Pollution, rubbish everywhere, bad roads, bad electricity, water, many things difficult. But," (and here his wonderful toothy grin erupts afresh), "every year, things improve. For so many years, all we do is fight war, avoid war, deal with war, recover from war. Everything is to do with war. Now, we build things, we make things. Finally we have good work to do. We are so happy to have good work. Every year things improve."

From a Western perspective, they have a mountain of tasks. But it's a mountain without a war being fought on it for once, so they love the scenery. I stand for our parting handshake, and he practically shakes it off my wrist. Outside, Mr Tuk-tuk leaps to attention.

"Thank you, Mr Sab. It's good doing business with you."

"Thank you, Miss Eileen! I hope we see you next year."

I hope so too. This is now my favourite tourist attraction in Phnom Penh.

Bella Vista: Month Three

It's month three in my saga. Thailand has had a change of season and a change of attitude. Usually the challenge this time of year is a stifling hot, muggy stillness. Now, however, the weather is stormy and windy, yet every bit as hot. It is provoking short tempers.

It's been like this for days. Few boats are running, and I'm delayed getting back. The backlog of freight stacked on piers is towering. Out on a smaller pier, a lone bald monk in bright saffron holds his mobile phone up to the dark grey sky, seeking a connection via divine intervention.

Finally, the ferry decides to go. The crossing is terrifying, nauseating, and longer than usual. We're all grateful to crawl back on land. After the traditional taxi mayhem, I'm soon on the road back home to Mai Bay Village.

Delightful memories give me butterflies as soon as I see familiar palm trees.

I'm doubly pleased with my completed visa run, giving me an added thirty days permission to stay, and further progress in my continual refusal to go home for real, or to be realistic in any way. We "do the hill", and I merrily leap out of the truck onto the patio. There's nobody there, which surprises me. It's nearly lunchtime when it's usually heaving. The taxi is gone.

"Hello? Sawadee-ka?"

Taa emerges from the kitchen, unsmiling and not very talkative. She can speak enough English to get across that Nic and Noo are delayed in Bangkok for business, and also now the baby is sick and is in the hospital. The older girls are at school at the moment. Normally now she'd ask if I want to eat. She doesn't. She stares, phone in hand.

"Can I have the key?"

"Key?"

"The key to my bungalow?"

"Bungalow?"

Oh no, please not this! This is my panic button! Please say I have somewhere to sleep tonight? This is high up my list of Top Ten Least Favourite Bad News.

"My bungalow? A bungalow? Is there a bungalow? Nic and Noo said I can stay."

General confusion follows. A phone call is made. It seems there may be a place for me. Taa and Pa encourage me to have a cold drink while they argue. They argue for rather a while. It's more than I've ever seen before, and with real feeling. Finally a padlock is produced, with a key that even works.

I'm assigned to the bungalow nobody knows the number of, the one nobody likes, at the bottom of the hill. It has only one window, no trees, no shade and no air. It's like an oven. Also, there is no table. This is akin to no water, for me. I rig up a table from a filthy old plank. It's slung across the two twin headboards with a thick towel over the splinters and the mud. I write this now, on that. Of course it's the last bungalow left. Low season and more choices come later. Fine. Any port in the storm.

Later on, a new resident explains that Nic and Noo wanted to be back from the city by now. Then the baby went into hospital. All three of them slept there, for all three days. Actually they didn't sleep much at all. Actually it's been a bit awful. Now they don't know when they'll return.

She also mentions that Taa and Pa spend a lot of time on the phone, with either Nic or Noo, disagreeing about how to run the place. Taa knows the kitchen and bungalows best, and she speaks a little English too. However, Pa is older, is blood family, and he owns the tool kit. It's a pecking order dispute. Nobody sounds happy. Generally the mood is sweaty, fed up, and overheated.

Meanwhile, I am forced into a new afternoon routine when I must escape my cell. It really cannot be survived during the hottest hours. It brings to mind those smaller metal versions used as torture chambers because of their sheer, devilish agony. When these sorts of thoughts bubble up, I crawl up to the café and beg for ice.

Even most Thais here are comatose in the most intense part of the afternoon, occasionally raising an eyelid to look at you as if they're thinking, "What's wrong with you? You don't have to broil like this. You don't need to be here. Go home. Go back where you belong."

So, every afternoon when I can't take it anymore, I do what is recommended as first aid for heat exhaustion: spray your clothes with water, wet your hair, and then fan yourself. Then I decamp to the café, the only place with both ice and a breeze. Sometimes I can borrow Pa's hammock, but sometimes he's in it and he stays there. Sometimes there is a babysitting gig, and sometimes there isn't. We are all too drooped to think. In heat like this, brains simply melt like candlewax.

It's official. There is trouble in paradise. The updated news is that Noo now has the beginnings of the terrible flu the baby is still getting over. They don't know when they're coming home. Pa and the girls miss them terribly, and the rest of us do too. The place is just not the same. Taa is a great cook, but they are great hosts and their absence is loud. There are fewer people here these days. There is very little Italian or English spoken any more. The two girls help in the café, after school and on the weekends, but they are too shy to approach customers to take an order. They deliver dishes mutely with a smile and run away as fast as possible.

I try to help where I can, but it's not much help. The rest of the time, when Taa is busy, Pa silently takes orders by gesturing for them to point to the dual-language menu. He holds that place with his finger, delivers this to the cook, who tries to read what's now covered with his finger. She scolds him, he snaps back, and so on. In short, people aren't hanging out here quite as much as before. Plus, tourist season is starting to wind down anyway.

It's still a hot evening, inviting late reading in the hammock – bugs or no bugs. The night becomes an absurdity when some party launches an astonishingly loud and distorted sound system. It's hard to tell what sort of function it is, but the main feature is extraordinarily bad karaoke. It goes on and on, well into the wee hours, trudging towards the grumpy dawn.

Near the end of this freaky all-night ordeal, a dozen local dogs join in, their howls echoing across the village and up the mountainside. The effect is crazed: wolf like, insomnia-producing and possibly supernatural. What a weird welcome back.

In the morning, I assume wrongly that The Usual, soup and internet, might be available sometime before noon. The soup, for once and once only, is both late and haughty. The internet is there but not for me. There is some new kid with his own set-up, and not sharing it either. He is petulantly searching for another trip. He is spoiled for choice. He has twenty-four hour pre-paid internet, and apparently he also has endless weeks and endless money to explore anywhere he likes. He is no more than twenty years old.

"Planning a journey?" I ask.

"Yeah," he shrugs, like it's a burden. "You know Thailand at all?"

"Yes. Some."

"You ever been up north?"

Ah. Now there's a question.

"Have You Ever Been Up North?"

On another occasion, a young man next to me on a boat mentioned his tour included going up north to Chiang Mai and Chiang Rai. He knew Thailand a bit, but not up there. I instantly sighed, and said, "Ah, it's lovely up there." I pictured it, smiling, drifting off.

"Why does everyone do that?" he asked, mildly irked or suspicious. "I say Chiang Mai and everybody goes 'Oo, ah'. They go all gooey. What is that?"

"Oh ye of little faith," I gently chided. "You're about to find out. It's charming. It's a lovely, lovely place."

Some cities, however crammed, have the friendly feeling of a big town, and Chiang Mai is very much like this. It has everything you might want in a city, and yet it doesn't feel dense. It is somehow incapable of frenzy. It's not a fraction as noisy or smelly as the capital.

329

There's greenery about, with mountains never far away, and there are more beautiful temples per square kilometre than anywhere else in the nation. There is certainly a laid-back attitude amongst most people I've encountered. Even the traffic's more reasonable, with less hooting, less craziness, less stress. I know that last bit will change, in time. I am so glad to be here now.

I prefer Chiang Mai to Bangkok for the same reasons I prefer Edinburgh to London. Some say it's like preferring Boston to New York. It's a city but not a megalopolis. It has plenty to do but isn't overwhelming. Most of it you can walk, and you'll have walked enough to feel nicely tired. I suspect Chiang Mai doesn't bother itself with what Bangkok gets up to, any more than most Scots care a damn what the southern softies in London think or do or say.

Priorities on my buying trips were similar from year to year. I'd replenish popular items, but not take as many. Novelty was what people always wanted. I was looking for things that would, for example, join the Joke and Prank department, to rival my top three:

1. Kenyan soapstone snake box – Slide open the lid, and a snake jumps out and nips you.
2. Guatemalan finger trap – not nearly as fiendish and impossible to get out of as the:
3. Chinese two-handed finger trap. That's devilish.

There were also all the novelty musical toys like the thunder drum, the rain stick, the wooden croaking frog, the squawking chicken, the bamboo slide whistles and loon calls – single, double and triple. The sillier the better, that was my motto.

On every trip to Chiang Mai, there were all sorts of different groups to see. Some were there year on year, and others came and went. There were chic, smart independent designers who collaborated with traditional groups: for example, buying long wheels of decorative trim in an ancient style that they fused into modern fashions, and sold to the upper middle classes and groovy youngsters.

There were also shops with royal, religious or charity/NGO sponsorship, and staffed by volunteers. They often sell only things that are strictly traditional and will not stylistically deviate in any way.

I worked with very different companies and groups, some very experienced and some not at all. Language barriers were everywhere, but so was generosity and goodwill.

I met a lady named Mrs Loom who organised a weavers' collective. She introduced me to the patchwork seamstress who did the trim on a lot of the bags and wallets I had sold the year before and now wanted more of. When she heard her stuff was in fifty shops across the UK, her smile started small and grew very wide. These are the moments I wait for.

There were also fine silversmiths. One old man in a loincloth supervised the whole clan in excellent silver jewellery making. They created straight traditional styles, and also all sorts of modern fusions. What I remember most about that visit was that a mobile phone rang, surprising us all, especially when he pulled it out of his loincloth to speak to his son who was selling their goods in some faraway market. A decade ago, of course, that wasn't possible, and landlines aren't coming out here anytime soon, if at all. The mobile phone revolution has been a boon for their business and countless others like theirs.

After Granddad spoke to his son, he handed the phone to his wife who cringed and wouldn't touch it. The daughters cracked up laughing. One said that Mum hates this phone, and also where he keeps it. They took turns saying hello to their brother, and Granddad put the phone back in his loincloth. I was all the more convinced that this was the place to buy earrings. Call it a hunch, or some kind of ironic comedy reward.

Another highlight was working with a young Burmese designer. She had all kinds of new jewellery ideas and samples, and wanted second opinions – especially from a European. Her idea was to mix silver with other materials like wood, coconut, textiles, beads, string and feathers. She was young. All the earrings were bold and huge – and fine if you're young.

We talked about thousands of possibilities. Versioning seemed to be the key. For example, we could take all her big bold designs, halve them and simplify them, or use them separately in simple pairs, rather than having four or five components to one piece. If we simplified and scaled down a bit, I'd be able to sell them to my middle-aged ladies. She could do all her wild stuff for the young as well as doing tamer versions. Thus she could double her potential appeal, all from the same basic designs and materials. She could use this idea for all kinds of future projects.

No sooner was that tree planted than it sprouted limbs and branches. By the time we were done, there were many more versions of everything she had, in all manner of sizes, materials and shapes. I think she was a bit mind-blown, but everybody was very happy with that meeting and its output.

I went everywhere with my radar tuned for new gift ideas, new samples, new things out on the market. I was also on the lookout for gifts for loved ones, and for me too. I was especially after practical travel clothes.

In Chiang Mai for the first time, my first wander down the road involved a classically simple Euro–Asian travelling dilemma. I asked for directions, got what sounded like nonsense, and followed it anyway, for their sake. Actually I wanted to go the opposite way, but they could see me. It is customary, when you ask a question here, for the local to talk total codswallop rather than say they don't know. They really must never say they don't know. That would be letting you down and embarrassing for all concerned. It's much better to say any old crap and send you on a merry chase. This particular merry chase took me past a small discount shoe shop, where I found a good new pair of well cushioned walking shoes. The shoes I was wearing were finished. Eventually I ended up in the Night Bazaar, which is a major tourist trap/attraction, depending how you look at it.

It was only late afternoon, and disgruntled but trendy young stallholders were just starting to arrive and unload all their crates, barely glancing at me or, if so, with barely concealed indifference.

I've done exactly this sort of work too, but not in a city centre on a busy pavement. I recalled the drag of setting up. This was my least favourite part of the process. Once I was set up and knew where food and toilets were, I was open for business and got on with it, usually on my own. Those were long hard days. I do not miss that sort of work.

I had seen all this stuff before, and of higher quality. This was a valuable recce, to see I need never step foot in there again. I need only go if I want a gander at how inflated things can get, what's "trending", how cheaply things can be copied, and other grotty, heartless research which makes me feel like I need an extra shower.

I saluted that perfect and uncool shoe shop, the one with no tourist appeal. The nice sales girl gave me a fifty baht (seventy pence, almost a dollar) coupon on my next purchase. I didn't tell her I was only there for a week, and this was my shoe budget for the next three years. I could always find some staff at the guesthouse who might want it.

My favourite of all is Chiang Mai's Walking Market. From my first time, I enjoyed it, writing in my journals: "This has tons of everything. Some of it is unbearably touristy and tacky, but it's well worth a trawl. Like all the best markets, contrasting things are jammed in together, and gems will surface where you least expect them. With some markets, I take a deep breath, gird my loins and stride apprehensively into the fray, wondering how long my limited energy will last. Not here. Here I wander in and am ready to enjoy admiring things." There is nothing like this in Bangkok.

The beer can wallet family was one I saw year after year, and it was always a lovely lift to see them afresh each time. At first it was only Granddad. Then it was him plus a daughter. Beer can wallets are just what they sound like. He cuts up beer and other metallic cans into rectangles, then flattens and stitches them into canvas-based novelty wallets.

I was sent here specifically to find gifts for men. This request came annually from, I believe, every single one of the hundred and fifty-plus shops that were then my customers. They all begged me to bring them something, anything, that might suffice as a gift to a bloke. A wallet made of beer cans seemed a reasonable solution. Maybe not for chaps, but certainly for guys, blokes, and lads.

The first year I grabbed all thirty of what he had, and later wished he'd had more. In the following years he increased the number of designs. I stayed away from all colas and imported cans, and stuck with Thai beers. Then I asked for everything he had.

He and his daughter would practically dance as they loaded bags. Each year I always told them how they sold out in the UK. Each year they were tickled their joke gifts travelled that far. I never asked for a discount and they always offered a fair one. Bargaining rules in Thailand are very different from the Middle East. Here, at times, if you act with quiet respect, and really expect nothing, sometimes a fat discount arrives on a plate.

There was also "a cute moment with a twelve-year-old tiny girlie who is minding the stall while Grandma snoozes in a lounger, two stalls away. I am collecting Shan earrings, and choose two pairs. Tiny doesn't know the price and calls to Gran, who calls back that it's eighty baht. I say OK. Tiny doesn't get that this is a sale. I get money out and she's thrilled, doesn't know how to make change and runs chattering to Gran, who explains, reassures and walks her through the process. It's a professional initiation. It's her first sale at work. I wave at Gran and she waves back as an equal old bag in respect. I show Tiny how to bag it up and say thank you in two languages in a row. It's been a banner day, most pleasing indeed."

In my later journals, after I returned several times to this Walking Market, things seem to have changed. "This used to be a sweet and family business sort of event, and a real antidote to the Night Bazaar, but now success is choking it. It's more sprawling, it's more cluttered, it's very difficult to move around, and it's stuffed, overcrowded, and uncomfortable. There's more commercial tat, more head cases, more rubbish, more plastic, more harshness."

My own shopping took me to Warorot Market, preferable in every way. It's on during the day. It's for Thais. It's normal. This is where the fabric shops are, which I so enjoy ogling. I tracked down the shop bearing last year's excellent non-wrinkle, allegedly 100% cotton. Whatever synthetics were in the mix were discreet, and these had worn beautifully in extreme heat. I wanted more of the same to take to the nice lady tailor whose daughter was now back to work after having a baby, and they remembered me from last time.

We had a routine. First she would advise me how much to get for each item. Then I would buy the fabric, feeling very brave, chaotic and local. Last time I bought the cotton mix from Mrs Redoubtable (née Scary), but she wasn't there this time. She'd sworn up and down it was 100% cotton, which it couldn't possibly have been.

This time it was her husband. He didn't remember the stuff, but I found it soon enough from his swatch book. I was sent to another branch with an elderly, wizened helper, who led me with a skeletal pointing finger to a corner stuffed with this high grade material. It was enough for good trousers for three years, I reckoned. I was happy as a hunter.

Back at Redoubtable HQ, Hubby agreed that this could never be 100% cotton, and there must be a little polyester in there, maybe 5%? It's utterly non-wrinkle. This is its forte. This is why I wanted it. Of course there's some poly in there. It can't be all cotton. His honesty tipped the scales in both our favours, funnily enough. By the way, he told me, they were getting sixty new colours in the following week, right after I was leaving town, possibly forever. That figured.

For now, I headed for their overflowing corner of cheap colourful chiffon, which my community centre back in Scotland wanted for making colourful banners with for their village hall. I had agreed to stump up the shipping, and they'd given me fifty pounds to spend on this and on bunting. We wanted a variety of bright solid colours, in cheap, sheer, yet durable synthetics. It always amazes me how hard it can be to find plain solid colours. I sifted through patterns, stripes, checks, dots, sequins, mirrors, lace, batik and more. Finally I found the seven solid colours of the rainbow, which obviously is a good metaphor for any community centre.

The bunting they requested involved a taxi across town to the temple décor area of the city. The temple specialist shops were packed with marigolds and smelled of incense. These shops only sell in cheap bulk, so for a pittance, this community centre now has enough bunting for a hundred miles' worth of events.

I was starting to feel loaded up, and this signalled the

end of my week here. Looking back on my rounds, I decided to open up a new folder called Wild Goose Chases, Cul de Sacs, Merry-Go-Rounds and Red Herrings. That should cover it. Here are the latest entries.

My favourite detour was into a nice jewellery and gift shop, which was not the one I was looking for. I was greeted warmly by an elderly lady claiming to be the young gentleman I was to meet. She was terribly sweet, spoke almost no English, and proudly showed me two large framed photos of herself at age seventeen. In one, she was in front of the Eiffel Tower. In the other, she was in front of Big Ben. These are faded pale pastels now. I was crass enough to ask her where this other shop was, but that was a bit undiplomatic, wasn't it? That's why her answer was to show me jewellery. I bought three pairs in the Shan style (cheap thin nickel) – a disc, a crescent moon and an elephant.

Another time, I wandered for fun into a government sponsored, regional industrial crafts promotion centre. No one asked me to leave, so I walked around. There was almost no one there, so I asked if they were open. "Yes!" shrilled a kind lady who eagerly showed me to where "you do shopping buying".

They called it a spa convention. The hall was devoid of humans, but filled with exhibits of soaps, herbal remedies, beauty creams, and massage tables. It was a trade show with no trade yet.

For comedy reasons, I was drawn to a company that made food-shaped candles like hamburgers, vegetables, and sushi. Everything was labelled Do Not Touch. I was scared to make any further enquiries. It's sad: Hamburger candles may never infiltrate the UK Fair Trade market.

I ended up at their tidy little snack bar, where a young woman was lying face down across a table, both arms outstretched, a twenty baht note clutched in her hand. At my one light cough she sprang up, lively and impressively eager to serve. Later on I found the toilet was hand-cuffed shut. Was that installation art, or improvised hardware? I remember wanting to get out of there quickly.

I couldn't help but notice a soap opera involving my neighbours at the guesthouse. It was one of those forays into the rent-a-girl world. By way of providing context, it's true that one does see every sort of interracial couple here. There are busy family people, the ones who seem like real couples. Then there are rentals that can range from monthly to hourly, and on any variety of terms.

I was guessing next door was a one week gig – and his first. I didn't think it was working to plan, as I noted in my journals.

They have nothing to say. She speaks English a little, but this is not the problem. He has set up his computer on the balcony table. She sits across from him, waiting, not knowing what to do or where to look or what to say. The other times they are on the balcony, they sit in either chair, facing each other, silent and embarrassed. Should he have gone for the hourly or overnight-only option?

Later that week, the maids were in action. Joe computer and lady joiner had checked out. Their rubbish bin was outside their door, now adorned on top by a single fresh red rose, still in its wrapper, untouched. Downstairs, they sat opposite each other, chewing. His gaze was fixed autistically down into his food. She looked sweet but in pain. I was thinking, she has to do this with dozens of clumsy clods like him? That's just crap.

Speaking purely as a distant outsider, I can say that over the years I have collected impressions. Judging by the hundreds of lady-bars I have passed by with the ladies on display, there seem to be three looks. I'd like to emphasise these are looks. These are merely appearances.

First, there are some right tough birds who look like they grew up where everyone whores or steals, and they are certainly unafraid of direct eye contact. Second, there are many with a metaphorical mask on and you will never know what they're thinking or feeling inside. Lastly, there are those who seem always on the verge of tears, longing to run home to their families, and possibly had no idea what they were being sent to do.

I can't imagine paying for sex. I can't imagine getting paid for it, and I can't imagine that world at all. It just sort of baffles me, and in the nastiest i.e most violent or enslaving scenarios, I deeply pity those who want out. That much I do know. Otherwise it's a world I will never know, even though here I am surrounded by men who visit this world all the time.

Around this time, I received news from my Zimbabwean traders that was both hopeful and desperate. There is nothing from that place that is not poignant. It said that my goods had been dispatched. I knew this was easier said than done, and they hadn't gone into much detail. That silence spoke volumes. It's better that way because everything they write is tracked. It could mean a wait of many months. It could mean they'd paid a fortune to get the goods out of the country, and lost whatever profit they might have had. It was very, very disheartening. They do great work and deserve to trade.

There's an ironic two-sided coin here. On the one hand, anything you send to Zimbabwe may get nicked before it gets anywhere near its destination, because of sheer poverty and desperate need. On the other hand, my experience was that because no one believed anything of value could be sent out, you got great service from a well-staffed but under-used postal service. Bizarrely I never lost a single box sent from Zimbabwe to the UK, and I sent dozens.

At the end of any trip, there were always things to send. The Thai exporter arranged the business stuff, and I arranged my personal stuff, which went separately through the excellent Thai postal service. I happened to particularly like the branch I got used to, which was right on the river.

Especially memorable was their manager, who reminded me of a Thai Ernest Borgnine. He was huge and impressive. He ran a tight ship, and was just scary enough to keep quality and efficiency extremely high, even amongst the customers. I also remembered the fellow who until recently worked the We Package Anything For You counter, at which he was extraordinarily adept. He, in his somewhat stoned looking way, would eye up a helter-skelter heap of grocery bags, turn in one motion to his shelf, select exactly the right sized box, assemble it with a flick, pack it to the millimetre, know the weight before he weighed it, and had all the prices in his head. He was a marvel. He spoke good English, and was especially sweet-tempered, diligent and patient. This time, though, he was not in his usual corner. Instead there was a young shy fellow looking lost.

"Hello," Ernest said to me, which startled me out of my reverie. "I remember you. You come every year. You send big things home every year."

"Yes, that's right."

"You like Chiang Mai?"

"Yes, I like it very much."

He smiled. He motioned to the boy. "You remember the man who worked there before?"

"Yes, I do. He was very good."

"Yes, he was very good. Very good. So it is very sad, that he died about two months ago."

"Oh no."

"He was not so old. But it was alcohol poisoning."

I was suddenly quite shaken. "I am so sorry to hear this. Oh this is so sad." I stood there shocked. Ernest put down his work and looked at me directly.

"He was a nice guy. He was a good worker. Everybody liked working with him. He worked here twenty years."

I suspected that this manager had been here even longer, and they may have had some excellent, brotherly beers together over the years. He nodded towards the new kid. "He will be OK. He only needs to learn."

Thais normally never do this, but he held out his hand for a European style handshake.

"I hope we see you next year," he said.

"Thank you," I replied. "Me too."

I do not usually leave a post office this emotionally in need of a hankie. I think a story like this is much less likely to come out of Bangkok, the Big Mango. This is why so many people smile warmly when you mention certain places. Chiang Mai is that kind of place.

A Short Word About Elephant Dung

In the world of art paper, there is some beautiful craftsmanship, and equally lovely materials – from the finest silky watercolour papers to strongest sculptable card. Somewhere in between are textured papers like saa paper, made from mulberry bark. Nowadays for some, it is less and less a world of paper from trees.

Other papers reveal sinewy, grassy textures. These may have passed through an elephant. Working in this business, I did not expect to learn about elephant dung paper, but it became one of my favourite substances of all time.

However I rack my brains, I cannot remember where I first heard about elephant dung paper. I imagine it must have been on a trip to Chiang Mai, where a nice side trip can take you to nearby Lampang and Thailand's national elephant conservation centre.

The elephant is Thailand's national symbol, but it's an endangered species. This place has a hospital, a maternity ward, and a troupe of about fifty or sixty fine beasts with their matching troupe of mahouts – the trainers and keepers.

Typically and traditionally, a young man and a young elephant get paired up and trained together, and spend a lifetime as a pair. Elephants often live about as long as people, and I imagine there are difficult partings at the end of such a long road.

Enter energetic Mr Wanchai. He's a keen admirer of these wonderful creatures, and lives near this sanctuary. Once upon a time, he used to often walk by a paper factory, and liked how simple it was to take natural tree fibres and make paper – high quality, hand-made art paper. On a trip to the elephant centre, a place filled with dung of course, he noticed how grassy and fibrous it was. He put the two ideas together. Elephant dung paper.

Elephants eat tremendous amounts of fibre that go right through them. They might eat two hundred kilos of food a day and produce fifty kilos of dung, which is mostly fibre and not that stinky, as dung goes. If it is smelly, the elephant is ill.

The dung is collected, then washed and boiled for hours before being disinfected. The fibres are spun and cleaned, at which point the result looks like fresh, if soggy, hay. This "hay" is tinted, weighed into balls of pulp, then spread across a screen and dried in the sun.

The paper is then peeled off and sanded, and either cut into pieces and sold as is, or made into cards and stationery. Chlorine is not used, and the paper is bacteria free.

One elephant provides the materials for a hundred and fifteen sheets of elephant dung paper per day. I sold masses of this stationery, which became known as ellie poo paper. I sold cards, memo boxes, notebooks, bookmarks, art paper and gift boxes. I had no end of fun explaining this to nice ladies with lavender hair and pearls. Bless the members of the Scottish Women's Rural Institute, every one of whom was up for a laugh. In a farming community, there is no squeamishness about dung.

Mr W almost got divorced because of his invention of elephant dung paper. After he learned about paper-making, he brought a carload of elephant dung to his home. At this stage his wife is reported as being amused and patient. He did many experiments. He needed to cut the fibres shorter, so he borrowed her kitchen blender. I believe this may have been where marital relations became strained.

Eventually she issued him an ultimatum: either to go back to work and forget dung paper, or to quit work and make dung paper his full time job. He did the latter, with the family's support, and to celebrate he bought her a new blender. He kept the old blender as a reminder to his kids that an idea may seem odd or nutty, but with courage and persistence it can succeed, as this one did.

He is now proud to run the workshop, which employs several people to make the paper and several more to assemble the products. He loves that this brings money to the centre, and to the elephants. He'll tell you that elephants have helped many centuries of Thai people and that each ball of dung that drops out of an elephant is a chance to help that creature in return.

The saying is true. Where there is muck, there is money.

Waiting for Hanoi; or, Some Shoes Never Drop

The tiny Vietnamese lady next to me was fierce-looking. She had Sumo-strength leg-locks on the twenty-seven carry-on bags at her feet, and in her sinewy arms she guarded what looked like a small fridge. She turned suddenly and bashed me with it, for the umpteenth time. There was no escape; I was trapped. This was not the fall of Saigon in 1967, and these weren't refugees running from burning villages. This was forty years later. It was 2007, and we were in Bangkok airport, waiting and waiting and waiting for our flight to Hanoi.

These hordes had not been fleeing. They'd been shopping. They were bringing home cheap Chinese and (not so cheap) Thai consumer goods. Mountains of materialism cluttered the crowded departure lounge. I say "lounge", but it wasn't lounge-like at all. Was even one person lounging? No. Thai airport departure lounges which are heavenly oases do exist, where you do indeed lounge like a sultan, while perfumed, angelic ladies caress you with wild orchids and bring you refreshing drinks and lovely snacks hand-sculpted into lotus flowers. This was not one of those. This was from the prison era. Here's what I wrote on that day:

> Vietnam Airlines. First impressions: not good, neither of staff nor customers. No smiles anywhere, plenty of aggressive pushing and shoving – and why are grannies always the worst? It's true the world over. The staff act as though they've only ever been employed by the military, and that's how they do everything in life, on duty and off. They bark out orders, like cliché Communist bullies, yet there's a modern twist: since they're now a commercial airline, female flight attendants (unbearably cool and graceful) are decked out in beautiful skin-tight red dresses, high Mandarin collars, buttoned down the front and slit up the side, with black silky pyjama trousers underneath. Somehow it suggests elegance, straightjackets, and prostitution, all at once.

Our crowd today was dominated by two large extended Vietnamese families, each with at least thirty or forty relatives, each person with their own household appliances and numerous carry-on items. They looked nervous, tired, and distinctly unhappy despite going home with goodies. What's wrong with this picture? I couldn't figure it. They just looked desperate to get there.

Bash. She did it again, Madame Fridge, methodically thumping each of my ribs in turn. I wondered if I dared say anything and, if so, how? Could I even say hello in Vietnamese? Possibly not.

On my other side it was calm as the desert, with no contact whatever from the two men in ill-fitting, outdated suits. I called them the Silent Russians. I say Russian, but I think I just decided that. They were very furtive. An odd couple: awkward. Not mates on holiday, not gays on holiday, more like work colleagues who neither knew nor liked each other. Spies.

They were particularly furtive with their passports. So was I. I was an American going to Hanoi, so of course I hid my passport. But I couldn't hide my accent. I didn't even try. I turned to Russian Number 1, eager to dissipate my boredom.

"Hello." (No answer.)

"Do you speak English?" (I tried an "isn't-this-a-silly-situation" kind of smile: totally misjudged.) He stared, thought, wrote something down, and looked around the room, like a radar sweep. He acted like I wasn't there. An invisible bird had dropped an Invisibility Cloak over me. It was unsettling, yet intriguing. Spies for sure. We can play with this.

"Are you on holiday?" (He stared.)

"Business?" (Not a blink.)

"Sorry, do you speak English? Deutsche? Russky? Polsky? Français, Italiano, anything?"

Nothing, not even a shrug. As before, as if I were not there, he conferred with his colleague in low muttering which sounded suspiciously like Russian. In unison, they returned to their newspapers which were – aha, in Russian! No, I made that up. I was so bored I was making up spy-story plots. They did seem a bit ex-KGB. I decided to test this theory during the flight.

This reminds me of a joke. Why do KGB agents always work in threes? One can read, one can write, and one keeps an eye on the Two Intellectuals.

Oddly enough, their behaviour over the course of the flight was so weird that, by the end, I really was sure they were spies, just very bad at it. That came later. For now, I waited and wondered.

Maybe they were Bulgarians who wished they could say "shut up" in English.

Maybe they were Martians, still getting the hang of things.

Maybe they were British public schoolboys who never learned how to talk to girls.

No, let's go with spies.

Still no news about the flight. Who else was going to be on board today? A few Japanese couples and small families, who kept to themselves. They'd be touring southeast Asia on their way back to chilly Tokyo. There were a few Thai couples and families off to visit their neighbours. They kept to themselves too.

Then there was me. I was to have just thirty-six hours in Hanoi, if we ever got there. The next day was a business day, perhaps some walkabout in the evening, and an early flight back the next morning. This delay was eating away at my precious day and a half, as I bristled.

A new group arrived. Americans. We heard them a mile off. Group package holiday. Only ten or fifteen of them, but they out-decibelled both Fridge Families put together. They found seats, unloaded and eventually settled.

Bash, another bruised rib. I attempted a mimed pleading gesture to Madame Fridge, but she wouldn't even do eye contact. She hid amongst her clan's Auntie line-up. The Auntie Brigade – so many families have them. With the next bash, I demoted her title from Madame to Auntie Fridge.

It was way past take-off time. Someone tried to approach the airline staff, but got The Look. You know the one. It stops you in your tracks. The question doesn't even get asked. The person slowly sits back down. That is power and I am in awe.

It's a gift. Military people have it. Certain teachers have it. Lots of mothers have it, and most black women have it. It is the authority to silence people *before* they even speak. I want this! Everyone at Vietnam Airlines has it. It must be in their training manual. They say "Please wait" in a tone that says "We have prisons; you will obey." We obeyed. We sat. We waited.

An hour passed, then another. Some retreated into books. Others chatted, fretted, muttered. Twenty languages fluttered about like many kinds of birds in a small field. With a big fence. And barbed wire. And towers with men wielding rifles.

Gradually, like a vast and slow ocean wave, the local baby population began to rise up. You could feel it, like a simmering volcano: they were revving up for a big collective howl. Mothers went on alert, others took shelter. I escaped into a tattered newspaper.

Top stories that day:

The Queen of Thailand defends the rights of southern Thai teachers to arm themselves against militant Muslim attackers near the border with Malaysia.

French President Jacques Chirac visits India, while Sikhs protest against turbans being banned in French schools.

The UN calls for the US to close Guantanamo Bay prison camp, accusing them of ill-treatment of prisoners. US Defence Secretary Donald Rumsfeld calls this "just plain wrong".

"Just plain wrong." Now there's a finely honed argument. This was all the news I could take.

The two Russians scrutinised everything I read. I thought of Glasnost, openly showed them and smiled.

They conferred with no smile and wrote things down, again as if I weren't there. Maybe they were delegates to an autism convention. A convention where no one communicates, I liked that idea. No, the KGB theory was still top. I named them Agents K and G; B had disappeared. Perhaps they'd bumped him off. That made them the Two Intellectuals.

Bash, more "incoming" from the East: a direct hit from Auntie Fridge. It looked like she was Auntie number five in their pecking order, and not happy with it either. But she piled on the lipstick and soldiered on, buying fridges and doing her duty.

I re-read my guidebook's chapter on "Dangers and Annoyances". Its categories, in this order, were: Theft, Beggar Fatigue, Violence, Scams, and Undetonated Explosives. Then came details of gun-fights in nightclubs, loads of ways to get hurt and killed, and way, way too many examples.

Why was I going to Hanoi? It wasn't for the danger, whether exaggerated or otherwise. I was on the Fair Trade trail, and that was as good an excuse as I needed. There were excellent baskets and textiles, from what I saw on the internet. Really, though, I was simply eager and curious to see the place. I could buy samples, look around and maybe satisfy some curiosity.

Could the flight be delayed until tomorrow? Then I'd have been stuffed. In two days I was to fly back to the UK, not to return for another year. No Hanoi, no deal, no looking around. Thousands of potential pounds of annual income were going straight down the Asian-style squat-toilet. Stop: that's panic-thinking. Change the channel this instant.

This trip was a last minute decision. I'd dithered for weeks, and nearly didn't come. It wasn't to do with business; it was to do with being American. There is still deep guilt felt by many Americans about what the US government did to south-east Asia, all those decades ago. There are plenty of Americans who still can't look a Vietnamese person in the eye and, until now, I hadn't realised I was one of them. In fact I was sweating and trembling. I was afraid of Hanoi, especially on my own. My stomach was in knots.

I was in primary school in the 1960s, during what we called the Vietnam War, and what they called the American War. Others called it the Indo-China Wars, because so many different nations and groups were involved, and because there was a series of these wars. That's what I remember: it seemed to go on forever. The same awful headlines, over and over, year after year.

I went on to junior high school and teenage years, and finally the headlines started changing, criticising the war, reporting mass protests against it, demanding that it end. Finally it did end, but only after years of grief and destruction and horror.

As a ten-year-old, I watched every young man around

get drafted into the army. There was a lottery, according to your birthday. All my cousins went. Fred, Rick, Ernie. We sent them letters and cookies, and there were parties when they came home. They actually did come home, so we were luckier than most.

It was said that fifty thousand US soldiers didn't come home, and almost the same number came back but committed suicide in the years that followed. I've heard that many times in many versions and contexts.

Bash and double-bash from Auntie Fridge. Why couldn't she put the stupid thing down? Who's going to nick it off her? I gave her a look. Not The Look, but the best one I had. No response. We stared at each other openly. She was about my age, fifty, and about my size too. Forty years ago, my cousins and her cousins shot at each other. Now we just wanted to get on the damned plane, with our respective fridges.

Bash, she nailed my last unmolested rib, lower right. She was nothing if not thorough. It seemed she was getting fed up with the waiting, and so was I.

Over on the Western front, surveillance duty continued with Agents K and G. Agent B still remained unaccounted for. I would never, ever find out what their story was, and this was to bug me throughout the flight to come. Or not to come.

I started to fantasise. They would put bars on this departure lounge, and stuff plates of gruel through small metal plate openings. Because I was American, they would make me empty the bedpans. I would die here and be thrown in the Mekong.

OK it was official, this was getting to me. Fine, let's do paranoia, and do it properly: what's the worst that could happen? I'd get beaten and robbed in the street, at night, alone and, as I called for help in my American accent, an old war veteran would hear me, freak out in a psycho-flashback of the war, pull out a pistol and shoot me in the head. It would all be over in seconds. That's better than the long torture version. I could be put in a cage with rats, like where they put Robert DeNiro and Christopher Walken in the film *The Deerhunter.*

Stop, I told myself. Chase away these thoughts. They are cockroaches in your mental shower. You will get there, you will. It will be OK. Just wait. Just wait. Just wait.

As it turned out, I would love my day in Hanoi. I would order baskets and textiles and they would indeed be lovely and sell well. During my visit I would also spend time seeing and hearing about historic photos of then US President Bill Clinton reopening trade with Vietnam after decades of embargo. (Bill towers over tiny seamstresses. Hilary admires baskets.)

The historic blending of the best of Chinese and French cultures was sublime. I would eat extraordinarily well, wander charming streets, and leave very eager to return. But none of this had happened yet. Now in that waiting-forever room, all I saw was drag and ordeal and war-guilt, and they'd probably blame me personally for Coca-Cola. I was stuck in time, imprisoned and waiting.

Bella Vista and Accidents Not Waiting to Happen

One night, I go to the café, but only find Pa gesturing they're closed. There's no way to find out why. I ask where Taa is, where the girls are, but he can only shrug and look lost. I and others eat elsewhere and wonder if everybody's OK.

The café reopens the next day. Everybody's not OK. Taa took Tia and Mia to the hospital following a motorcycle accident. Tia plus some guy took turns driving, and she certainly wasn't supposed to. They got no further than the bottom of Big Bastard Hill when they lost control and the bike went off the road. Today, Tia has a cast on her arm and Mia, the sidekick, has cuts and bruises. A shy new helper is now part of the kitchen team, introduced only as a cousin.

Taa took the girls (on her motorbike, without helmets, as always) to the local hospital. I use the word "hospital" very loosely here. It's more of a clinic or first-aid station. The cast looks crudely done. Her fingers are crushed together like a tight, unfolded rosebud. The scrapes and bruises aren't bad, though both girls look ashamed and shaken up.

Taa is stirring the wok with one hand and talking to Noo on the phone with the other. We sort of get the idea that Noo and Nic are desperate to get here as soon as they can. It's a long day, no matter how they do it, city door to island door. The baby is not over the flu, but is out of hospital. Noo is in the middle of her flu, and Nic has just started his. They are all feverish and comprehensively miserable, inside and out. They hope to be on some kind of night bus by the end of the day, if that's what you call a hope.

Late the next day, they arrive in a convoy with added relations in tow. They all look horrendously tired from night buses, early boats, flu, children breaking limbs, and possibly also arguing.

A tourist couple poke their heads in and ask if the kitchen is open. Noo nods, Nic gets the menus and does his best to host them warmly, but he simply lacks several months' sleep. Taa cooks, but wishes they could close, and this is written all over her face. The extended clan colonise the hammock deck in a large cluster with their backs to everyone else, murmuring to each other.

Nic sighs. "Tomorrow we must leave again. That thing on Tia's arm is no good. She has pain in all the fingers. We must go to the mainland to a real hospital, to get a new one, something which does not destroy fingers, like second accident." He sighs again, and takes a long drag on his cigarette.

"We close café tomorrow. You can eat in the village?"

"Sure. We all can. Anything I can do to help?"

"Not really. Well, maybe. Please, how you say – please look after this place? Take care, our home, when we are away?"

"Sure."

"Thank you." He sighs again, stubs out the cigarette, searching immediately for another.

This makes me turn to thoughts of home, naturally. It's obviously time to move, but I don't know where. It could really be anywhere on earth. I don't even know which continent. Do I really have to decide this right now? When my belly feels panic and my knees go weak, like the ground just moved and not in a good way, I remind myself I am not in Zimbabwe, where I witnessed great suffering handled with great dignity. Therefore, my rubbish too can be dealt with, somehow or other.

First things first. I do know one thing for sure: When I get back, I have to vacate that cold, swampy, slug and frog farm with the drafty windows and exorbitant heating bills. Once I get back, I'll start slimming down for a move. All six rooms of business clutter is the mountain to be moved.

Meanwhile, over here – in terms of the symbolic party being over – it's as if I've glanced at the clock and located my high heels, but haven't put them back on, and am nowhere near booking the cab. In truth, I have booked nothing at all, but I know I'll need to soon.

A couple of days pass, and the family returns from the mainland. Everyone looks awful but relieved. The cousin brigade has gone back to the city, but phone calls are frequent and lengthy between all concerned.

The new arm cast looks much better. Tia can actually move her fingers. We all shudder at the idea of it crushing her hand like that for several weeks. She can't play pool, but she can play dangle the baby's feet. Mia has decided that she will upgrade to grown-up pool games where you don't try to break each other's fingers. Woman to woman, I initiate her into the ways and rules of eight ball. Let's forget for the moment that it's on a tilted, uneven snooker table, surrounded by pillars. This is a rite of passage. We're all glad for some distraction and it's nice to see a few smiles flicker about, here and there.

In the morning, a surprise awaits me.

Well, what do you know? Today's emails deliver a new twist. Here's a note from a friend back home. Months ago, just before I came here, I told her I wanted a warmer home and I wanted to live in town, not so isolated. She said she'd keep her ears open. She has only gone and stumbled into exactly what I'm looking for, which is a good little house in town. A positive word has been put in, I'm told, and I am being head-hunted, which is uplifting. She also gives me a rough idea of the catalogue of awful previous tenants. In this context I am a great catch.

If I can see it within the month, the landlady will hold it for me. Did I read that right? She can be flexible? Heavens, that would work out perfectly. I don't know how to move six roomfuls of stuff into three, but there's a month to work that out.

Right: now we downsize this business. We prioritise jewellery and sell off all bulky stuff, starting with baskets, textiles, stationery and anything heavy or annoying. We have a plan. Surprise! I haven't had any of those in a while. I'd almost lost all belief in their existence. Dad would approve, and I don't even have to ask.

At a nearby table, Nic totals up a fistful of medical bills on a calculator, studying the total. Then he takes a stack of menus, and one by one pencils in higher prices. Within a week, the place is empty.

"At least it happens in low season. We are nearly closed anyway," says Nic, still looking concerned. The season's over from their point of view, and the party's over for us. It's time to go home – or to start looking for one.

I wish I could live here for good, someday, somehow. I've had this dream for a long time. I used to draw pictures of palm trees and dream I could live near them. I've done this since I was a small child. I've always hankered after warmth and tropical fruit from a young age. At breakfast the following day, Nic is in the same pose: at the table with the calculator, as if he's been there all night. He holds a different set of paperwork in his hands though. They don't look like birthday cards.

"From the second hospital?"

"No," he seethes, "this from third and fourth hospital."

"What?"

"My dog. He bite the boy, Boo."

"The dog bit Boo? Oh no. Is he OK?"

"He's OK. He needs some injections. Also the dog needs tests and injections. There is no rabies, but it is all very expensive, and I am angry."

"It costs that much?"

"Before, you get this for free! Injections, small operations for nothing, no money, from foreign vet volunteers. Also, government do this too – but only one day each year. Now is too late. Now I really pay. Is no problem. Is just stupid. I hate to pay." This could be the concluding outcry of so many stories.

There's interesting news in today's email. The owner is eager to end her ten years of bad luck with tenants who piss on the carpet and don't pay their bills. She wants me write back to confirm.

I write back. I confirm. I book my airline ticket to go back home, now that it finally feels like home again. I don't have to sleep on it this time. I'm also desperate to come back here next year. I hate thinking there might be places I will never see again.

Ciao and No, You Cannot Come Back

This morning I am at the calculator working out my bill, at the same table as Nic, who is listening to a lengthy, boring phone call where he doesn't get to say much. Taa is shredding carrots, Noo is showing Bee her toes, and Boo is hanging from a beam like a monkey. Nic hangs up the phone.

"It's that stupid skinny couple, you know, the soap opera twins, who shout at night. I am the daddy sometimes, also the bartender and priest and therapist for some people. They need to talk so much about their problems. Oh, is bad sometimes! But, some people, not difficult like this."

Noo is tugging his sleeve, urging him to say something, and finally he does, a bit reluctantly. "Tell me. When you came here three months ago, you had a lot of stress, yes?"

"Yes."

"But, you no want talk about this. You want to forget the shit, not talk about shit."

I laugh. "Exactly."

"You just want to get healthy and strong again. And now you are. Yes?"

"Yes."

"Good."

"Yes! Very good! Thank you, for everything."

"You are welcome. By the way, everybody says you look ten years younger. Everybody except Giulio, who says you look twenty years younger."

"That man is drunk all day, and you know it."

"OK, but he mean this nice."

There is a delightful morning errand to run. I need a trip into town for last minute tasks, at the end of which, I meet my new pal Joy at the pier. She's just returning from her visa run – the Kuala Lumpur version – and will arrive with the big fat ferry. We'll share a taxi-truck back to the village. Joy is fine company. Joy is indeed a joy.

I see her waving from the back of the queue, looking fine and trudging along contentedly behind the more impatient ones. Because we once joked about meeting people with signs, I've made one for today. In a child's notebook, in large red cross-hatched letters, is the word JOY filling the whole page. There's plenty of time to hold up my sign and offer joy to everyone on that boat, whether they want it or not. It's not every day you get a chance like that. They all look JOY straight in the face and walk right past it, not comprehending. I did that for months, but not now.

Back at the café, I drink my last coconut for a while. Now comes the final question.

"Noo, can I have a bungalow next year?"

"Not sure."

"Not sure? I can pay now."

"Sorry, no, cannot." She runs out of words. She appeals to Nic to explain further.

"First, sometimes people pay and cannot come. This is no good. So, if you come back—"

"Not if. When. When I come back."

"OK, in future, here is the point. We might not be here."

"What?"

"Is long story. Contract here nearly finished. We talk to the landlord many times, but do not agree. This place did badly before, but now it's doing very well. So now they want more rent. Much more. Is problem. Maybe we can solve. But also we look at other places we can go."

"But where? You mean on this island?"

"Sure, on this island if we can. In this business, is difficult, over time. You begin in a quiet, beautiful place. Then everybody comes, and ten years later it's not so quiet or beautiful. There's money to be made, more people come, rents go up, then you decide: stay or go?"

He takes a deep drag on his cigarette. "Sometimes, you need a new island." Noo stands beside him, nodding with a small sad smile.

Pa gets out of his hammock, remembering something to do, and offers his place to me. Boo soon joins me for a few monkey games, but his mood is subdued. He climbs down from the ropes, and lays his skinny self across my belly. We just sway gently and quietly, and I rub his back. His mother leans out of the kitchen, sees him, smiles and goes back in. That's very touching, suddenly, to be trusted with someone's child. I'm sure he felt my heart lurch.

It's finally time to go. I look and feel as pathetic as poor Guido did when he had to go back to his old life again. It's hot, so most of what goes on is bleary and wordless. I've returned the bike. Mr Truck is waiting by the entrance, and gestures I can take my time and he can take my bags.

Here, suddenly, my eyes fill with tears, so I look up at the sky and slide them back into my head for later. Mia and Tia are away at a friend's house, so I give Noo their gifts, which are matching water pistols. I also give a pink and blue, his-and-hers set to Noo and Nic, who are very pleased, and immediately look as though they have plans for later.

Noo reminds me that the baby is still a little sick, so I put her kiss goodbye on the tip of my finger and transfer it to Bee's hot pink cheek.

Noo struggles to say, "Next year, we say you, we say you..." and here she nudges Nic, who has the words to finish her thought.

"Next year, we find new home, we say you. When we know where we are, we say you."

Noo beams, "OK?"

"OK. Thank you. Mille grazie. Kab-kun, ka."

"Sure. Prego. Ka."

They have loaded the first two old bags, and now they load the third old bag which is me. Pa and Nic wave. Noo blows a kiss with the baby's hand. Taa is whispering something into Boo's ear. She has to prod him a little. Finally he lifts his head and chirps like a bird.

"Bye-bye, Kun Yai."

"Pope-gan-mai, ka!" I yell back, which means "see you again".

Our truck lurches forward. Sometimes you need another island.

Recommended Reading – Things Thai

Dream of a Thousand Lives (originally published as *Touch the Dragon*) by Karen Connelly. Canada, Seal Press, 1993. A seventeen-year-old Canadian girl receives a scholarship to attend a Thai secondary school for one year in a small northern rural town. Her memoir of that time is poetic, insightful and sweet.

From Condoms to Cabbages: An Authorised Biography of Mechai Viravaidya by Thomas D'Agnes. Bangkok, Post Books, 2001. This half-Scottish Thai MP brought fun and comedy to sex education and condom use, and is famous for his work in many areas of development as well as for his dedication to the ideal of eliminating poverty.

Mai Pen Rai Means Never Mind by Carol Hollander. Boston, Houghton Mifflin, 1965. I suggest this to those who can read only one book about Thailand. She was a very unprepared American housewife who followed her husband to Bangkok, taught at a Thai university in the 1960s, befriended more Thai people than most do, and wrote about these years with wit, deep affection and tremendous intelligence. It gets better every time I read it.

Peoples of the Golden Triangle: Six Tribes in Thailand by Paul and Elaine Lewis. Bangkok, River Books, 1998. History and photographic record of the larger hill tribes of northern Thailand.

Phra Farang: An English Monk in Thailand by Phra Peter Pannapadipo. London, Arrow Books, 2005. This is a sincere and thorough look at life as a foreign monk in this particular monastery, written by an earnest man who describes many unfamiliar things very well to the uninitiated.

A Photographic Guide to Snakes and Other Reptiles of Peninsular Malaysia, Singapore and Thailand, edited by Merel J. Cox et al. New Holland Publishers, Sydney, 2006. This is all too relevant, unless you are enjoying armchair-based, creature-free travel.

Travelers' Tales Guides: Thailand, edited by James O'Reilly and Larry Habegger. San Francisco, Travelers' Tales, 1993, new edition 2009. This anthology has a good range of high quality writers, and has only improved with age.

Welcome to the Bangkok Slaughterhouse: The Battle for Human Dignity in Bangkok's Bleakest Slums by Father Joe Maier. Hong Kong, Periplus Editions, 2005. The author is the founder of the Human Development Foundation in the Klong Toey slum where he's lived for 30 years.

Non-Thai

Belching Out the Devil by Mark Thomas. London, Ebury Press, 2008. He originally wanted to call this *Gary Glitter Likes Coca-Cola*. This entertaining satirist does a serious exposé of this corporation's alleged worst behaviour around the world. Also recommended by the same author is *As Used on the Famous Nelson Mandela* (London, Ebury Press, 2007), in which he goes undercover inside the UK's arms industry.

Far From Home: Twenty Years in Exile by Htet Aung Kyaw/Democratic Voice of Burma. Thailand, Irrawaddy Press, 2006. Memoirs of a freedom fighter.

Fighting the Banana Wars and Other Fairtrade Battles by Harriet Lamb. London, Rider, 2008. This is a good introduction to and history of the Fair Trade food movement.

Island of the Blue Dolphins by Scott O'Dell. New York, Houghton Mifflin, 1960. This children's novel is based on a true story of a girl who survived for many years alone on a desert island off the coast of California.

McCarthy's Bar by Pete McCarthy. London, Hodder and Stoughton, 2000. Never walk past a bar with your name on it. This is how he meanders all over his beloved Ireland, even though he was English-raised, and this complicated theme is much on his funny mind as he goes.

The Tao of Pooh and the Te of Piglet by Benjamin Hoff.
"Te" means virtue of the small. This explanation of
Taoism via the world of Winnie-the-Pooh presents the
ancient philosophy as Very Useful Things to Know.
This is worth a read for an infinite number of reasons.

There are so many. I'll bring more to the blog in due
course.

Top ten thanks go in alphabetical order to:

All those who lent me a spare bed or storage space. I hope I plied you with enough bribes, samples, alcohol, or whatever it took.

All those who sent moral support when I was far away and when it was needed most.

All those who wrote things like "Hurrah for more lizard stories! Yes please, more stories!"

BAFTS – The British Association for Fair Trade Shops and Suppliers and its many members with whom I had the pleasure of doing good business. You are fighting a good fight, and consumer information is a fine tool. www.bafts.org.uk/

Editor Tamsin Shelton, who gave this story the tune-up it needed to run smoothly.

Lockerbie Writers, who heard many of these stories before anyone else did. (I just can't not thank them.)

Rimini Bungalows and Fish Restaurant. Best fish on the island, and also your local Italian club. *https://www.facebook.com/RistoranteRiminiBungalow?ref=ts&fref=ts*

Rokpa Women's Workshop of Nepal. We hand-produced hundreds of ornaments, splitting the tasks, and piling finished products into a large basket. Each sundown, in a circle, together we looked at them all and divided them into three groups: sell, repair and sell, don't sell. No blame, just practicalities. Thank you. I'll now try to apply this method everywhere. *http://www.rokpauk.org/*

The good folk at the gift shop Traidlinks, in Wirksworth, UK. One of my favourite former customers, they later bought my old website and stock. So it's not advertising my wares, but theirs. *www.traid-links.co.uk* and/or: *www.eileensimports.co.uk*

Zimbabwe's Mothers of Disabled Children workshop, in Harare, makers of textiles, cards and earrings – against all odds. They start each day in a circle, in which they have a prayer, a song and a dance. This practice is highly recommended. *http://batsiranai.com/*

There are more thanks rolling in all the time. They'll appear on the blog and in volume two.

Links

www.wfto.com The World Fair Trade Organization
www.bafts.org.uk The British Association for Fair Trade
Shops and Suppliers
http://www.elephantdungpaper.com Just what it sounds
like.
http://www.thaicraft.org Represents producer groups from
all over Thailand.
http://www.ttcrafts.co.th Thai Tribal Crafts, based in the
North, representing many groups, known for consistent
quality, and one of the founding groups in the nation.
http://phatriceblog.com/tag/saori-welfare-centre-thailand
More about the tsunami survivors' group.
http://www.ywamthai.org/hopecards and
http://www.hopecards.net/about More about the Hope
Cards group.
In Vietnam: *http://www.craftlink.com.vn/*
In Cambodia: *http://www.rajanacrafts.org/*

The Thansila Hotspring Resort: that nice place to stay in
Ranong, south-western Thailand:. Ask about the Night
Market.
*https://www.facebook.com/thansilahotspringresort?fref=t
s*

www.noodletrails.com. Author's website with present day tales of icky fauna, life in a jungle hut, and noodle shaped journeys through other topics too

About the Author

Eileen Kay is a former comedienne who went around the world working in Fair Trade.

She's worked on London's stand-up comedy circuit in send-up magic act Dork and Tacky, and was KISS-FM radio co-presenter Carmen Ghia, of whom the *Guardian* newspaper said, "She can make the Hanger Lane Gyratory sound like a deviant sexual act. Put her in charge of all radio jingles immediately."

She's done TV voiceovers, directed the comedy sketch show pilot *Spontaneous Combustion*, and her dramatic film *Refugees* won praise and prizes at international festivals. Her stage play *Little White Lies* was produced in 2013 in Scotland. This is her first book of memoirs. A second is in progress.

For eight years she was the entire staff of Eileen's Imports.co.uk, and worked with groups in Nepal, India, Zimbabwe, Cambodia, Vietnam and Thailand. Many were abandoned wives and mothers living near the poverty line, so it was reassuring how much giggling went on, and mealtimes were always a revelation.

Born and raised in the USA, she fled as soon as possible. She was educated at Oberlin College (music and English), the Suzuki "Talent Education" Institute in Japan (music education), and London Film School (distinction in

editing). She's done a miscellany of other studies and jobs, and those stories are waiting in the wings.
She lived in the UK for nearly thirty years and is now a sickeningly proud British citizen. She is currently wandering around Thailand.

Happy trails until then.